D0594073
STRAND PRICE
5.00

The Dignity of Youth and Other Atavisms

The DIGNITY of YOUTH and OTHER ATAVISMS

By EDGAR Z. FRIEDENBERG

BEACON PRESS BOSTON

The author gratefully acknowledges permission to reprint as follows: "Truth: Upper, Middle and Lower," reprinted from *Commentary,* copyright © 1960 by the American Jewish Committee; "Neo-Freudianism and Erich Fromm," reprinted from *Commentary,* copyright © 1962 by the American Jewish Committee; "Society and the Therapeutic Function," published in September 1956 *Adult Leadership* by the Adult Education Association of the U.S.A., 1225 19th St. N.W., Washington, D.C.; "The Image of the Adolescent Minority," *Dissent*; "The Modern High School: A Profile," reprinted from *Commentary,* copyright © 1963 by the American Jewish Committee; "Why Students Leave Science," reprinted from *Commentary,* copyright © 1961 by the American Jewish Committee; "The Gifted Student and His Enemies," reprinted from *Commentary,* copyright © 1962 by the American Jewish Committee; "An Ideology of School Withdrawal," reprinted from *Commentary,* copyright © 1963 by the American Jewish Committee, also published in Daniel Schreiber (ed.), *The School Dropout,* Washington, D.C., National Education Association, 1964; "The School as a Social Environment," reprinted with permission from *College Admissions 10: The Behavioral Sciences and Education,* College Entrance Examination Board, 1963; "The Purpose of Liberal Study versus the Purposes of Adult Students," published in May 1958 *Adult Leadership* by the Adult Education Association of the U.S.A., 1225 19th St. N.W., Washington, D.C.; "Intimations of Mortality in the Literature of Public Education," first published in *Social Problems,* Vol. 11, No. 3, 1964; reviews of *The Uses of the University, The Education of American Teachers,* and *The Hiroshima Pilot,* reprinted by permission of *The New York Review of Books,* copyright © 1963 and © 1964, The New York Review, Inc.; review of *The Educational Decision-Makers* by Aaron V. Cicourel and John I. Kitsuse, Vol. 29, No. 5, October 1964, pp. 773-774; "The Mature Attitude," published in February 1957 *Adult Leadership* by the Adult Education Association of the U.S.A., 1225 19th St. N.W., Washington, D.C.; reviews of *The Schools* by Martin Mayer, *The Adolescent Society* by James S. Coleman, *Values and Ideals of American Youth,* edited by Eli Ginzberg, *Mental Health in the Metropolis* by Leo Srole *et al., The Children of Sanchez* by Oscar Lewis, first published in *Commentary* and reprinted by permission of the American Jewish Committee; review of *An Introduction to the Sociology of Education* by Karl Mannheim and W. A. C. Stewart, published in *Social Research,* Vol. 29, No. 4, Winter 1962.

Library of Congress Catalog Card Number: 65-23468
Published simultaneously in Canada by Saunders of Toronto, Ltd.

Beacon Press books are published under the auspices
of the Unitarian Universalist Association
Printed in the United States of America

For BENNETT: *fidèle Berger*

CONTENTS

The Dignity of Youth and Other Atavisms

Preface

When I was a very small child—small enough to require some measure of assistance, reassurance, and coercion to get me into the bathtub, my old aunt who lived with us and cared for me devised a stratagem that worked when nothing else would. There was, at the time, a well-known football player at Centenary College named Mexico Farrell, whose picture was always in the paper, and whom I adored, although I had, of course, only seen him from a distance. My aunt used to clip his picture out of the paper and pin it on the wall above the tub where I could sit in the bath and enjoy it. This solved the problem of motivation all through the autumn. During the spring I must have been a mess most of the time. I have never cared for baseball.

I don't recall these pictures exactly, of course; but I do remember that Mexico Farrell had a friendly, expressive face and a rough-looking body—not brutal, but warm and creaturely. A little boy in a predominantly feminine household could, and did, imagine him as almost a tactile presence, and a protective *genius loci*. I never did meet Mr. Farrell, who, the last I heard, was practising law in Wyoming, and who must be pushing sixty now. But I am grateful to him for unwittingly molding my character, and making me aware from childhood of the feelings and obligations that were to form its central core. Though this is not a biographical essay, I have begun it with a memory, simply to emphasize that my life and work have been built from the beginning on the same emotional foundation. This has never been altered; the only way to alter it would have been to throw the baby out with the bath. If this policy was considered, it was never executed.

The essays in this book illustrate various stages in the development and elaboration of this fixation on, and concern for, youth. Some take the form of enquiries into the social circumstances that bear on youth; some deal directly with the plight of youth in confronting these circumstances. They also illustrate, of course, the deficiencies in my grasp of the actual situation of American youth at the time that I wrote about them. It is one of these deficiencies and limitations—so far as I have come to comprehend it—that I wish chiefly to discuss in this essay.

There has been, I believe, a certain naïveté in my conception of human identity itself. I have always assumed that the injunctions of Socrates and Polonius to know yourself and live according to your nature were universally valid moral admonitions. I still regard them as absolutely binding on people who share our cultural tradition; but I have become more aware of that tradition's limits—largely through belated acquaintance with Marshall McLuhan's brilliant work. Consequently, I must grant that the central assumption—explicit in *The Vanishing Adolescent* and implicit in most of my work—of my thought is likely to be a double source of trouble. It contributes to a kind of obsolescence. And, more seriously, it leads me to make what may be internally inconsistent demands on youth in relation to society.

I had noted in *The Vanishing Adolescent* that the crucial developmental task of adolescents is self-definition—establishing who they are and what they really feel. I had also noted that this could not occur and be recognized as appropriate to a distinct period of life except in a society that prized individuality and individual dignity. Among primitive people who had formulated no such concepts and among organization men who had abandoned them, there could be no adolescence. All this is true enough. But I had failed to grasp, in spite of having read George Herbert Mead, that this sense of one's own identity, which I think of as the core of human dignity, may also be regarded as a kind of alienation. This is a near miss; in the early paper "Society and the Therapeutic Function," included in this collection and still, I think, one of the best things I ever wrote, I come very close to seeing this point. But it took McLuhan in *Understanding Media*[1] to finally get it through to me that the kind of person whose existence gave meaning to mine was already a product of a considerable degree of alienation simply because he was aware of his strength and pride and of his origins in a way that only people who stand aside from their experience and examine it in the light of various symbols can be. What I have been calling integrity is really the integrity of a print-oriented, individualized people; and the very self-awareness that I have conceived as the source of their nobility is also, it seems, the instrument of their estrangement which saps their vitality.

If McLuhan's thesis is right—and, in general, I think it is —then the kind of youngster I cherish most must be rare, not only because he is being counseled and organized out of existence but because he is an unlikely combination to begin with. This disturbs me. I don't much mind having devoted my life to trying to keep in production what may, by the standards of the organized future, be an obsolete model of human character. Nor do I mind the obvious fact that the values by which I judge youth, like all values, themselves express a cultural pattern no more permanent than any other. If they don't make them like that any more, I am all the more fortunate to have lived while they still did, and if nobody can tell the difference now anyway, I am glad I still can.

But I do mind having devoted my life to demanding that the young develop qualities that perhaps just don't go together —that is the sort of thing an old-fashioned, print-oriented character *would* mind. My ideal youngster is very much like E. M. Forster's favorite kind of person, as described in "What I Believe" in *Two Cheers for Democracy*:[2] sensitive and plucky, humorous and warm enough to be able to accept and delight in his body; delicately robust. Phineas in John Knowles' *A Separate Peace*[3] is exactly the kind of person I mean; and all my work has been devoted to trying to say in more detail and on the basis of more convincing evidence what Knowles said with greater economy and grace. I have also been trying to make it clear that such as Finny face extinction and must be preserved, and to make it less likely that Gene Forrester, who is so very able, will destroy Finny every time there is an encounter between them. But McLuhan suggests to me that the decent young executive, Gene, who never makes a false move or wastes an ounce of hostility is really who I have been harboring all the time, that *he* is the really self-aware one, the boy who could define himself and who tells his own story, knowing it to be the story of Cain. Finny, though maimed by Gene's beautifully timed unconscious attack so that he quite literally falls from grace, dies at the moment he becomes self-aware because he cannot bear the knowledge of his own existential plight. He could never have told what was happening in and to him; if he could have there would have been no story.

McLuhan further suggests that the new suburban type of youth, narcissistic and shallow but emotionally labile and responsive, may be more like Finny, and less like Gene, than I have given him credit for. Both are *innocent;* though Finny is prelapsarian and the suburban youngster exists in a paradise in which the idea of guilt has never been permitted to develop and serpents and policemen are defined as friendly, though calling them so does not make them so. If I understand McLuhan's argument correctly, anyone who loves Finny and fears Gene must either welcome the suburban youngster as the contemporary embodiment of such of Finny's virtues as are still functional, or admit that what he really wants is Nietzsche's blond beast, whose integrity was unmarred by any degree of self-consciousness at all.

Nietzsche's blond beast, as anybody who has read Nietzsche knows, is neither beastly nor necessarily blond. The Nazis would have hated him, but he was already dead when they discovered him and stuffed his skin with their ideas. It may have been something very like him that I saw when, at the age of four—before the Nazis had been heard of in North Louisiana, at least by that name—I gazed up at Mexico Farrell's picture. It was an expressive beast, passionate and direct, that was very good at what it did and consented to do nothing it did badly; it would have been jolly and gentle with little boys. Even when angry, it would have been forceful and direct; the blond beast never nags. Well, it *is* dead and therefore beside the point, and, as McLuhan says, it could never have learned to read, so it would only have been in the way. I cannot disparage it; but I must consent to its burial.

The memory of it, however, still involves me in what, I suspect, are certain conceptual confusions; at any rate, my affection for it has established in my mind certain categories that contemporary reality does not always fit very well. The recent tremendous increase in rebelliousness and social action among college students, for example, leaves me with more mixed feelings than I would have expected. On the whole I am delighted with it; I respect the youngsters of the Free Speech Movement and their peers around the country and see them as the hope of the nation, if it has one. I also like them; but, against my common sense and better judgment, I sometimes like the fraternity boys and jocks who oppose them, if not better, at least more immediately and spontaneously; I don't mean by this that I have any doubt which side I'm on—I'm on the Free Speech and Civil Rights side and actively so—but I am also put off by its nagging hostility and portentousness, and its sentimental assumption that a victim is made morally superior by having been victimized. "Rescue the drowning, and tie your shoestrings," Thoreau advises. "Take your time, and set about some free labor. . . . Do not stay to be an overseer of the poor, but endeavor to become one of the worthies of the world."

I really would rather see a bunch of fraternity boys playing exuberant sandlot ball or just horsing around than a group of civil rightists, or uncivil leftists, sitting in the administration building or praying loudly by the roadside. I know that the civil rightists are more usefully occupied, while the fraternity men oppose most of what I stand for. But I am not expressing an opinion; I am describing a reaction. I know that, stereotypically, jocks and other collegiate types are not supposed to be as bright as their politically active antagonists and are often anti-intellectual. But this does not put me off, much. I prefer big, sunny, surf-ridden people to small, nervous, hagridden ones; and if there is any thinking to be done, I would rather do it myself than bother them.

But I distrust my reaction, and quite properly. Again, I am almost sure that I am looking at Gene and seeing Finny because I need to see him—not because he is there. The fraternity man may look exuberant and expressive when he is playing ball, and there may be real tenderness in his touch as he washes his car. But when you get to know him it is likely to be *he* who seems hagridden and nervous, using the fraternity house as a social situation in which to make contacts and learn manners; it isn't a castle, and he isn't a knight. I have yet to recover from the irony of having participated as a speaker at a Big 10 Interfraternity Council and Panhellenic meeting last year, at which I turned out to be the only speaker who defended the right of fraternities to an elitist position and suggested that their most useful educational function might be precisely to shelter specialized—not racial—minorities who were bound together by common feelings and experiences and strong ties of personal affection, even though this would keep them exclusive. The more liberal kids were bewildered, shocked, and indignant. The other speakers had either predicted a dark future for fraternities unless they became open to all social classes, or had defended the system as already being more democratic than it got credit for, and I had been invited because the youngsters who were emerging to leadership in the fraternity of tomorrow had assumed from my strong endorsement of student freedom in *The Vanishing Adolescent* that I would join them in the struggle to make fraternities open up. There is, in the thinking of both liberals and conservatives in this country—especially among youth—an endemic confusion between civil liberties and civil rights to which I must return later. But for the moment, I want to stick to the evidence that the fraternity system is less romantic than I had supposed it to be, though the audience of local chapter officers —as distinct from the speakers who had come to exhort them —did glow as if I were describing what they had been looking for in fraternity life without knowing it.

Conversely, I have twice been a speaker at national meetings of the United States National Student Association. This remarkable organization is very little known, and I think it would be a public service to describe it. It is in U.S.N.S.A. that I saw the kind of comradeship, exuberance, and emotionally disciplined competence that I think fraternities ought to have but probably do not. There were students taking part in these meetings who really did resemble Phineas or, at any rate, Coningsby, whom Disraeli described in terms not unlike those Knowles applied to Finny and who certainly found in Eton the warmth and community I should like to attribute to fraternity life if I could. Yet the U.S.N.S.A. is commonly and on the whole accurately counted a progressive organization, has usually been dominated by its liberal wing, and by the time this is published (it meets in late August) will have had to take a position on Berkeley and other arenas of student conflict that I expect to be libertarian.

U.S.N.S.A. is an organization of official student governments. It is not open to individuals, and is limited to "democratically constituted" student governments though no student government in the United States is really that in my judgment. Nevertheless, though none is truly independent of the administration, there are many that are neither dominated by nor rebellious against the administration. At the better liberal arts colleges and more independent state institutions the student government is a genuine part of the power structure which enjoys rather more autonomy than its possesses on paper because its services are indispensable in organizing the complex pattern of non-academic activities which bear heavily both on student morale and public relations. Fraternities, likewise, as Howard S. Becker has found in a study of undergraduate life at the University of Kansas, on which publication is pending, exercise great influence though they usually manage to exercise it smoothly. They do train their members in executive-type social skills and organizational norms, and act as a major channel for academic demands; they keep the grade-pressure on both for prestige and for power, since a fraternity must maintain a pool of members who meet university eligibility requirements for athletic and social participation in order to make the scene. But they also defend certain conventional freedoms for their members. Universities depend on the fraternities both for housing and social coordination, and must, in return, protect them from some of the more intrusive forms of community puritanism; the system requires a certain amount of beer and sex and freedom of association to keep it going at all. These are earthy and concrete, but not necessarily trivial, forms of freedom that in Kansas, and elsewhere, are easily lost.

Since fraternities and sororities often dominate student governments and always affect them strongly, and since a school can only send delegates to U.S.N.S.A. if its government has voted to join the organization and has been accepted within it, the young men and women who make up a U.S.N.S.A. annual meeting must often be fraternity types themselves. The meetings are large-scale enterprises. U.S.N.S.A. has member institutions, I believe, in all fifty states, and the larger ones send several delegates. Delegations also include alternates and there are observers from non-member schools, foreign youth organizations, organizations with youth programs that are not centered in any particular school, and, of course, also from the press. There are workshop meetings prior to and concurrent with the general meeting: for student government officers and student newspaper editors—even for deans and administrators, who are also permitted to observe any session, though floor privileges are strictly limited to delegates. This all adds up to a couple of thousand people—mostly college students—and goes on for about a week of regular sessions with workshops having started a week before that.

The atmosphere at these meetings is unique. The agenda is huge, and there is a highly formal and complex committee structure for dealing with it: drafting proposals and ordering their precedence, ultimately bringing them to the floor of a plenary session for action. As this proceeds, the political maneuvering preceding the election of the next year's officers gathers momentum; so does that related to revision of the formal *Codification of Policy* that governs U.S.N.S.A.'s activities from year to year. There is a small and poorly paid permanent staff in Philadelphia which carries out the mandates of the national meeting during the year; these mandates direct the organization either to inform governmental or educational bodies of certain policies that have been adopted, or to raise certain issues with them, or to gather data pending some specified further action. I do not recall any that directed the national staff to collaborate with any other organization, and as a tax-exempt body it is prohibited from certain kinds of direct political action. All that is really at stake then is the expression of certain opinions and candidacy for certain offices; the U.S.N.S.A.'s actions are not, as such, formally binding even on the student governments that compose it. As described, the project sounds, I am sure, tedious and boring.

It is not tedious and boring; neither is it, in the usual sense, exciting and interesting. These are not the right dimensions along which to place the experience, which is psychedelic rather than intellectual. Within a few hours, as the emotional pressure of the meeting gradually builds up, other aspects of reality lose their power to distract; to break off from the meeting would produce an aesthetic shock, a sense of incomplete closure. It is true that the issues discussed are interesting if one is interested in the life of middle-class late adolescents, as I am. But they are also familiar: speaker-bans and freedom of the student newspaper, the insistence of colleges that they stand *in loco parentis* and student objections to that position; H.U.A.C., the bomb, and student participation in the civil rights movement in the South. (There are many Southern schools in the U.S.N.S.A. and even some that are publicly supported—the University of North Carolina was one of the most active during my two meetings—and these Southern colleges are generally among the most articulate supporters of civil rights for Negroes.) American foreign policy is usually hotly discussed.

These are all matters of fundamental importance, but the U.S.N.S.A. cannot directly implement decisions about any of them and can hardly influence the more global ones at all. Furthermore, there is very little debate on the actual issues. Except for the delegation of an occasional religious-affiliated girl's college, nobody argues in favor of more restrictions on students or their political freedom; they argue about what would be practical on their campuses and oppose actions that would be embarrassing to them at home even though they can think of no arguments against them—just like U.N. delegates. There is some difference of opinion on the more global issues, but most U.S.N.S.A. delegates are liberal, and the American student right is so intransigent that it stumbles over itself and falls down on the way to the meeting room. The last U.S.N.S.A. meeting I attended, at Indiana University, was picketed by Young Americans for Freedom and other neo-conservative groups who had indignantly pulled the University out of the U.S.N.S.A. during the previous year, thereby making themselves ineligible to express their position in the meeting itself, when it took place on their home campus.

What, then, makes a U.S.N.S.A. meeting so compelling? For one thing, style: personal and political style. U.S.N.S.A. delegates play politics not like professional politicians but like tough amateurs of a sport at which they excel. Victory does not change the course of history, and they know it; but they mean to win and they play for keeps. They put—the cliché is precise—body and soul into it.

Their bodies contribute a lot to their general expressiveness, too. This is a serious, but not a ceremonious, occasion, and it is held in the hottest part of summer; the procedure is exhausting and the meeting rooms are crowded. The convention often runs right through the night when it is winding up. The kids dress for comfort, and at their age to dress for comfort is to dress for effect. I do not mean simply that this makes them more attractive, though it certainly does; but that the whole feeling-tone becomes more authentic; gestures are more revealing, the whole emotional weight of the delegate seems to flow more easily into what he is saying. If this seems like mere personal fantasy, I would suggest that you imagine Senator Dirksen attempting to carry his point while dressed in a T-shirt and a pair of Bermuda shorts and sandals. There are students at the University of Illinois, however, who can do this quite effectively.

But the soul is equally involved. The test of its commitment to any secular enterprise is, I should say, self-discipline for the sake of self-expression; which is what good violinists, for example, must develop. At U.S.N.S.A. the medium of expression is parliamentary procedure; and before I had attended one of their meetings I could not have imagined that parliamentary virtuosity could be interesting or moving. I do not mean rhetoric—American youngsters don't develop much skill at this—and I certainly do not mean political maneuver which, at U.S.N.S.A. as elsewhere, is concealed as much as possible. I mean sheer precision in the use of parliamentary technic to make it possible to transact an enormous and complex volume of business, every step of which is involved in controversy, expeditiously. U.S.N.S.A. adheres so strictly to parliamentary procedure that when a speaker is speaking too softly to be clearly understood the delegates don't call out "Louder!" but "Privilege!" since, strictly speaking, they must be recognized on a point of personal privilege before they may complain that they can't hear. And since there is not much informal debate, ideas are usually expressed by proposing amendments to motions. There are amendments to amendments, undebatable motions of the previous question at a time when a less expert body would have become completely confused as to just what such a motion would bring before it. Any lapse in the Chair's attention or dexterity creates chaos, but I have seen this happen only once or twice. When it did the delegates regarded the chairman as adolescent drivers do a housewife who backs her car out of the garage without first opening the door.

As the meeting wears on, it develops the tone of a marathon. The general effect is clearly athletic. There is continually heightening tension, excitement, and partisanship; but there is not much hostility and no *ressentiment* at all. The undertone of pleasure is not an expression of good sportsmanship, which is not, I think, a common quality among Americans, who care much more about winning than playing the game. It is due, rather, to comradeship; to what these young people share as experienced campus leaders and members of a student corps that has more informal cohesion than is sometimes recognized. Beneath its liberal ideology U.S.N.S.A. is upper-middle-class; the more prestigious colleges are disproportionately represented among its members, and their more prestigious students are disproportionately represented on their delegations. The organization is expensive to run; registration fees are higher than for most learned societies. It is legendary at U.S.N.S.A. that whoever is elected president will, regardless of his political views, be offered a choice of executive training posts when graduation makes him ineligible for office.

It is this elite quality, rather than its dominant social attitudes, that distinguishes U.S.N.S.A. from the Free Speech Movement and its counterparts. To the critical general public both look like red rebels. When U.S.N.S.A. met at Ohio State University in 1962 it was attacked in the local press for permitting the Young Communist League to maintain a booth in the display section of the meeting hall along with all other youth action groups which had applied. After this report, and U.S.N.S.A.'s refusal to turn the group out of the booth it had rented, news of the meeting was effectively blacked out, though local reporters were more nearly omnipresent than before. An address by Congresswoman Edith Green, the Chairman of the House Committee on Education, to a plenary session of U.S.N.S.A. was briefly reported, but from day to day none of the organization's constructive actions got in the local papers, one of which has a regular teen-age section. I recall that this section carried, during one of the days when U.S.N.S.A. was not mentioned or barely mentioned, a large photograph and detailed story on a local farm boy who had grown a prize ear of corn—a commodity from which the U.S.N.S.A. is, among political organizations, uniquely free. My impression is that while the convention was going on it received more coverage in the *New York Times* than in the *Columbus Dispatch*, and I know that the *Times* carried a favorable, illustrated account of it in a later edition of its magazine.

It will be interesting to see whether attitudes toward U.S.N.S.A. will alter this summer, after a year of student political activity directed toward much more realistic intervention in off-campus issues than U.S.N.S.A. attempts. U.S.N.S.A. has for some time enjoyed the amicable interest of the American political establishment, whose motives for such interest are not clear to me; probably, it was just looking. But the attitude of the Columbus press seems ironic in the light of the telegram of congratulations addressed to the meeting by the late Congressman Francis Walter, of the McCarran-Walter Act; and by Attorney General Kennedy; my own appearance at the 1963 Indiana meeting was informally arranged by a member of Mr. Kennedy's staff. All the U.S.N.S.A. delegates I ever met had, and needed, a good sense of humor and a strong sense of self. As American youth goes, they tend to be unusually secure, having been validated both in their sense of personal competence and often in superior social status as well. But even though U.S.N.S.A. is rooted in the official structure of student government and received a considerable amount of informal support from other official sources it seems to me about as free-spirited as any group can be. These youngsters are true to themselves and they do what they feel to be right for *them.* In taking account of themselves, they also take account, among other factors, of their life-style and unconscious class-patterns; it would be just as phony for them to pretend to be proletarians or revolutionaries as it would be for them to fink out on their political interests altogether.

But they are playfully political: tough amateurs, as I have said, knocking themselves out but not betting much on the outcome. This is enough to gain my affection and respect; but I am not sure it will still be enough to keep up their self-respect. Even in 1963 delegates who had participated personally in the civil rights movement, white and Negro, were heard with the superior deference and respect they had earned; in 1965 it may just not be possible for youngsters to display their political interests and acumen in so artificial an arena without feeling that this, in itself, is an evasion of the dangers and responsibilities their peers have faced up to in the San Francisco Bay area and the South. Many delegates, of course, will have done both, and political activism in real life where it counts will surely be in itself one of the most highly contested issues at the next meeting, since colleges often forbid student governments to adopt a position on "off-campus" issues. It will be ironical if the one national student organization that had maintained good working relationships with the establishment without losing its freedom or its integrity—and been ignored as juvenile and suspected as left-wing for its pains—should be forced into a position of militancy because the establishment has never troubled to make itself even the least bit trustworthy or defend even modest claims to student autonomy. The University of California Regents and Administration for example, have placed responsible student leadership in this country in a position analogous to that of the N.A.A.C.P. Cooperation with the administration is itself a rather suspect activity, and finkhood has become an ascribed, rather than an achieved, status of those who work within the system.

Participation in genuine political conflict undoubtedly contributes more to maturity—at least for those who survive—than the more sheltered, restricted, and self-restricted activities of U.S.N.S.A. can. As Frank Musgrove has stressed in his recent *Youth and the Social Order,*[4] our resolute and, I should say, hostile determination to exclude youth from any real share of power in the social order they are called upon to defend and maintain infantilizes them; adults, and school personnel particularly, then use their immaturity as an excuse for further immobilizing them. "Responsible" is a favorite adjective among deans and other officials who assume jurisdiction over youth; in fact, they punish real responsibility and seek, insofar as possible, to deny the young any occasion to practise it. Youth should be commended and supported in its social and political commitments, not obstructed, harassed, and imprisoned. Nevertheless, excessive commitment to political action also seems to me to be damaging. Even the fully adult ought to avoid centering their lives on the quest for power in a complex, egalitarian society; it is just this quest, after all, which has made administrative officials the kind of people that youth is coming, quite properly, to loathe. It is so difficult to gain much power in the American social system without becoming personally contemptible that the risk probably should not be taken while young.

In stating this I am, of course, going directly counter to the liberal view that the only way to improve politics, public, corporate, or academic, is to get good people into it. Politics and sex, it is held, are dirty only because people think they are and higher-minded individuals contribute to their debasement by their reluctance to plunge into them without reserve. This seems to me naïve. Neither is naturally dirty, but both become so when society is organized in such a way that you have to deceive, flatter, and exploit weak, helpless, and often uncomprehending people in order to make out with them. Our society is like this, and for reasons so basic that I do not think they can be remedied by application of the processes of reconstruction that have been built into it. Since revolution does not appeal to me on the basis of its previous record, and is certainly not a responsibility to be imposed on the young, the alternative seems to me to be to emphasize private, personal, and particularistic relationships—I follow E. M. Forster on this, too—and regard political action as an essential, highly skilled, but specialized activity like meat-packing. People who share this attitude with me are, it is true, less likely to be permitted to withdraw from the political process than they are to end up as meat, and this is why I like them to be both amateurs and tough.

This preference for the private sphere commits me to take a different attitude toward civil liberties than toward civil rights, which is yet another obstacle to my identification with the more progressive contemporary student groups. Both they and I, to be sure, support both civil liberties and civil rights, but they usually seem to believe that the two are so related that actions which advance the cause of one also advance the cause of the other, and that it is therefore not necessary to consider seriously that in any particular case a gain in one may be costly to the other. Since in practice there is usually such a conflict, in practice a choice must be made; and these youngsters usually put civil rights first. I am personally more concerned about civil liberty, though I cannot always allow myself to be guided by this preference.

External reality, among other things, is a more important determinant of alternatives than personal preference. As a Southerner, for I still feel myself to be that for whatever honor or guilt attaches, and in the South, I would strongly favor civil rights; their abuse is simply the more crucial problem. Moreover, the Southern authorities have themselves abandoned civil liberty in order to protect its violators and sometimes murder its defenders; and in such a situation civil liberty can only be retrieved by a firm establishment of civil rights, and disestablishment of the delinquent authorities.

Nevertheless, the issue raised by many reluctant though non-violent white Southerners, that the advance of civil rights will curtail their previous freedom of association and lead to intrusion upon cherished and formerly private areas of human interaction, seems to me perfectly valid. This will occur, and a valuable and distinctive intimacy will be lost from Southern life. Well, let it go. One cannot allow Negroes to be treated as they have been treated in this country for a century, even if they would permit it. Justice is not always a higher value than intimacy; but when the injustice has become so great, and the quality of the intimacy so poor, justice is obviously more important. So, all honor to the kids who march to Montgomery. They love freedom, and they are building a great Freeway, binding the concrete with their own freely given blood. They are right to do it, but they are being a little less than candid about what Freeways do to the surrounding countryside. It isn't all good.

In less desperate circumstances, where the existing roads are not so narrow and sunken, and the forests, though private and enclosed, are responsibly-tended and kept free of bandits, the choice is more evenly balanced, and harder to make. Where it hinges on race it is easy enough to make since the concept of race is itself absurd and there is no benefit whatever to be derived from making distinctions on an absurd basis, however traditional it may be. Where it hinges on social class, and thus serves to perpetuate the consequences of earlier injustice, the choice is particularly hard; but I sometimes make it in a manner contrary to that of a civil rightist. The difficulty—one might almost say paradox—is that generally speaking the lower one's status and hence the more desperately one needs civil rights as guarantees, the more likely one is to be an enemy of civil liberties. Consider the roots of Senator McCarthy's support; consider the British constituency in which a working-class electorate recently went Conservative, thereby unseating an incumbent who had been slated for a cabinet post under Mr. Wilson, because the Conservatives campaigned in favor of restricting West Indian immigration. Consider particularly the favorable position of academic freedom both for faculty and students in well-established private universities in this country as compared to State universities. There is not much difference in the by-laws and procedures under which these institutions operate; none is ultimately governed by its faculty or students and most have fairly reliable provisions for tenure. But there is a great difference in the degree to which such institutions feel themselves to be subject to the popular will, and to the degree that they are so subject, liberty is assumed to be curtailed. Everything mean, petty, or constrictive that occurs in the University of California, from cheap and ugly architecture and inadequate travel grants to regulation of student expression, is justified on the grounds that Sacramento would insist on it. Perhaps it would; it was certainly the Governor, in his official capacity, who ordered the arrest of the protesting students who sat in Sproul Hall last year. He is governor of the whole state, yet I doubt that his commitment to law and order would have made him feel obligated—or even free—to do the same thing at Stanford. Conversely, we have by now forgotten that Stanford students at this very period managed to defend their liberty and get rid of an offensive group of deans without creating such a fuss—largely, I feel sure, because their style was more controlled and their administration had more respect for them and had built this respect into their system.

Students in America are rarely treated with this respect; both in high school and college they almost always find themselves in the custody of officials who oscillate between trying to win their good will and betraying their confidence in order to retain that of the public which supports and controls the institution. This, I believe, is why American youngsters assume that civil liberties and civil rights are, if not identical, coterminous. The public, by and large, has no respect for either; it has been repeatedly demonstrated, as in the Stouffer report[5] and, among high school students themselves in Remmers' survey,[6] that the Bill of Rights would not stand a chance if these constitutional amendments had to be submitted for adoption today. Those students who do become concerned about personal freedom have, like their peers, spent all their formative years in the hands of adults who impartially deny them both civil rights and civil liberties, and may never have experienced any privacy or sense of their own dignity and right to freedom from intrusion. Having dealt with this issue at length both in my two books and in three of the papers included in this collection—"The Modern High School; a Profile," "An Ideology of School Withdrawal," and "The Image of the Adolescent Minority"—I shall not expatiate further here. Things may get a little better; *The New York Times* last winter carried a series of prominent and sympathetic reports on the fate of a fifteen-year-old Connecticut boy, Edward T. Kores, Jr., whose parents finally enrolled him in a private school they could ill-afford because they were facing prosecution for contributing to his truancy after the public school had suspended him for refusing to get a regulation haircut that they would not force upon him. The Connecticut Civil Rights Commission refused them a hearing, which proves that it, at least, understood the difference between civil liberties and civil rights; but I doubt that its action helped to clarify the distinction for Edward Kores, Jr., himself. But the kind of regulation he objected to is common in American high schools today, and if, as educational officials usually maintain, this is an inevitable expression of the democratic will, then only youngsters who have been partially sheltered from its expression by a position of comparative privilege are likely even to become aware that they have any civil liberties to defend. Mr. Kores, Sr., is, to be sure, not an executive but a carpenter—the history of Christianity suggests, however, that these have always been given to rebellion on matters of principle. It has gotten pretty hard these days, though, to find a good carpenter when you need one.

Nevertheless, the Kores made the news, and this is a somewhat hopeful sign. I am not, however, reassured by the response that beleaguered educational administrations are now choosing to make to the wholesome scent of rebellion in the air. We hear a great deal nowadays about the trouble being that schools are too big and impersonal—which they are—and the need for better communication between faculty, administration, and students. We hear that faculties contribute heavily to student discontent and create a sense of abandonment because they devote themselves to their research and publication instead of to their students. This is true, and important enough to be worth examining; but I doubt if the remedy is necessarily to make institutions more personal. They are too personal already; it is bad enough having a friend at Chase Manhattan and the devoted service of the Internal Revenue Service without having the dean and the faculty be a pal to your boy as well. I wish they could be, but this has to wait, not just till schools can be made smaller, but till different kinds of people choose academic careers for different reasons than they usually do now. The basic intent is still to control the young and prevent them from becoming a threat to good public relations, rather than to cherish them and further their growth. Small, personal, clinically sophisticated prisons are even worse than huge, impersonal ones; and the same, I fear, is true of schools if their major function is to recruit personnel for an industrial bureaucracy and maintain the existing state of order.

Even feeling as I do about students, I sometimes enjoy writing more than teaching: though not if I have a class of attentive, quarrelsome students who have participated enough in their culture to understand what I am talking about. But I rarely do, and current trends in both the demographic climate of the schools and colleges and in the way the educative process has come to be defined make it less and less likely that I will. Precisely because of the growing burden of the "disadvantaged" there is an increased emphasis on teaching technic: on getting students who see no sense in school to stay there long enough to learn a body of skills that may never mean much to them but will make them useful to somebody else. A major part of this usefulness lies in acquiring a credential that will reassure prospective employers that the candidate has been fully socialized—they don't know enough about what they want him to do to really worry about competence and, in my area, sociology, real competence would frighten many of them. The student-teacher relationship, of which so much is suddenly to be demanded, has become in most cases a tacit agreement that neither party will disturb the other in pursuing his career, since both need the *form* of the institution in order to do it: the student needs a corporate body empowered to grant his degree and an active and competent placement service; the teacher needs a corporate employer to sign his grant applications and administer the funds with which these provide him. Under these circumstances, the real satisfaction is bound to shift more and more to the research the grant makes possible, which has now often become the more honest part of the job. "Publish or perish?" How difficult it would be to choose, if one really had to make such a choice. Vital—or more precisely, mortal—statistics suggest that the alternative is not, however, quite correctly stated. Publish, rather, that one may perish in good conscience; and always with awareness that a deadline is properly so-called.

1. New York: McGraw-Hill, 1964.
2. New York: Harcourt Brace, 1951.
3. New York: Macmillan, 1959.
4. Bloomington, Indiana, Indiana University Press, 1965.
5. S. A. Stoffer, *Communism, Conformity and Civil Liberties* (New York: Doubleday, 1955).
6. H. H. Remmers, ed. *Anti-Democratic Attitudes in American Schools* (Evanston, Northwestern University Press, 1963).

Truth: Upper, Middle and Lower

Truth surely is complex, but there is one dimension of truth that is especially useful in distinguishing among the different approaches to conviction that occur most frequently at different social class levels. This is the dimension that we sometimes call "subjective-objective"; it has to do with whether truth is thought to be primarily an aspect of inner experience, unique and essentially incommunicable, or whether it is thought rather to lie in consensus, and to consist primarily of what all honest and technically qualified observers can agree on.

Common sense tells us, to be sure, that no one can hope to live through the day unless he accepts both kinds of truth as valid. Yet, it makes a profound difference to the total personality and to the meaning one finds in life itself whether the subjective or the objective approach to the world predominates; or whether, to speak in more fundamental terms, one's sense of who one is in relation to the rest of the universe is felt to depend ultimately on one's inner qualities, or on one's dexterity and precision in responding to observable features of the environment.

Of course, we must all rely on both, and with the exception of a small number—these, at least, do not constitute a group—of schizophrenics, we all do. But most people find that one approach—the subjective or the objective—tends rather consistently to make them feel calmer, stronger, and better defined, while the other tends to make them feel more anxious and vulnerable. Pressed by circumstances, any of us might go against his inclination, but it is difficult to imagine Baudelaire or Beckett serving as Chairman of a Committee on Political Arrangements, or Dale Carnegie in solitary confinement scratching a poetic masterpiece into the walls of his cell. Each of us develops a pretty stable tendency to see the truth primarily as internal and subjective—though meaningful, of course, only in relation to external realities; or as primarily empirical and verifiable—though subject, of course, to much mutability and bias.

Generally speaking, the subjective approach appears to be more congenial to and commonly found among members of the extreme social classes—both upper and lower—while objectivity is more frequently the posture congenial to members of the middle classes. It should astonish no one to find greater similarity between upper- and lower-class individuals in this respect than between either of them and middle-class individuals. This is no novel insight; carried to extremes it constitutes the familiar D. H. Lawrence postulate in literature, in which the rich and mighty hold the poor to be somewhat more spontaneous, more tender, and more real than the legions of middling functionaries who are engulfing them. This point of view, perhaps best illustrated in contemporary life by the Ginsberg howl and the truculent assumption that one cannot read poetry, let alone write it, in a Brooks Brothers suit, is often applied very sentimentally. Like all sentimentality it can lead to incredible brutality; as in the infatuation of many Germans of high status with the sleek, violent, proletarian irrationality—as they saw it—of early Nazism. But there is a core of truth in this perception, nevertheless.

Take, for example, attitudes toward alcohol. Physiologically one of the most harmless of drugs, it owes its appeal to its power to weaken and depress the objective—that is, the critical, the rational, the judging and calculating—components of mental life, giving much freer scope to the subjective. The emotions alcohol releases may not be pleasant or comely; the behavior to which they lead may be seriously antisocial. But people who like to drink like it because it makes *their* feelings seem more important to them, in comparison to the rest of reality. For the moment, they don't mind doing what they really feel like doing, or they mind it less. They are less cautious. Fine discrimination, motor coordination—logical acuity—such powers as these are impaired. On the other hand, flashes of wisdom and insight—even perceptions of reality previously blocked by anxiety—which the sober individual would never permit himself may break through to him while he is drunk.

In upper class and in lower class, people may take alcohol or leave it. It is generally regarded as an amenity both by gentlemen who wish to indulge themselves euphorically at dinner after a day they are rather proud of, and by those who, in their destitution, must try to sleep on a subway platform and see no profit in being needlessly aware of their condition. A minority dislike alcohol and avoid it; it floods them with feelings they find uncomfortable; or it blunts perceptions that they would rather use to make their own poetry fresh—these are the heroes who enjoy taking reality straight. But people in lower class and in upper class are very unlikely to *disapprove* of drinking or to regard it as, of itself, a problem. The unguarded moment, the missed opportunity, the danger of being a public spectacle, the future sacrificed to momentary pleasure—these are not what upper- and lower-class people fear.

Middle-class people do. For them, there is little *veritas* in *vino.* Their kind of truth is something to be stalked, captured, and appraised. Their churches condemn rum from the pulpit at lower levels, or accept alcoholism as a problem for group therapy and rehabilitation at slightly higher ones. They mean no insult to the Christ in taking Holy Communion from sanitary thimble-cups of grape juice; this is their way of assuring Him that they are worthy of His help, because they always keep their eye on the ball. By keeping it there they reach higher status and, somewhat ironically, discover drinking among the status symbols they are teaching themselves to use; they find comfort in the slight loosening of constraint they gain from scotch or bourbon—once they are reasonably sure which drink is "in." But they know better than to lose control; if they nevertheless do, their most effective defense against guilt is to push their drunkenness over into the empirical sphere by regarding it as a symptom to be treated from a quasi-medical viewpoint.

Empiricism—indeed, science itself—is essentially middle class. As such, it has certainly a very long history; Adam and Eve were the first experimental scientists. Their results, which, true to the tradition they were about to found they immediately published and placed in the public domain, were so startling as to divert attention from the novelty of the process by which they had obtained them. Yet it was the process, rather than their findings, to which God objected. He had hoped to people Eden with a calmer and more inward race, able to take itself and its place in the world for granted. Finding Himself faced instead with an anxious and ambitious Jewish couple who believed that the clue to themselves lay in their relationship to the environment, He was obliged to create downward mobility, which has remained ever since the true anathema of the middle classes.

God having set his countenance against it, science did not really flourish or take on the institutional form that has become familiar until the Reformation, at which time He apparently consented to a number of alternative administrative arrangements. All of them had in common the consequence of opening the social order and turning man loose within it to rise or fall according to his wit and his conscience. Not all at once, of course, and certainly not equally. But this was the fundamental issue. One may approach the opening social order first as the rise of Protestantism, making each man his own priest, responsible for his own understanding of the Scriptures, encouraged and even obliged to master the skills—from literacy to accounting—that would make him master of the earthly destiny through which God might reveal he had pleased Him. One may approach it as the rise of capitalism, severing the connections between wealth and the time, place, and personal relationships in which it had been created—making wealth available elsewhere and at another time when it might be more efficiently employed by better businessmen. One may approach it as the rise of the national state: that guarantor of contracts and protector of commerce and property, the codifier and registrar of the impersonal agreements on which earthly expectations depend. Or one may approach it as the rise of the natural sciences, providing the method and the attitude through which one could work the natural world over with the confidence that one would learn how it operated and how to operate it, and predict with increasing accuracy what the results would be and make them increasingly the results that were wanted.

It would be fruitless to speculate as to which of these components of the sixteenth-century reorientation came first; but the growth of science is surely inconceivable apart from the simultaneous rise of a middle class able to profit by progress and of fiscal and governmental institutions able to insure the material future well enough to encourage investment. To a landed gentry or aristocracy, more effective mastery of the external world offered little promise of a better life, at least until other peoples' progress began to make it a military necessity. They were more likely to see it as a threat, and not only to their vested interests. The whole idea must have seemed uncouth and intrusive, a violation of nature both through manipulation and, more subtly, by altering completely what was held to be important about the natural.

Of course, many upper-class individuals were interested in science and favored its development; in sixteenth- and seventeenth-century England science was largely a rich man's toy. The Royal Society was founded by Charles the Second; its first presidents were Wren and Newton. But science has always been costly in equipment and education; and the point was that it *was* a toy, whose source of wonder and delight lay in its very objectivity, its intrusiveness and its outwardness and detachment. Francis Bacon, dying of pneumonia contracted while trying to freeze a chicken in a snowbank, is not a proper precursor of either Clarence Birdseye or modern cryoscopy. For the seventeenth-century intellectual, to look at the world he had always taken for granted through a telescope or a microscope was a novelty and a joy. But he could hardly have realized that he was participating as well in the beginning of an ethical and epistemological revolution; that the kind of truth whose novelty delighted him would quickly come to be regarded as truer than other kinds because it led to a profitable mastery of the environment and hence to a competitive advantage in life and ultimately to lifemanship as a technical specialty. Machiavelli so shocked the ruling Medici—though this was not easy—by treating the dynamics of government with scientific detachment that they placed him permanently on the Index Medicus and his name has ever since been, quite erroneously, taken as a synonym for political chicanery. Offense, however, was the furthest thing from his intention; he sincerely respected empirically effective political technique and was interested in the principles on which it might be based. Machiavelli was, quite simply, a professional political scientist before the social role existed. The Medici couldn't take him; capable of extremes of roguery, they were yet incapable of coolly plotting a course from general principles.

The most salient characteristic of the modern world, in contrast to that of four or five hundred years ago, is the range of activities and relationships that *are* now carried on by coolly plotting a course from general principles—empirical principles, that is, not ethical or doctrinal principles. Only this kind of approach could make a world efficient enough in a productive sense to begin to support its present and growing population. But the change has of itself done much to bring about a social and even a political revolution. The rise of empiricism, that is, has led to and has required a complete revision in the concept of authority. This is not a question of power and status, or of the kind of person who achieves it—the familiar spiral that has led from the gentleman or nobleman through the captain of industry to the executive. It is a question rather of authority in the sense of confidence and legitimation—of what we put ourselves through before we can feel reasonably sure of ourselves and of what we are doing.

The essence of scientific truth is that it is as general as possible. The test of it is that it works and works the same way no matter who is looking at it, assuming a certain high minimum of intelligence and technical competence. It is important that smallpox vaccination work with all kinds of people, including those who do not believe in it and whose moral convictions are violated by it. It is important that those whose vested interests, economic or characterological, lead them to deny a newly found scientific truth, be subject *in culture* to the discipline of a method which *tends,* at least, to make their biases ineffective. We have this, and we ought not to underestimate its value. The integrity, or even the intellectual honesty, of cigarette manufacturers does not matter much because science has the manufacturers by the short leaves. In our culture, there is no really effective answer to a clear, classical, conventional demonstration that an empirical relationship exists. The industry has been reduced to trying to fight science with other science; that is, to hiring scientists to prove scientifically that there is no demonstrable relationship between cigarette smoking and cancer. This is probably impossible to do effectively, because scientific integrity, in the sense of not falsifying data or suppressing them or drawing false inferences from them, is one of the kinds we have left. Scientists are honest about science, less out of a sense of principle than a sense of role. The ones who are willing to shave a few points don't, usually, have enough status to do their seducers any good.

The elders of an Indian village opposing modern methods of hygiene, or even the British peasant of fifty years ago opposing modern methods of agriculture, did not have to deal with this problem. It is not very threatening to be proved wrong unless your culture has indoctrinated you with respect for scientific proof. Only after other traditional sources of authority have abdicated in favor of empirical validation need conservatives claim to be *right.* They can claim rather that the meaning of life, as they have come to understand it, is more important to them than being right. The South, till the press of recent events exacerbated old fears, could generally manage to accept anthropology; a reasonably secure Southerner will admit very cheerfully that there are no grounds whatever for regarding Negroes as inferior to white people. It costs him nothing to do so, since he has never regarded his racial attitudes as conclusions from data.

The shift toward empirical dominance, then, has been a social and political as well as technological and epistemological shift. It has not only yielded—more abundantly than could possibly have been anticipated—the promised technical mastery of the environment. It has led into positions of mastery those who have most effectively committed themselves to an empirical posture toward all experience—who have either silenced their inner voice or taught it, when a choice must be made, to defer to the facts and to the kind of reality which can be treated factually. "How many divisions has he got?" Stalin asked of the Pope, and we are shocked—not at his contempt for moral authority, but at his administrative naïveté. This is the sort of mistake a power politician just doesn't make.

It is not so much that the shift to empirical dominance has made conditions especially propitious politically for those untroubled by inner doubts and undistracted by the meaning of their own experience. This has always been true, for power is always largely an empirical problem. What is more significant is that the authoritative roles and statuses have come to be defined in empirical terms and to arouse empirical expectations. The bad guy, we really feel, is the man who rocks the boat. Such people, under any system, are regarded as irritating and dangerous; what seems to me new is our conviction that they are *out of role,* sick, egocentric. When they do win—rare as this is—it is usually because their superordinates, righteous in their empiricism, simply could not take them seriously at all.

They don't win, though, very often; and when they do, they have perhaps a certain impact on the structure in which they are operating, but usually none on the assumptions on which it rests. Their victory is attributed to their bosses having underestimated their empirical competence; they were better operators than they got credit for. They made a shrewder estimate than expected of their chances for victory. That they may have had to behave as they did for internal reasons, quite apart from the probability that they might influence the outer world effectively, is no longer really believed.

Much that we call anti-intellectualism in the modern world is really anti-subjectivism. Nobody seems disgruntled about the intellectual activities of engineers, or physicians, or scientists as long as they do not involve themselves in the value-consequences of their work. What is feared and avoided is really the intellectual activity of humanists, who still depend to some extent on internal validation to give them confidence in what they say. Poets, composers, novelists—essayists, perhaps, even more since they are invading a field now thought to belong properly to the empiricists—find themselves trapped in a noose-like circularity. Nobody can listen to them until they demonstrate their empirical *kashrut* by becoming successful; and since of course they cannot become successful until people listen to them, they depend to a large degree, I am afraid, on blind luck to even get started.

If nothing succeeds like success, then the successful become the only power elite; and the empirical knowledge that brings success drives all other knowledge out of the market. *Noblesse,* certainly, cannot *oblige* if the noble are too poor to meet their obligations and have too little status to influence anybody else to meet theirs. Yet, all this has a Gresham's Law type of effect, for empirical knowledge is, in some ways, worse knowledge and cheaper knowledge than the kind that it replaces. Its very scorn of inwardness and subjectivity makes it, by definition, finally unconvincing; one is not even allowed to raise the question of conviction about it—to doubt that which has been, for all practical purposes, proved. "One can be practical even in Hell," says Lavinia in *The Cocktail Party.* One can be practical *especially* in Hell. Indeed, there is nothing else left to be. Elsewhere, and earlier, there are alternatives: to be generous, to be extravagant, to be affectionate, to be lazy, to be oneself.

Hell is not Hell for demons; they live there. It is the environment to which they are adjusted, and which offers them greatest opportunity for growth, advancement, and fruitful interdemoniacal relationships. But it is Hell precisely for those from above who must regard their presence there as evidence that their self-betrayal was more serious than they had feared, and not merely a temporary expedient. The self-betrayal of the Western upper classes has been, on the whole, very thoroughgoing, and their characteristic perception of truths has largely been sacrificed. Few indeed are gentlemen—in our culture, perhaps, there is a large proportion of ladies—with the inner serenity and strength to go on believing they are right even when they lose; that their own inner sense of validity, if self-consistent, is an adequate source of norms. There are still a few such, as there have been for years, in the State Department, which is perhaps not the safest place to keep them; but for the most part, today's upper-status individual uses his status in order to run the middle-class show according to middle-class rules.

Lower-status individuals are exposed to less temptation than upper-status individuals; their souls are not thought to be worth as much and they receive fewer and poorer offers. What happens to them depends, naturally, on whether they nevertheless accept one of these offers. Most do; they settle down, that is, into the working-class routine of life, which can best be tolerated if one learns to make a virtue of monotony. It is easy to forget that a plurality of those who share the urban Western world spend one-third of their lives doing noisy, repetitive, uncomfortable work at a rate they do not choose and toward ends that they cannot usually really envision. In the rest of their lives they insist equally on discipline and familiarity. Children are expected to be obedient, wives chaste; the TV runs in its accustomed channels.

For such people the test of an experience or a proposition is likely to be its conventionality. Subjectivity would be suicidal; a high level of sensitivity to external reality would be equally so. These people cannot afford to open their senses or their hearts to new perceptions or new sensations. If they ever become simultaneously sensitive to reality and aware of its possibilities, they are done for. Their routines prevent their being overwhelmed with rage, envy, and despair; undoubtedly, under our economic system, the continuous seductive din of the mass media requires that those who cannot afford to join the safari to suburbia develop a very high threshold of irritability or lose their self-esteem. Insensitivity, indeed, is hardly enough; the razor strop still protects the authoritarian father, fatigued from his day on the assembly line, from children who wish to have the blandishments of TV commercials translated into reality.

Social psychologists disagree as to whether working-class authoritarianism is genuinely rooted in character or is largely an adaptive response to a highly constrictive situation. There is not much doubt about the data; these are indeed the people who go down the line with the items on the F-scale, whip their children for the kind of sex play which induces a frozen paroxysm of permissiveness in middle-class parents, and who worshiped Senator McCarthy until his behavior began to lose its veneer of conventionality under the glare of TV and the masterful direction of Mr. Welch. There is also not much doubt that a middle-class father who threw his weight around as much as a working-class father generally does would be a lot sicker in general; so would a middle-class mother who bought the same jolly greeting cards of fat red Santas and cute little teddy bears. But hostility to novelty, wit, and taste in the sense of a flexible perception and response to the individual qualities of materials, situations, and persons may be real and intense without being psychopathological. The working-class individual is most easily convinced by what is least disturbing to the order to which he has submitted. If disturbed, nevertheless, he is likely to withdraw or to turn nasty.

But what of those who spurn all meager offers for their souls and receive no generous ones, who are absorbed and preoccupied with the exigencies and the satisfactions of daily living under conditions that make it very difficult and often useless to try to plan for more than a day at a time—conditions that, *faute de mieux,* encourage spontaneity? These exist—the true lower class below the working class. Its members are not as numerous as those of the working class, though one reads more about them in the papers, and their colorful, violent lives tend to overshadow the short, simple, gray annals of the decent poor. But nearly a sixth of our population is truly lower class, even though our ideology of comfort and success tends to treat them as exceptional. So, indeed, they very often are.

In today's affluent society, a reasonable degree of social mobility from lower class is very easily achieved; indeed, it is the norm rather than the exception. In order to stay in lower class today one must either be committed to and absorbed in it as a way of life, or have a personality that either makes one entirely rigid in the face of any prospect of change or arouses such hostility in the rest of society as to excite continual punishment. That is, one must either be beat, a virtual psychotic, or a delinquent or criminal. Otherwise, one can expect to be picked up and wafted upward a certain distance merely by the technological shift that is doing away with manual labor and simple clerical work, and by the refinements of an economy that can only keep going during peacetime if nearly everybody consents to share in the rudiments of gracious living. Economic convection is not going to carry anybody quite to the top, but it does easily land people in lower-middle unless they are so oddly shaped that they break the flow.

The beat, the psychotic, and the criminal all tend to be highly subjective; they are idiotic, in the classical Greek sense. And all these types are relatively abundant in lower class. Drifters and criminals are lower class almost by definition, while psychosis is the form that severe mental disturbance takes in lower-class in preference to middle-class psychoneurosis; the lower-class individual, beset by unbearable experience, finds reality not worth distorting and abandons it. This statement is in no sense meant as derogation of the lower class or its members. "Beats" and psychotics can be just as nice as anyone and often much nicer. So may criminals; it is not necessarily a sin to commit a crime. But all these people tend to be idiotic, and, while (using Rebecca West's distinction) I much prefer idiocy—overabsorption in and preoccupation with one's private world—to lunacy—irrational subjugation to external influences—which is the official disorder of the middle classes, idiocy still has its limitations.

The worst thing about the idiotic way of life is that it just cannot be generalized at all. It is not merely that it does not teach those who live it general propositions that can be applied to other people and places. It cannot even lead to a sense of calm, inner coherence; an idiot cannot learn by experience. Idiocy at its best—that is saintly, or Dostoevskian idiocy—can lead to something else of exquisite value, to moments of truth so penetrating and luminous that the rest of life is brightened by them. But these moments cannot be ordered; one cannot speak of a series of moments of truth since there is nothing serial about them. To be valuable, idiocy must be complemented and restrained by another sort of subjectivity: by artistic discipline, which is a respect for the actual properties of one's medium, whether that medium be a musical instrument, or a medium of communication, or simply oneself in one's social role. If one is to grow, one cannot simply feel and act out. One has to feel what the *inherent* possibilities are—an entirely different matter from the operator's preoccupation with what the external consequences may be.

The lower-class individual today does not usually have enough sense of the stable properties of life to temper his subjectivity. Unlike the middle-class man, he can still listen to his inner voice, and he knows no better source of truth. But he has no basis for telling when it is talking nonsense, or for tuning it out when it is jabbering away incoherently about the miscellaneous agonies of the past and present. Education would help with this, but we have no lower-class education—only a system by which lower-class youngsters who want to can be admitted to lower-middle-class schools.

Lower-class truth is likely, therefore, to remain even in adulthood quite purely idiotic. Like upper-class truth, it is essentially subjective. But it is much weaker in its sense of time. It is weaker in its sense of causality. Above all, it is deficient in symbols, so that there are almost no possibilities of abstraction. The result at its worst is the *Lumpen*-proletarian, whose passion is merely violence and whose love is merely lust, who is lost and helpless in a mechanical world where the machinery is hardly ever right out where you can see it. To the lower-class man, this can be destiny.

Still, in the terminology of Norman Mailer and his co-workers, he is hip rather than square; so, perhaps there is hope for him. His problem is to learn to order his experience, and to do so without turning it into a set of maxims or reducing it to purely instrumental terms. The most blatantly and continuously advertised rewards, however, become available to him only if he does just this; so those lower-class individuals who notice the larger world are peculiarly tempted to surrender to it. Can many survive to become a modern Villon or a Colin Wilson, without making a commercial production out of being an outsider? It seems unlikely. Poverty and low status in the twentieth century are dangerous drugs, containing within them, perhaps, the seeds of delivery for some; but for most people they are, in truth, far more destructive in their effects than is alienation under comfortable circumstances.

More hopeful, it seems to me, is the growing middle-class tendency to insist on more variety and on uniqueness. This is not only a discernible, but a conspicuous social trend; if I am a little skeptical that it will soon have fundamental consequences, it is because I believe that the security to trust inwardness must ordinarily be developed early, in a home and family life that puts no undue emphasis on other persons' expectations. Can one really internalize the pragmatic? Can one come to feel that tentative solutions to the problems of a shifting universe are not only real and trustworthy, but one's own?

Well, some can, some do.

People do grow in the suburbs as well—or nearly as well—as elsewhere. The better sort of modern suburbanite may actually be a genuine follower of John Dewey, creating new knowledge out of open-ended experience and making it not only his own but a part of himself. And at this he had better be very good indeed. The future, as one of the most perceptive contemporary exegetical critics of modern empiricism has stated in the title of one of his best works, lies ahead.

1960

Neo-Freudianism and Erich Fromm

Of all the psychoanalytic theorists who have tried to formulate a system better suited than Freud's to problems of contemporary life, none has been more productive or influential than Erich Fromm. No psychoanalytic thinker approaches him in the power or consistency of his effort to apply the values and insights that derive from his position as a therapist to major social and political issues, from the nature of human liberty in general to the prevention of atomic disaster in particular. Fromm has had no medical training; this is perhaps one reason why his approach to the neurotic personality in a sick society has been moral and committed, rather than detached and empirical. The texture of his thought is really more like that of Martin Buber than of Freud.

Fromm has become to a degree both the conscience of the psychoanalytic movement and its most articulate and consistent advocate of social policy. Nevertheless, and surprisingly, he cannot really be said to have become a controversial figure. Disagreement and sometimes snide criticism there have certainly been,[1] as well as occasional complaints by classical Freudians that Fromm is either really repeating what Freud has already said—as, of course, anybody writing about psychoanalysis often must—or is wrong. But there has been rather less of this sort of thing than so prominent a lay analyst might expect; especially in view of his great and sustained success as a popular writer.

Yet, it is not so simple to pin down exactly where his uniqueness lies. Fromm is not a great creator of systematic doctrine. He has been notable rather for his continued assertion, in a variety of contexts, of a few fundamental moral ideas drawn from and supported by his experience as a psychoanalyst. These moral ideas are of fundamental and immediate concern to all who share the modern, technically developed world; if, as Fromm maintains, man may prevail to create a better one, Fromm's influence and intellectual attraction might well diminish sharply. The sacrifice would be worth making.

To understand Fromm's *raison d'être,* both as a scholar and an institution, it is therefore even more necessary than usual to look at the social context in which his thought has developed and to ask what changes in the human condition since Freud's high period have made the neo-Freudian revision in general, and Fromm's version of it in particular, a practical necessity. Fromm was born in Frankfort in 1900; his first popular work, *Escape from Freedom* (called *The Fear of Freedom* in Britain) was published in 1941. It has been followed by *Man for Himself* (1947), the publication of his Terry Lectures on *Psychoanalysis and Religion* (1950), *The Sane Society* (1955), *The Art of Loving* (1956), *The Forgotten Language* (1957), *Sigmund Freud's Mission: An Analysis of His Personality and Influence* (1959), *Psychoanalysis and Zen Buddhism* (with Daisetz Suzuki and Richard de Martino, 1960), *Marx's Concept of Man* (1961), and, most recently, *May Man Prevail?* (1961).

The chronology alone is suggestive. America's malaise in the position of power and responsibility it has occupied since Pearl Harbor has become a cliché, but it is also a fact. These years, and those of the Great Depression that World War II, in true Marxian style, finally terminated, brought about the changes in social climate in the United States that made classical Freudianism seem obsolete and neo-Freudianism flourish. Erich Fromm shared these years with us. Having taken his Ph.D. at Heidelberg in 1922 and begun training at the Berlin Institute for Psychoanalysis in 1923, he returned to Frankfort and became associated in 1929 with the Psychoanalytic Institute and the Institute for Social Research of the University there. The Institute for Social Research is best known to Americans as the organization from which the leading German social scientists, driven into exile, ultimately came to America where they produced the landmark investigation of *The Authoritarian Personality*.[2] Fromm, however, came in 1933 in response to an invitation to lecture at the Chicago Institute of Psychoanalysis, and has remained in this country, occupying highly respected positions in the psychoanalytic institutes associated with the neo-Freudian schools of both Karen Horney and Harry Stack Sullivan. In 1951, he accepted a professorship in the Universidad Nacional Autónoma de México which he still holds, dividing his time between Mexico, Michigan State University, and short-term lecture courses at the New School for Social Research and New York University.

Fromm's personal experience with the remarkable moral potentialities of Western capitalist democracy not only includes participation—as a lifelong democratic socialist of no particular party affiliation—in the circumstances of German life that culminated in the rise of Nazism; it also includes participation in our own economic collapse and later reluctance to accept responsibility for our victories in terms more profound than those of nuclear dominance and resistance against Communism. His participation, moreover, has remained sufficiently marginal to permit him to look at his world somewhat as if he were down there on a visit. No social scientist has been more outspoken politically than Fromm, especially in his most recent work and pronouncements. But his capacity to consider social and economic trends in the light of their humanistic consequences seems to have made Fromm especially perceptive of their concreteness. Hitler and McCarthy were not only totally loathsome to him; they were the predictable consequences of the social and psychological trends that constituted his central concerns and the basis for his life work. Fromm, unlike most of Hitler's and McCarthy's potential victims, attached sufficient importance to what they threatened to gain foresight; he saw them coming, and had established a defensible base elsewhere before they arrived. This is to his credit; yet in reading Fromm, as in reading Buber, one is sometimes a little troubled by a feeling that the psychological and moral systems they have erected—though noble and complex—suffer a certain loss of authority and detail of feeling from their comparative exclusion from the tragic events of our time.

Fromm's basic patterns of thought are intensely Jewish;[3] he himself remained Orthodox to the age of twenty-six. Specifically, his central concern is with the social and psychological processes in human beings that destroy their productivity; and with the alternative ways in which people might grow if society gave them a fair chance to become capable of love and productive life. He is, however, justifiably skeptical of both the power and the inclination of secular authority to further the ends of love and human justice, and for this reason has been a consistent and vocal opponent of Zionism, which he sees as a most unfavorable exchange of moral authority for secular power.

The waste of human potentiality under the social and economic conditions of modern life is a common theme to the neo-Freudians, as is the conception that more benign social arrangements are possible.[4] The new social arrangements envisaged are, at least implicitly, more liberal, though the neo-Freudians vary greatly in their degree of explicit concern with social institutions. My own choice for the greatest of the neo-Freudians, Harry Stack Sullivan, sticks close to the clinical context in his writings, though his *Interpersonal Theory of Psychiatry* and other work makes it clear that he attributes failures in individual development to the eclipse of genuine interpersonal relations by anxiety. For Sullivan, what he calls "arrest of development" is then also a failure in socialization; though he never presents as Fromm and Horney did a typology of such failures that—like Fromm's "receptive," "exploitative," "hoarding," and "marketing" orientations of character—can be attributed to specific institutional traits of our society.

But it is here that a subtle yet crucial issue begins to separate Freudian thought from that of the neo-Freudians, and perhaps of Fromm most of all. The issue also explains, I believe, why the chronology of Erich Fromm's life and publication has had a great deal to do with his success. It is hard to imagine that, prior to 1941, many Americans would have seen Fromm's thoughts as relevant to any very serious problems we faced. During the depression, by and large, we did not take any form of psychoanalytic thought to have serious social implications, but tended to dismiss it as a rich man's toy. Whatever defects of character the rich might have, the poor were seen simply as the victims of their failure, as healthy and even noble, but betrayed. Chatterley may have been a neurotic; Mellors was a natural man. The Joads, surely, could never have had a daughter like Lolita.

World War II and its aftermath put an end to this sort of sentimentality, at least as an effective intellectual force. Nazism had its Thyssens, but it was clearly rooted in the hearts of the common people as well as of the rich and the bourgeoisie. In this country, racial hatreds, the paranoid suspicions aroused by the Communist label, and worst of all, the apathy and alienation with which many failed to respond to the destruction of their neighbors and of presumably cherished civil rights, made it very clear that people in general were not merely entrapped by wicked leaders in evil institutions, but had badly deteriorated in a captivity that had been imposed with their partial consent. The shoddiness and dominance of mass culture expressed an emptiness and hostility in which everyone was implicated.

Such grisly phenomena could hardly be explained by any theory of individual psychopathology. They required, instead, a kind of psychology which retained its psychodynamic character: its concern with the effect on individual growth, in all its complexity and uniqueness, of ubiquitous social conditions. Here Fromm's conception (as stated in *The Sane Society*) of the "socially patterned defect" is essential:

> There is, however, an important difference between individual and social mental illness, which suggests a differentiation between two concepts; that of *defect*, and that of *neurosis*. If a person fails to attain freedom, spontaneity, a genuine expression of self, he may be considered to have a severe defect, provided we assume that freedom and spontaneity are the objective goals to be attained by every human being. If such a goal is not attained by the majority of members of any given society, we deal with the phenomenon of *socially patterned de-*

> *fect.* The individual shares it with many others; he is not aware of it as a defect, and his security is not threatened by the experience of being different, of being an outcast, as it were. What he may have lost in richness and in a genuine feeling of happiness, is made up by the security of fitting in with the rest of mankind—*as he knows them.* As a matter of fact, his very defect may have been raised to a virtue by his culture, and thus may give him an enhanced feeling of achievement.

This paragraph seems to me to be the cornerstone of Fromm's position. What all his work deals with essentially is: (1) an appraisal of the loveless economic nexus that links modern men and of the Nessusary fabric of their social relationships; (2) an analysis of the psychodynamic impact of these relationships on individual growth toward the goals of freedom and spontaneity; and (3) more recently, an examination of certain factors in the current situation that might help us to achieve them, ranging from Zen Buddhism to disarmament and sanity in foreign policy. Fromm offers no panaceas and, indeed, no systematic social theory; but he is consistent in his insistence that modern life makes it impossible to maintain love and disciplined spontaneity as common human experiences, and that deprivation of these causes such widespread deformation and stultification as may well lead us to put ourselves out of our misery and into that which the next war will leave in its place. In *May Man Prevail?* he offers specific and very sensible suggestions for political action intended to make peace and world preservation more likely, and he tries to pitch these suggestions at the modest level of sanity of which our society may still be capable.

Fromm adverts to the conflict between his thought and Freud's through much of his work as well, of course, as in *Sigmund Freud's Mission.* But I am not convinced that he ever gets to the bottom of it. The source of conflict may be approached by starting from the phrase in *The Sane Society* I have already quoted: "provided we assume that freedom and spontaneity are the objective goals to be attained by every human being." This assumption is absolutely central to Fromm's position; and I think Freud would have been sadly amused by it. The just old man who commented, after the storm troopers had despoiled his apartment in Vienna, that he himself would never have dared charge quite so much for a single professional visit, might have felt that it did not express his world view.

The difference between Freud and Fromm is not really a disagreement, but a different moral reaction to the nature of society. And both may be right, because the moral relation of the individual to society did in fact change crucially in the two generations that separated them. Freud at eighty could face the storm troopers secure in the conviction, built up over a lifetime of hard struggle, that man and society are two tough adversaries who can still respect each other's dignity. The Nazis must have seemed to him a contemptible, though not an astonishing, aberration. Fromm, at thirty-five, would have known that Freud was extrapolating the 19th century too far. The Nazis were not an aberration; there was no longer anything effective in Germany, and not much in Western culture, to which they might be scornfully contrasted. They were not an aberration; they were a miscarriage.

Freud would not have assumed that freedom and spontaneity are the objective goals to be attained by every human being, because he had already made the prior assumption that these values are *partially* mortgaged under the terms of the social contract that is presumed to safeguard the individual in his enjoyment of the residue of freedom and spontaneity left him. This is the central theme of *Civilization and Its Discontents.* In this respect, Freud is a pure Hobbesian. But if a state of nature provides no arts, no letters, no society, and, what is worst of all, continual fear and danger of violent death, and the life of man is solitary, poor, nasty, brutish, and short; then how shall we describe the contrasting civilization of Auschwitz?

A cheerful but not an optimistic man, Freud was certainly under no illusion that society or, indeed, reality is benign. He takes no position in *Civilization and Its Discontents* as to whether the game is worth the candle; he merely points out that it cannot be played in the dark and the individual must pay what the candle costs. His toughly compassionate reservations about using psychoanalysis to treat working-class patients suggest that he felt that, for most individuals, the candle really did cost more than the game would be worth; and that people who in reality had very little opportunity to lead richer lives might better be left with their defenses and illusions. Freud knew that the social contract was too hard a bargain for most of the people who were subject to it, and that they would have very little freedom and spontaneity left after meeting its terms. What he may not quite have grasped as Fromm did, was that we had entered an era in which society was dominated by people whose sense of self is so weak that they cannot be trusted to keep even those bargains that are grossly to their advantage; so that no social contract is possible.

This explains, I think, why it is so difficult to respond to Fromm's assumption with freedom, spontaneity, and joy of one's own. We do not make this assumption freely ourselves; we come to it as to a counsel of despair. Freedom, spontaneity, and a genuine feeling of self are not goals, and none become redder of tooth and claw than those who pursue them as if they were. They are—as Fromm, of course, emphasizes throughout his work—conditions, attributes, consequences; not the ends of growth and love, but the evidence that the processes of growth and love are going along reasonably well. In a society that establishes conditions in which they go conspicuously badly one struggles in agony to achieve them, just as respiration rate rises dramatically during a heart attack, in an effort to compensate for the inability of the blood stream to carry oxygen to the tissues by forcing more oxygen into the blood.

This is not meant as a criticism of Fromm's position, but as an explanation of the insuperable difficulties it faces; and also of one reason why his work does not seem to me as joyful or exuberant as Freud's is, in its own grim way; though its message is surely "be joyful or perish." Fromm does not underestimate the difficulties. His social criticism is radical; and it is certainly most appropriate and even perhaps helpful for a psychoanalyst deeply concerned with the failure of society to sustain growth and love to plan in some detail for a better one. His understanding of the plight of modern man seems to me nearly flawless. But I think he then reifies from his analysis of that plight the qualities that would be necessary to extricate man from it, even though we have got into it precisely because these qualities do not operate in the kind of situation we are in.

More specifically, I think, Fromm makes an unanswerable case for the existence in all men of very strong tendencies toward free and spontaneous growth; the same tendencies toward health, undoubtedly, that Carl Rogers and the client-centered therapists have found so dependably present in even the sickest patient when the therapeutic situation permits him to lower his defenses. Fromm is perfectly right in emphasizing that what is repressed into the unconscious and forced to manifest itself in sickness and in symbols is, in our culture, as likely to be the patient's most constructive and expansive tendencies as it is any impulse that he would be afraid or ashamed of. He is right in noting that the guilt against which we defend ourselves by repression is today more likely to be the existential guilt of having betrayed our best selves than any fear we may have of our worst. Dr. Jekyll's problem is no longer Mr. Hyde, but the way he really feels about himself for going ahead and joining the AMA anyway.

The trouble is that when the social contract weakens or lapses, restrictive though it may have been, people cease to believe that doctors are *bound* to care for the sick, or stockbrokers to abstain from manipulating the market, or ethical drug manufacturers to manufacture drugs ethically. If they don't—well, that's the way the self crumbles. And under these circumstances, there is hardly a chance that freedom and spontaneity will come to be associated with a genuine sense of self. There is no reason to suppose that people are less honest than they used to be; this is merely one of the delusions associated with Goldwater fever. In fact, the rogue on a heroic scale has disappeared along with the other heroes, to be replaced by a collective administrative policy. But we do seem to be shiftier than people used to be; less able or less inclined to assume responsibility for the outcomes of the processes we take part in. The corporate form, the professional organization, and the committee are far more sophisticated and effective at concealing the reality of a decision than the blank cartridge traditionally placed in the musket of one member of a firing squad.

If we cannot trust our commitments to our social roles, we are thrown back upon ourselves as individuals; but our selves are weaker than they would have grown to be in a less shifty and impersonal social order. It has been rather widely noted by practicing analysts that, since the time of Freud, there has been a major change in the kind of difficulty that brings patients into therapy. There is now a much smaller proportion of hysterical or obsessive-compulsive neuroses, and a much larger proportion of what are called "character disorders." What this means, among other things, is that a far larger proportion of Freud's patients than of those of a contemporary analyst felt their symptoms to be ego-alien; felt, that is, that they had a self of their own to which the symptoms were alien. They came to Freud to have their real self restored, and this is what he undertook. Their paralyzed leg, their terror of horses, their impotence were somehow *not like them at all.* They were, of course, deceiving themselves, and could only be helped by being brought to face their own deceptions. But the point is that they had a self to deceive—a self that was much more real to them than their symptoms, and whose life the symptoms had disturbed.

But a character-neurotic does not feel his problem to be the intrusion of the repressed upon an otherwise functional, established self. His whole life is a symptom; he is miserable, not because his symptoms make him so, but because they interfere with his perception of reality and keep him from getting the satisfactions he needs. He is not exactly fooling himself; his self is still immanent. This, to be sure, is exactly Fromm's point in noting that the character structure which develops in interaction with social institutions like ours suffers from its very incapacity for freedom, spontaneity, and love. Moreover, he is perfectly consistent in then seeking the roots of the difficulty in an unwholesome society, rather than attempting merely to treat the individuals who have been, and will continue to be, its victims.

But the sick society is, of course, an expression of the present needs, accommodations, concessions, and mutual arrangements of its victims in their present state; all there is to work with is what we are now. Fromm is right in maintaining that those who fear freedom, however numerous, are gravely ill and have usually been gravely mistreated. But this does not make it less likely that they will atrociously mishandle freedom. It makes it more likely.

This is a political issue of the first priority; though, perhaps, no question of fundamental policy is involved. I do not believe that one man or one social group "gives" freedom to another; morally, it is not his to give or withhold; and, practically, he usually does withhold it as long as he can profitably remain dominant—and no longer. What is presented as a decision to abdicate, or grant national sovereignty, or extend the franchise is usually a belated rationalization of social and economic changes that occurred some time before; there has been an interaction of social forces, but not a decision. Moreover, these forces bear no consistent relationship whatever to the moral issues involved or thought to be involved. Since the world is even now rational enough that people who have a great deal of anything which is difficult to get and hold on to usually must want it badly—the converse of this statement is emphatically false—then the power elites of most societies are quite probably even sicker than the people they dominate; since power over others and enormous wealth are not greatly coveted by healthy people. This reasoning tends to support the moral implications of Fromm's position, since even the sickest and most frightened or truculent slaves are likely to be more rational and healthier than those who would willingly have reduced them to such a condition.

Nevertheless, if a French restaurateur with a family business in Oran, or a white Southern bus driver were to complain to me that he had been feeling a little nervous lately, I think I should be inclined to sympathize. And I am not sure that I would recommend Erich Fromm's work to him in order to get him to look forward more enthusiastically to the joys of general liberation and spontaneity. Liberation and spontaneity are more valuable than anything else I could name; and more of them for one individual means more for all, rather than less, which is a desirable property in itself. But they can be very costly, too; especially if large increments of them come to be distributed in strange and unwieldy ways in a society that is unfamiliar with them in these particular forms.

Even morally—as well as practically—the restoration of freedom and growth is not a simple issue. For me, the perfect paradigm of Fromm's work is *The Tempest*. Many of his subtlest and most telling points are illustrated in Shakespeare's treatment of both character and incident. It is wholly Frommian, for example, that we should see Ariel as just as much a victim as Caliban; though Prospero thinks that he loves the one and hates the other, he uses both for his own purposes and permits neither his own freedom to develop. Ariel, in some ways, is worse off. For he knows that he wishes to be free but does not question even in his own mind Prospero's assertion that he is being treated lovingly. Caliban at least snarls back and plots revenge, though in his pathetic dependency and need for affection he sets the drunken Trinculo and his fellows up as objects of worship and mistakes his bondage to them for freedom from Prospero.

Explicit in *The Tempest* is the power of human love to resist enchantment and delusion—the healthy mortality of Ferdinand and Miranda, who are not really a very intelligent young couple, is enough in the end to induce Prospero to abjure magic in favor of rational authority; not for their sake but for his own. In the epilogue he can say: "Now my charms are all o'erthrown/And what strength I have's mine own," and return to Milan to claim his just heritage as Duke. *Rational authority*, in contrast to authority based on pretense, charisma, or intimidation, is a very positive concept on which Fromm places great emphasis. The power to distinguish and accept rational authority, based on the authoritative individual's actual competence and derived from his responsibility to use his competence for mutual social benefit, is for Fromm an important sign of maturity.

For just this reason, *The Tempest* seems to me to illustrate the limitations of Fromm's position, so far as it has yet evolved, as well as its subtlety and strength. For Caliban's tragedy is not really softened when the play ends. Prospero's magic is enough to enslave Caliban; but once he has done it his own reversion to rationality and growth cannot free Caliban again. Slavery and degradation are not reversible experiences.

The actual parallels are a bit too close to modern life for comfort:

> CALIBAN: This island's mine, by Sycorax my mother
> Which thou takest from me. When thou camest first,
> Thou strokedst me and madest much of me, wouldst give me
> Water with berries in't, and teach me how
> To name the bigger light, and how the less,
> That burn by day and night; and then I loved thee
> And showed thee all the qualities of the isle
> The fresh springs, brine-pits, barren place and fertile:
> Cursed be I that did so! . . .
> For I am all the subjects that you have
> Which first was mine own king: and here you sty me
> In this hard rock, whiles you do keep from me
> The rest o' the island.
>
> PROSPERO: Thou most lying slave,
> Whom stripes may move, not kindness! I have used thee,
> Filth as thou art, with human care, and lodged thee
> In mine own cell, till thou didst seek to violate
> The honour of my child.
>
> CALIBAN: O ho, O ho: would't had been done!
> Thou dids't prevent me; I had peopled else
> This isle with Calibans.
>
> PROSPERO: Abhorred slave,
> Which any print of goodness wilt not take,
> Being capable of all ill! I pitied thee,
> Took pains to make thee speak, taught thee each hour
> One thing or other: when thou dids't not, savage
> Know thine own meaning, but woulds't gabble like
> A thing most brutish, I endow'd thy purposes
> With words that made them known. But thy vile race,
> Though thou dids't learn, had that in't which good natures

Could not abide to be with; therefore wast thou
Deservedly confined into this rock
Who hadst deserved more than a prison.

In the end, of course, Prospero does free Caliban; that is, he tells him he is free, and leaves him on the island that once was his. "I'll be wise hereafter," Caliban pledges, "and seek for grace." Prospero departs with his daughter and handsome son-in-law, for Milan. A more prophetic Shakespeare might, perhaps, have made him Duke of Brussels.

Neither Fromm nor any other qualified therapist would take Caliban's pledge as reliable evidence that the goals of therapy had been achieved; though, in any case, if we turn a child into a monster by mistreating him we certainly have no right to justify our continued mistreatment as self-defense. If we treat one another in such a way as to turn human beings into Furies, we must learn to live together as Furies, though it isn't a very rich life. But the problem remains. Let us grant that the impulse to growth, love, and freedom in human beings is more basic than the impulse to evil, perversity, and fixation, in the sense that it appears earlier and would never be replaced by darkness and stagnation if love and freedom were accepted and cherished in our society instead of exposing the child to rejection, anxiety, and pain. More basic does not necessarily mean stronger, or even in the long run, preponderant. Caliban and Ariel are Prospero's victims; at their worst, they are not as bad as he is in the full panoply of his sorcery. When he leaves, they are better off without him. But they will never be what they might have if he hadn't happened to them. They may transcend the experience, use it to grow on, and be greater, but they may also turn on each other and destroy the island in impotence, terror, and hatred. Most likely, they will handle their fear of freedom by trying to be as much like him as possible, which will prevent them from making the island their own. Caliban may yet people the isle; but his eldest son will be named Prospero.

At bottom Fromm seems to me to be a Manichean. Manicheanism is the most appealing of the ancient Alexandrian heresies, and there is probably no more reason for a Jew to avoid it than any other part of the friendly persuasion of Christianity. But it certainly makes him very different from Freud. Manicheanism is complicated, but Rebecca West in *St. Augustine* adequately states the central point at issue:

> The myth . . . has grandeur and profundity. Light and darkness, good and evil, are the same pair under different names . . . Mani . . . being an artist . . . gave the kingdom of light a personal ruler who was God, and put the kingdom of darkness under the lordship of Satan and his angels.
>
> For long the two kingdoms were unaware of each other. Then Satan made war on the kingdom of light, and God begat Primal Man on his consort to be His champion and defender. But Primal Man was vanquished and thrown into captivity. God himself then took the field, routed evil, and released the captive. But meanwhile there had been wrought a malicious and not easily reparable confusion of the two kingdoms. Seeds of darkness had been scattered widely in the soils of light, innumerable seeds of light found themselves sown deeply in the darkness. These elements must be sorted and returned to their own. For this purpose the universe was created. It is planned as a means of deliverance for the stolen particles of light. . . . On earth man plays out a peculiar drama of the division. He is the work of Satan, who placed in his dark substance all the particles of light he could steal, so that he could control them. Man is, therefore, a house divided against itself. . . . When all the particles of light are liberated the kingdom of light will be perfected, the good angels who maintain the present universe will withdraw the prop of their power from it, and it will collapse into fiery nothingness.

Nothing goes quite as planned; and there is some reason to believe that the good angels may be going ahead with the final stages of their program before the earlier ones have been quite completed. To this, Fromm strongly objects. But his doctrine still falls afoul of the basic theological objection to Manicheanism, which is that it implies that God and Satan are evenly matched, and that the outcome of the struggle between them is, in effect, the responsibility of man. If man can overcome the division in himself and fulfill his Primal nature, light will triumph. Since even heretics mean God to win in the end,

Manicheanism, in effect, *demands* a greater optimism about the nature of man than the record, at the time Augustine was fighting it, seemed to warrant. Sixteen hundred years later, it still does.

Optimism is not a very sound basis for love; love is not love . . . which bends with the remover to remove. Love, too, is partly a dark business; mastery of the art of loving leads lovers to accept each other as wholes and as ends in themselves. They delight in their mutual growth; but they do not expect it—lovers are not much concerned about the future. They do each other evil, and hurt each other, too; but they do not forgive or accept each other's faults; for a whole cannot accept one of its own parts. Love grows, but it does not progress. Paolo and Francesca go to Hell together; but not to White Sands Proving Ground. Love and Life never triumph, and are never wholly defeated; they just *are,* and being is not a form of strategy.

1962

---

1. I find John H. Schaar's *Escape From Authority* (Basic Books, 1961) unbearably snide, even though I agree with many of his conclusions.

2. T. W. Adorno and others, Harper, 1950.

3. See Jakob J. Petuchowski's "Erich Fromm's Midrash on Love," *Commentary,* December, 1956.

4. Martin Birnbach, *Neo-Freudian Social Philosophy* (Stanford University Press, 1961) is a superb and intellectually dexterous source on this.

Society and the Therapeutic Function

The psychoanalytic movement has now had a reasonably stable theoretical, institutional, and administrative framework for something over half a century. Its development, though turbulent and bitterly opposed, has been rapid and continuous. I know of no other development, technical or conceptual, which has ever done so much good over so short a time.

And it is clear that most of the benefits society has derived from psychoanalysis have not come from the treatment of individual psychoneuroses. Benefits have come largely from an influence on the humane professions and on advances in the conception of leadership and administration. In medicine the general practitioner has become aware of the emotional function of his patient's symptoms. He recognizes that illness may be an essential part of the strategy of life. There are lawyers and even judges—though not a very large proportion—who perceive the incongruity between the conception of truth underlying the rules of evidence and the way human memory actually works.

Education, counseling and guidance, and social service as professional specialties have grown up in the climate of psychodynamic thought. They are in contrast to the instructional and philanthropic practices of earlier days precisely in those characteristics which show most clearly the influence of dynamic social psychology. Theological seminaries now include the rationale and technique of parochial counseling in their training programs. The *quadrivium* of professions cited by the Lord Chancellor in *Iolanthe*—the Army, the Navy, the Church, and God knows, the Stage—have all been transformed by the influence of psychoanalytic thought and its derivatives. So susceptible a Chancellor might well judge it wise today to withhold the famous pattersong in which he recounts his dream, even though his repose would then continue to be tabooed by anxiety.

That so controversial a body of concepts should so rapidly and effectively permeate the intellectual and administrative apparatus of a timid world is remarkable. But when we think about it, we are inclined chiefly to acclaim the victory of psychodynamic thought or to protest that our lives have been invaded by it. We less frequently ask ourselves why the victory occurred just when it did, or why the invasion has been so complete.

Yet the answer to these questions depends, I believe, on certain social factors which it is particularly important that persons in a position of group leadership recognize and understand, if they are to continue to do more good than harm by the application of psychodynamically derived procedure in their work. It is these factors—this changing social context, which I think tends increasingly to subvert therapeutic processes—which I wish to examine here and of whose consequences I wish to take account.

I do not think there is any ambiguity as to what the function of psychotherapy is—call it psychoanalytic, client-centered, or what you will. The function is to free men to take more account of the meaning of their lives. All of us have been terrified enough by the conditions of modern life to induce a degree of emotional necrosis. Those most severely affected have lost much of their capacity to feel with and for people, including especially themselves.

The psychotherapies make it possible for them to re-establish some supply of feeling in the deadened areas of experience. This is an exquisitely painful process, but unless it occurs we remain somewhat dead to ourselves and others, and we poison ourselves further with the emotional products of our personal decay. Whether therapeutic intervention is necessary is a matter for individual clinical judgment; but when it is, this restoration of emotional function is always its purpose. In modified and related form this purpose underlies the psychoanalytic contribution to social work, education, and just about everything else.

It is a thoroughly noble purpose, but it is hard to understand why it should be a novel one. What seems paradoxical is that the psychotherapeutic function should have had no effective institutional form prior to the beginning of this century. I am not talking about technical theoretical limitations at all—that is another matter—but about the absence from earlier culture of a conception of the *kind* of help a psychotherapist gives, today, however primitive the resources for offering it might have been.

Let me illustrate specifically what I mean by this absence, even though in order to do so I must resort to a device which I think has become distasteful to many thoughtful people—that of plucking neurotics out of history. Once there were two very wealthy and influential English people—man and daughter—who were very seriously disturbed. They were given to fantasies of grandeur and of persecution, during which they perpetrated acts of egregious cruelty on those who had been closest to them.

Their sexual lives were dreadfully impaired, although in contrasting ways. They were often miserable themselves; and before Henry and Elizabeth died, and the Tudor line with them, they had completely altered the social fabric of the world in which they lived—whether for good or ill, indubitably for neurotic reasons.

Now, the point I am making is that the realm of which they were monarchs included no resources whatever—however ineffective—to which they could have turned for help. It was not merely that there was no adequate theory or technique on which to base a therapeutic system. There was not even a conception of the problems created by the psychoneuroses in their effect on the individual's participation in life and society, though these were as manifest and as sweeping as they are today.

This is totally different from the problem created by lack of technique. When Elizabeth was physically ill she could call a physician. He would come to her with virtually none of the resources available to his modern counterpart, *but with an identical purpose.* The conception of the physician and his function were there for her to use. Similarly, if Henry wanted to go up to Hampton Court from Westminster, he could get in a boat and be taken there. His court could not have conceived of British Railways, but it could conceive of transportation.

It had no idea, however, that the things Henry felt and did were related in such a way as to require a kind of expert help if his life and theirs were to be spared; and it had no provision at all for such offices. It had provision for dealing with madmen, of course, but a man who murders his friends, his wife, destroys churches, and starts civil war is not necessarily mad. He is, however, in some kind of bad trouble; and by the time of Sigmund Freud western culture was about ready to establish an administrative basis on which such trouble could be recognized and dealt with.

How did the intellectual climate of nineteenth-century Vienna, hostile as it was to psychoanalysis itself, differ from that of Elizabethan England in a manner which made the function of psychoanalysis more acceptable? In several significant ways.

It was, in the first place, a much more empirical climate. In these three centuries most of the development of modern science had taken place, and one of its most pervasive consequences was a disposition to regard any kind of misery or dysfunction as a problem to be solved.

The academic world of the nineteenth century did not like the way Freud presented the problem of emotional disorder, but it was quite accustomed to the idea that such conditions were problems, and that the best way to lick a problem was to attack it scientifically. Not only was Freud on the firmest possible ground in operating as a scientist attacking a problem; he was even, it seems, somewhat handicapped by the strength of his own conception of himself as a scientist and of what science must be like. After he had solved problems he wasted quite a lot of time and effort in trying to couch his solutions in terms consistent with the science of his day. Freudian psychodynamics do not, for example, require that *libido* be conceived as a kind of caloric fluid. But it is much easier to see that this is not necessary in the light of twentieth-century physics than of nineteenth.

But the scientific attitude contributed something more precise than empiricism and an orientation toward problem-solving to the formulation of the therapeutic function. This was its peculiar objectivity. Freud contributed not only genius, courage, and technique; but the institutional form which permits a person, in order to help himself and under skilled guidance, to treat himself utterly and in most intimate detail as an object. That he must do so is, in effect, the basic rule of analysis. And that he shall permanently regard himself—in greater degree than before—as an object, is one way of stating the fundamental purpose of analysis. "Where id was, there shall ego be" surely means that the patient is to learn to stand aside from his impulse-life, perceive it more nearly as if it were a part of external reality, and gain in his ability to channel its force toward his own ends as he would other sources of energy.

I do not imply that in analysis the patient learns to look at himself coldly. The contrary is true; psychotherapy does not work in a cold climate. The emotional attitude pervading a working analysis, variable as it must be, more closely resembles that established by two youths working to repair and tune up a hot-rod belonging to the younger. If youngsters did not love hot-rods they would, as Freud teaches us, call them something else. But the patient and the analyst can be effective only by being objective; their feelings are the source of data about what is wrong, and must be pushed out into the empirical field for examination. If, instead, the patient handles his feelings *subjectively* he is said to be "acting-out," which delays or forestalls therapy.

This distinction is what I think was absent from the culture of the Tudors. In a world altogether less empirical, any powerful fantasy was either simply controlled or acted out. Raleigh or Mary of Scotland might have hoped that Elizabeth would restrain herself out of principle or compassion. But they could hardly have expected her to police-up her feelings by examining their relationship to reality.

It would never have occurred to them that a person could set out purposively to do this. If it had, the idea might have frightened them a good deal more than Elizabeth did. Very few of us, then, would have risked running into ourselves suddenly in a dark alley. But by the late nineteenth century people began to take such risks; indeed, to set out in search of themselves. Analysis provided the organization of the search, and the technique of illumination; but it cannot of itself account for the fact that people began to be willing to undertake it.

Why did they? What finally induced them to submit their individuality to scientific surgery? Very much the same thing, I suppose, which leads anyone to submit to any surgery: the existence of an intolerable condition, and confidence that the surgical intervention will be undertaken for their own welfare.

The power and prestige which empirical and objective attitudes had by then derived from the triumph of science certainly suggested the therapeutic function. But they did not make it less painful. What drove people to seek it? What had become intolerable for many people, and was about to become so for vastly more?

The answer to these questions is, I think, that they felt their identity undermined by continuous and devastating subversion. The source of this subversion lay in the nature of society itself, and it was effective enough to hurt badly. From those most sensitive—Kierkegaard, for example—there had been complaints for some time. And things were getting worse.

The late Victorian era appears to have been the Golden Age of capitalism—an age golden as the autumn harvest or the setting sun. In its development capitalism had profoundly affected the place of man in the universe. It had, in fact, told him that he had no place except that which he might make for himself by individual, competitive achievement against persons whom he might otherwise have loved, hated, or related himself to in some complex but equally personal way. Nineteenth-century man—at least middle-class man, such as found his way to Freud's consulting room—had by and large come to a way of thinking which made his personal significance almost completely dependent on his skill in wresting symbols of identity from an impersonal environment.

He had, therefore, to be good at it; to learn to keep himself healthy, happy, and emotionally fit. Such unhappiness as had always been the common lot of mankind was now perceived as an added threat to success on the job or in what is called—sometimes without the ghost of a smile—interpersonal relations. Henry and Elizabeth knew very well when they were miserable. But they were not aware that this made them inefficient, and if they had known, they would not have cared.

In the rigidly stratified world of the Tudors, status was defined by the circumstances of birth. For most people, it must have afforded little satisfaction, and less anxiety. It was not immutable, certainly; there were many opportunities for the adventurous to get on in the world. Men whose origins had been humble, or at least very curious, did achieve a place in the pageantry of the age.

But the life of the times did not lead people to expect that this would in general be their destiny, or despair of themselves if it were not. Any man could without dishonor accept the definition of himself which came with his social role, and which often fit him very snugly.

As assessed by modern values, the costs to society and to individuals of this system of rank and privilege were enormous and insupportable. Real competence and real human potentialities were not so much discouraged as stillborn; there was little impetus to progress as we define it; the physical condition of the poor was appalling by any standard.

The very brutality of life sickened people of all ranks, physically and emotionally. There was much neurotic devastation, and doubtless much anxiety. But people seem to become aware of anxiety as the fundamental factor in their plight only when they feel isolated by it—and they only feel isolated by it when it stems primarily from problems of status and identity.

What seems to me both inescapable and ironical is the inference that mankind never objected to neurotic devastation strongly enough to identify it as a problem until it had become not merely destructive but manifestly inexpedient as well. Men have always needed help in becoming free to take account of the meaning of their lives, if they were to live richly and lovingly. They have always gotten such help from the arts, which attest beyond doubt that the emotional dynamics of human misery and human happiness have remained substantially the same throughout the scope of Western culture.

The arts attest also that the basic insights expressed in psychoanalytic theory are, as Freud maintained, ancient; and have therefore been available since antiquity. But no therapeutic process could be devised until man consented to use these insights in order to look at himself objectively for his own purposes. He never thought of it, until he had been initiated into such objectivity by isolation—by a century or so of hard usage as an object by others for *their* purposes—and had consented to judge himself by his effectiveness as an operating instrument.

There is a growing literature, much of it neo-conservative, which expresses our mounting conviction that this existence as an isolated object, this sense that one has no antecedent or inviolable claim on a place in the universe and is solely responsible for the kind of place one makes, is the most agonizing condition possible to man. *L'âme humaine est morte; vive l'humanité!* is the existentialist cry.

In such a crisis the therapeutic function is the most profoundly moral source of real help. It keeps the victim from panic, and it keeps him from settling down into the role of a victim. If man is to be an object, it sustains him as he designs himself to be his *own* object for his *own* ends; he becomes, at least, more self-possessed.

At most, he becomes tremendously more—a love-object, capable of strongly cathected object-relationships. When this is accomplished, the existentialist cry is stilled, for the therapeutic process has then broken through to the human soul; finding it neither dead nor much the worse for wear, but trembling with rage, and wont to complain that analysis has taken the devil's own time. Well, it does.

But the morality of the therapeutic function does depend

unalterably on the joint purpose of analyst and patient to restore and maintain the patient's integrity and identity. The function of psychotherapy is precisely to do so. This is exactly what the problem of freeing men to take more account of the meaning of their lives has at present become.

At other times and places this problem has been one of preventive medicine, nutrition, or economic production. For us it is a problem of the restoration and maintenance of human identity. Psychotherapy arose as very nearly a last-ditch defense of the human spirit against usurpation as a means rather than an end, in a society increasingly preoccupied with means and negligent of ends—even of its own.

As Trilling points out in his recent essay on *Freud and the Crisis in Our Culture*, psychoanalytic theory, while supplying the basis for a process of incomparable value to the individual in functioning more effectively in his culture, does indeed postulate the most basic kind of conflict between the individual and his culture. It helps the individual survive the more crushing cultural demands.

I think there are strong indications, however, that the therapeutic function has altered appreciably, and is continuing to alter in the same direction. The professional therapist has not changed his goals; but the patient, by and large, has. He is likely to come now for help in building an identity *acceptable to the demands of society* rather than in *maintaining his own character productively in the situation which these demands create.*

The social developments which took the economic form of capitalism, the religious form of protestantism, and the political form of nationalism provided immeasurable and unprecedented opportunity for individual self-advancement. They also shifted to the advancing individual the responsibility for handling himself objectively and with conscious respect for his human properties; he could no longer take himself for granted.

Democracy may be defined as the kind of social order in which this responsibility is universally shared among all persons. Each is entitled to respect as a human being. Each must define for himself his own identity and the meaning of his life. It was, in essence, the need of such men which psychoanalysis was designed to meet.

It is true that psychoanalysis is essentially a middle-class technique; or, more precisely, that it addressed itself to the solution of a peculiarly middle-class problem: the problem of the successful puritan who had lost himself in his effort to master his environment. The psychotherapeutic function is still the restoration and maintenance of identity and integrity. But the problem has changed. The way in which it has changed may be elucidated by considering a rather striking development in individual psychotherapy.

It has been rather widely noted by practicing analysts that since the time of Freud there has been a major change in the kind of difficulty which brings patients to the couch. There is now a much smaller proportion of hysterical or obsessive-compulsive neuroses, and a much larger proportion of character disorders. This is not merely a technical change, but one which has important and I think rather sinister implications.

What this means, among other things, is that a far larger proportion of Freud's patients than of those of a contemporary analyst felt their symptoms to be ego-alien—felt, that is, that they had a self of their own to which their symptoms were alien.

They came to Freud to have their real self restored; and this is what he undertook. Their paralyzed left arm, their fear of going out in the streets, their impotence were somehow *not like them at all.* They were, of course, fooling themselves and could only be helped by being brought to face their own deceptions. Nevertheless, they had a self to fool—a self which was much more real to them than their symptoms, and whose life the symptoms had disturbed.

But a character-neurotic does not feel his problem to be the intrusion of the repressed upon an otherwise functional, established self. His whole life is a symptom; he is miserable, not because his symptoms make him so, but because they interfere with his perception of reality and keep him from getting the satisfactions he needs. He too is, as Freud said of his patients, a fool. But he is not exactly fooling himself. His self is still immanent.

He is much harder to treat than the hysteric, for the ego must be not merely strengthened but, in effect, newly constructed. A large proportion—much larger than in the classical cases—of the therapeutic effort goes into the building of the self, so much so that classical Freudians regard some of the newer psychoanalytic schools, which were largely molded by the necessity of treating character disorders, as merely "ego-psychologies."

Why has this trend occurred? The answer given depends upon one's particular training and vantage point. But one way of putting it is that, while our social and economic institutions have supplied more and more of us with the resources to become conscious of self, these same institutions have so straitened our lives as to deny us the occasion to do so. We possess the fiscal means for growth and lack the experiential. The therapeutic function of freeing men to take account of the meaning of their lives presupposes a life in which experience has meaning; not in which people move about in a kind of soap opera.

The therapeutic function, in short, can be shared only among participants in what Lippmann calls the public philosophy. It is restricted to responsible people. And our society seems increasingly to discourage individual responsibility.

If one accepts the conclusions of such social critics as C. Wright Mills, whose analysis I find quite convincing, responsible human perception and action are diminishing in frequency and effectiveness at all levels of society. It tends to lead to the systematic exclusion of the responsible individual from the councils of decision just at the period in history when more and more decisions—if, indeed they are that, and not simply the residuals of adaptation—are made in councils rather than by individual self-determination.

It is true that we have lately redressed some of the more extreme sanctions against independence of mind and spirit recently imposed in our country. A new norm of nonconformity seems to be emerging as a pattern for the promising junior;

there must be embarrassing inventories of uncut grey flannel in the workrooms of J. Press and Chipp. However, it is questionable whether this mild reassertion of individual initiative reflects a deep and widespread awareness of a dangerous defect in our way of life and a gentle determination to correct it; or merely the response of a society committed to co-operation as one of the higher virtues and deeply fearful of any real conflict, to the discovery that it has gone too far. We seem to be retreating from an extremely vicious assault on human dignity in the State Department and elsewhere, not because it was vicious, but because it was extreme.

So long as social institutions are directed by individuals who participate in the preference for a responsible and meaningful life, and serve at least a working minority of individuals who also do, the influence of psychodynamic thought on their operation will be beneficial—yielding more humane courts, more flexible and perceptive schools, more decent administrative processes.

But to the extent that psychodynamic thought must operate through persons who lack dignity themselves and despise it in others, it can contribute nothing to the therapeutic function. It can actually be used to obscure the meaning of life; contributing through the mass media to more effective manipulation; imposing a norm of adjustment on gifted and spontaneous children; guiding consulting firms in their search for a purple pimpernel on the bottoms of junior executives. It is used for these purposes today, and we are none the better for it.

The therapeutic function may, in fact, be a short-lived aspect of social transition. A society in which men derive their identity from their status, and their status from the circumstances of their birth, cannot formulate it. A society in which identity must be ratified by an artificially stimulated popular endorsement cannot maintain it. The Western world has come a long way from the former, and seems to be approaching the latter.

In a strange way, the journey has been circular. Once more, we are approaching a condition in which *who* a person *is* is determined almost by his place in society, and much less than before by his personal craftsmanship. But there is a barrier; all the neo-conservative nostalgia in the universe cannot readmit to Eden a populace which has become cynical about how the place operates, and self-conscious about getting to be an archangel.

I do not know how much those who are responsible for administering the therapeutic function in their various professional or administrative roles can do to preserve it. Teachers, counselors, social workers, lawyers, psychiatrists, and everybody else are of course a part of contemporary culture. Not only are we all subject to its vicissitudes, but our values and power to perceive what is happening are themselves largely culturally determined. Certainly, we cannot get far by training to maintain professional service to such people as wish to be individuals as a kind of picturesque specialty, like blacksmithing. Society probably does have the power to make us a part of the huge manipulative apparatus whose function is to seduce the anxious into consent, and perhaps this is what society needs if it is to run smoothly without ever making anybody feel guilty or embarrassed.

The public has come to expect therapy to reduce tension and improve adjustment. Many professional workers concur in this without much question. But this has never been the function of therapy; it is the precise opposite. Therapy arose rather to help people maintain a taut psychic balance and provide themselves with rational alternatives to adjustment instead of destructive ones in those situations where adjustment would have meant a gross insult to their humanity.

If we take the therapeutic function seriously, I believe we must continue to do as much of this as is humanly possible, whether or not it is what contemporary social policy demands, or what the community has come to expect. The democratic tradition demands it, and we expect it of ourselves.

1956

THE IMAGE OF THE ADOLESCENT MINORITY

IN OUR SOCIETY there are two kinds of minority status. One of these I will call the "hot-blooded" minorities, whose archetypical image is that of the Negro or Latin. *In the United States, "Teen-agers" are treated as a "hot-blooded" minority.* Then, there are the "long-suffering minorities," whose archetype is the Jew, but which also, I should say, includes women. Try, for a second, to picture a Jewish "teen-ager," and you may sense a tendency for the image to grate. "Teen-agers" err on the hot side; they talk jive, drive hot-rods and become juvenile delinquents. Young Jews talk volubly, play the violin, and go to medical school, though never on Saturday.

The minority group is a special American institution, created by the interaction between a history and an ideology which are not to be duplicated elsewhere. Minority status has little to do with size or proportion. In a democracy, a dominant social group is called a majority and a part of its dominance consists in the power to arrange appropriate manifestations of public support; while a subordinate group is, by the logic of political morality, a minority. The minority stereotype, though affected by the actual characteristics of the minority group, develops to fit the purposes and expresses the anxieties of the dominant social group. It serves as a slimy coating over the sharp realities of cultural difference, protecting the social organism until the irritant can be absorbed.

Now, when one is dealing with a group that actually is genetically or culturally different from the dominant social group, this is perhaps to be expected. It is neither desirable nor inevitable, for xenophobia is neither desirable nor inevitable; but it is not surprising.

What is surprising is that the sons and daughters of the *dominant* adult group should be treated as a minority group merely because of their age. Their papers are in order and they speak the language adequately. In any society, to be sure, the young occupy a subordinate or probationary status while under tutelage for adult life. But a minority group is not merely subordinate; it is not under tutelage. It is in the process of being denatured; of becoming, under social stress, something more acceptable to the dominant society, but essentially different from what its own growth and experience would lead to. Most beasts recognize their own kind. Primitive peoples may initiate their youth; we insist that ours be naturalized, though it is what is most natural about them that disturbs adults most.

The court of naturalization is the public school. A high school diploma is a certificate of legitimacy, not of competence. A youth needs one today in order to hold a job that will permit even minimal participation in the dominant society. Yet our laws governing school attendance do not deal with education. They are not *licensing* laws, requiring attendance until a certain defined minimum competence, presumed essential for adult life, has been demonstrated. They are not *contractual;* they offer no remedy for failure of the school to provide services of a minimum quality. A juvenile may not legally withdraw from school even if he can establish that it is substandard or that he is being ill-treated there. If he does, as many do, for just these reasons, he becomes *prima facie* an offender; for, in cold fact, the compulsory attendance law guarantees him nothing, not even the services of qualified teachers. It merely defines, in terms of age alone, a particular group as subject to legal restrictions not applicable to other persons.

Second-Class Citizen

Legally, the adolescent comes pretty close to having no basic rights at all. The state generally retains the final right even to strip him of his minority status. He has no right to *demand* the particular protection of *either* due process or the juvenile administrative procedure—the state decides. We have had several cases in the past few years of boys eighteen and under being sentenced to death by the full apparatus of formal criminal law, who would not have been permitted to claim its protection had they been accused of theft or disorderly conduct. Each of these executions has so far been forestalled by various legal procedures,[1] but none in such a way as to establish the right of a juvenile to be tried as a juvenile; though he long ago lost his claim to be treated as an adult.

In the most formal sense, then, the adolescent is one of our second-class citizens. But the informal aspects of minority status are also imputed to him. The "teen-ager," like the Latin or Negro, is seen as joyous, playful, lazy, and irresponsible, with brutality lurking just below the surface and ready to break out into violence.[2] All these groups are seen as childish and excitable, imprudent and improvident, sexually aggressive, and dangerous, but possessed of superb and sustained power to satisfy sexual demands. *West Side Story* is not much like *Romeo and Juliet*; but it is a great deal like *Porgy and Bess*.

The fantasy underlying this stereotype, then, is erotic; and its subject is male. The "hot-blooded" minorities are always represented by a masculine stereotype; nobody asks "Would you want your *son* to marry a Negro?" In each case, also, little counter-stereotypes, repulsively pallid in contrast to the alluring violence and conflict of the central scene, are held out enticingly by the dominant culture; the conscientious "teen-ager" sold by Pat Boone to soothe adults while the kids themselves buy *Mad* and *Catcher*; the boy whose Italian immigrant mother sees to it that he wears a clean shirt to school every day on his way to the Governor's mansion; *Uncle Tom*. In the rectilinear planning of Jonesville these are set aside conspicuously as Public Squares, but at dusk they are little frequented.

One need hardly labor the point that what the dominant society seeks to control by imposing "hot-blooded" minority status is not the actual aggressiveness and sexuality of the Negro, the Latin, or the JD, but its own wish for what the British working classes used to call "a nice game of slap and tickle," on the unimpeachable assumption that a little of what you fancy does you good. This, the well-lighted Public Squares cannot afford; the community is proud of them, but they are such stuff as only the driest dreams are made of. These are not the dreams that are wanted. In my experience, it is just not possible to discuss adolescence with a group of American adults without being forced onto the topic of juvenile delinquency. Partly this is an expression of legitimate concern, but partly it is because only the JD has any emotional vividness for them.

I would ascribe the success of *West Side Story* to the functional equivalence in the minds of adults between adolescence, delinquency, and aggressive sexuality. Many who saw the show must have wondered, as I did, why there were no Negroes in it—one of the best things about Juvenile Delinquency is that, at least, it is integrated. Hollywood, doubtless, was as usual reluctant to show a member of an enfranchised minority group in an unfavorable light. But there was also a rather sound artistic reason. Putting a real Negro boy in *West Side Story* would have been like scoring the second movement of the *Pastorale* for an eagle rather than flute. The provocative, surly, sexy dancing kids who come to a bad end are not meant realistically. Efforts to use real street-adolescents in *West Side Story* had to be abandoned; they didn't know how to act. What was depicted here was neither Negro nor white nor really delinquent, but a comfortably vulgar middle-class dream of a "hot-blooded" minority. In dreams a single symbolic boy can represent them all; let the symbol turn real and the dreamer wakes up screaming.

Adolescents are treated as a "hot-blooded" minority, then, because they seem so good at slap-and-tickle. But a number of interesting implications flow from this. Slap-and-tickle implies sexual vigor and attractiveness, warmth and aggression, salted with enough conventional perversity to lend spice to a long dull existence. Such perversity is a kind of exuberant overflow from the mainstream of sexuality, not a diversion of it. It is joyous excess and bounty; extravagant foreplay in the well-worn marriage-bed; the generosity of impulse that leads the champion lover of the high school to prance around the shower-room snapping a towel on the buttocks of his team-mates three hours before a hot date, just to remind them that life can be beautiful.

Experience Repressed

When a society sees impulsiveness and sexual exuberance as minority characteristics which unsuit the individual for membership until he is successfully naturalized, it is in pretty bad shape. Adolescents, loved, respected, taught to accept, enjoy, and discipline their feelings, grow up. "Teen-agers" don't; they pass. Then, in middle-age, they have the same trouble with their former self that many ethnics do. They hate and fear the kinds of spontaneity that remind them of what they have abandoned, and they hate themselves for having joined forces with and having come to resemble their oppressors.[3] This is the vicious spiral by which "hot-blooded" minority status maintains itself. I am convinced that it is also the source of the specific hostility—and sometimes sentimentality—that adolescents arouse in adults. The processes involved have been dealt with in detail by Daniel Boorstin, Leslie Fiedler, Paul Goodman, and especially Ernest Schachtel.[4] Their effect is to starve out, through silence and misrepresentation, the capacity to have genuine and strongly felt experience, and to replace it by the conventional symbols that serve as the common currency of daily life.

Experience repressed in adolescence does not, of course, result in amnesia, as does the repression of childhood experience; it leaves no temporal gaps in the memory. This makes it more dangerous, because the adult is then quite unaware that his memory is incomplete, that the most significant components of feeling have been lost or driven out. We at least know that we no longer know what we felt as children. But an adolescent boy who asks his father how he felt on the first night he spent in barracks or with a woman will be told what the father now thinks he felt because he ought to have; and this is very dangerous nonsense indeed.

Whether in childhood or in adolescence, the same quality of experience is starved out or repressed. It is still the spontaneous, vivid and immediate that is most feared, and feared the more because so much desired. But there is a difference in focus and emphasis because in adolescence spontaneity can lead to much more serious consequences.

This, perhaps, is the crux of the matter, since it begins to explain why our kind of society should be so easily plunged into conflict by "hot-blooded" minorities in general and adolescent boys in particular. We are consequence-oriented and future-oriented. Among us, to prefer present delights is a sign of either low or high status, and both are feared. Schachtel makes it clear how we go about building this kind of character in the child—by making it difficult for him to notice his delights when he has them, and obliterating the language in which he might recall them joyfully later. This prepares the ground against the subsequent assault of adolescence. But it is a strong assault, and if adolescence wins, the future hangs in the balance.

The Adolescent Girl

In this assault, adolescent boys play a very different role from adolescent girls and are dealt with unconsciously by totally different dynamics. Adolescent girls are not seen as members of a "hot-blooded" minority, and to this fact may be traced some interesting paradoxes in our perception of the total phenomenon of adolescence.

Many critics of the current literature on adolescence—Bruno Bettelheim[5] perhaps most cogently—have pointed out that most contemporary writing about adolescents ignores the adolescent girl almost completely. Bettelheim specifically mentions Goodman and myself; the best novels about adolescents of the past decade or so have been, I think there would be fair agreement, Salinger's *The Catcher in the Rye,* John Knowles' *A Separate Peace,* and Colin MacInnes' less well known but superb *Absolute Beginners.* All these have adolescent boys as heroes. Yet, as Bettelheim points out, the adolescent girl is as important as the adolescent boy, and her actual plight in society is just as severe; her opportunities are even more limited and her growth into a mature woman as effectively discouraged. Why has she not aroused more interest?

There are demonstrable reasons for the prominence of the adolescent boy in our culture. Conventionally, it is he who threatens the virtue of our daughters and the integrity of our automobiles. There are so many more ways to get hung up on a boy. "Teen-agers," too, may be all right; but would you want your daughter to marry one? When she doesn't know anything about him except how she feels—and what does that matter when they are both too young to know what they are doing; when he may never have the makings of an executive, or she of an executive's wife?

For this last consideration, paradoxically, also makes the *boy,* rather than the girl, the focus of anxiety. He alone bears the terrible burden of parental aspirations; it is his capacity for spontaneous commitment that endangers the opportunity of adults to live vicariously the life they never manage to live personally.

Holden, Finny, and the unnamed narrator of *Absolute Beginners,* are adolescent boys who do not pass; who retain their minority status, their spontaneous feelings, their power to act out and act up. They go prancing to their destinies. But what destiny can we imagine for them? We leave Holden in a mental hospital, being adjusted to reality; and Finny dead of the horror of learning that his best friend, Gene, had unconsciously contrived the accident that broke up his beautifully articulated body. The Absolute Beginner, a happier boy in a less tense society, fares better; he has had more real contact with other human beings, including a very satisfactory father, and by his time there is such a thing as a "teen-ager," little as it is, for him to be. On this basis the Beginner can identify himself; the marvelous book ends as he rushes out onto the tarmac at London Airport, bursting through the customs barrier, to stand at the foot of the gangway and greet a planeload of astonished immigrants by crying, "Here I am! Meet your first teen-ager."

Political Disinterest

There are still enough Finnys and Holdens running around free to give me much joy and some hope, and they are flexible enough to come to their own terms with reality. But the system is against them, and they know it well. Why then, do they not try to change it? Why are none of these novels of adolescence political novels? Why have their heroes no political interests at all? In this respect, fiction is true to American life; American adolescents are notably free from political interests. I must maintain this despite the recent advances of SANE kids and Freedom Riders; for, though I love and honor them for their courage and devotion, the causes they fight for are not what I would call political. No controversy over basic policy is involved, because nobody advocates atomic disaster or racial persecution. The kids' opponents are merely in favor of the kind of American society that these evils flourish in, and the youngsters do not challenge the system itself, though they are appalled by its consequences.

Yet could they, as adolescents, be political? I don't think so; and I don't know that I would be pleased if they were. American politics is a cold-blooded business indeed. Personal clarity and commitment are not wanted in it and not furthered by it. I do not think this is necessarily true of all politics; but it becomes true when the basic economic and social assumptions are as irrational as ours.

Political effectiveness in our time requires just the kind of caginess, pseudo-realism, and stereotyping of thought and feeling; the same submergence of spontaneity to the exigencies of collective action, that mark the ruin of adolescence. Adolescents are, inherently, anti-mass; they take things personally. Sexuality, itself, has this power to resolve relationships into the immediate and interpersonal. As a symbol the cocky adolescent boy stands, a little like Luther, an obstacle to compromise and accommodation. Such symbols stick in the mind, though the reality can usually be handled. With occasional spectacular failures we do manage to assimilate the "teen-age" minority; the kids learn not to get fresh; they get smart, they dry up. We are left then, like the Macbeths, with the memory of an earlier fidelity. But Lady Macbeth was less resourceful than ourselves; she knew next to nothing about industrial solvents. Where she had only perfume we have oil.

The Girl as Woman

This is how we use the boy, but what about the girl? I have already asserted that, since she is not perceived as a member of the "hot-blooded" minority she cannot take his place in the unconscious, which is apt to turn very nasty if it is fobbed off with the wrong sex. Is she then simply not much involved by our psychodynamics, or is she actively repressed? Is she omitted from our fantasies or excluded from them?

It may seem very strange that I should find her so inconspicuous. Her image gets so much publicity. Drum-majorettes and cheerleaders are ubiquitous; *Playboy* provides businessmen with a new *playmate* each month. Nymphets are a public institution.

Exactly, and they serve a useful public function. American males are certainly anxious to project a heterosexual public image, and even more anxious to believe in it themselves. None of us, surely, wishes to feel obligated to hang himself out of respect for the United States Senate; it is, as Yum-Yum remarked to Nanki-Poo, such a stuffy death. I am not questioning our sincerity; the essence of my point is that in what we call maturity we feel what we are supposed to feel, and nothing else. But I am questioning the depth and significance of our interest in the cover or pin-up girl. Her patrons are concerned to experience their own masculinity; they are not much interested in her: I reject the celebration of "babes" in song and story as evidence that we have adolescent girls much on our minds; if we did we wouldn't think of them as "babes." I think, indeed, that in contrast to the boy, of whom we are hyperaware, we repress our awareness of the girl. She is not just omitted, she is excluded.

The adolescent heroine in current fiction is not interpreted in the same way as the adolescent hero, even when the parallel is quite close. Her adolescence is treated as less crucial; she is off-handedly accepted as a woman already. This is true even when the author struggles against it. *Lolita,* for example, is every bit as much a tragic heroine of adolescence as Holden is a hero—she isn't as nice a girl as he is a boy, but they are both victims of the same kind of corruption in adult society and the same absence of any real opportunity to grow up to be themselves. Lolita's failure is the classic failure of identity in adolescence; and Humbert knows this and accepts responsibility for it; this is the crime he expiates. But this is not the way Lolita—the character, not the book—is generally received. Unlike Holden, she has no cult and is not vouchsafed any dignity. It is thought to be comical that, at fourteen, she is already a whore.

A parallel example is to be found in Rumer Godden's *The Greengage Summer*. Here the story is explicitly about Joss's growing up. The author's emphasis is on the way her angry betrayal of her lover marks the end of her childhood; her feelings are now too strong and confused, and too serious in their consequences, to be handled with childish irresponsibility; she can no longer claim the exemptions of childhood. But what the movie presented, it seemed to me, was almost entirely an account of her rise to sexual power; Joss had become a Babe at last.

One reason that we do not take adolescent growth seriously in girls is that we do not much care what happens to people unless it has economic consequences: what would Holden ever be, since he never even graduates from high school; who would hire him? He has a problem; Lolita could always be a waitress or something; what more could she expect? Since we define adulthood almost exclusively in economic terms, we obviously cannot concern ourselves as much about the growth of those members of society who are subject from birth to restricted economic opportunity. But so, of course, are the members of the "hot-blooded" minorities; though we find their hot-bloodedness so exciting that we remain aware of them anyway.

But girls, like Jews, are not supposed to fight back; we expect them, instead, to insinuate themselves coyly into the roles available. In our society, there are such lovely things for them to be. They can take care of other people and clean up after them. Women can become wives and mothers; Jews can become kindly old Rabbis and philosophers and even psychoanalysts and lovable comic essayists. They can become powers behind the power; a fine old law firm runs on the brains of its anonymous young Jews just as a husband's best asset is his loyal and unobtrusive wife. A Jewish girl can become a Jewish Mother, and this is a role which even Plato would have called essential.

Effects of Discrimination

Clearly, this kind of discrimination is quite different from that experienced by the "hot-blooded" minorities and must be based on a very different image in the minds of those who practice it and must have a different impact upon them. Particularly, in the case of the adolescent, the effect on the adult of practicing these two kinds of discrimination will be different. The adolescent boy must be altered to fit middle-class adult roles, and when he has been he becomes a much less vital creature. But the girl is merely squandered, and this wastage will continue all her life. Since adolescence is, for boy and girl alike, the time of life in which the self must be established, the girl suffers as much from being wasted as the boy does from being cut down; there has recently been, for example, a number of tragic suicides reported among adolescent girls, though suicide generally is far less common among females. But from the point of view of the dominant society nothing special is done to the female in adolescence—the same squeeze continues throughout life, even though this is when it hurts most.

The guilts we retain for our treatments of "hot-blooded" and "long-suffering" minorities therefore affect us in contrasting ways. For the boy we suffer angry, paranoid remorse, as if he were Billy the Kid, or Budd. We had to do our duty, but how can we ever forget him? But we do not attack the girl; we only neglect her and leave her to wither gradually through an unfulfilled life; and the best defense against this sort of guilt is selective inattention. We just don't see her; instead, we see a caricature, not brutalized as in the case of the boy, to justify our own brutality, but sentimentalized, roseate, to reassure us that we have done her no harm, and that she is well contented.

Look: she even has her own telephone, with what is left of the boy dangling from the other end of the line.

A Lonely Ride

This is the fantasy; the reality is very different, but it is bad enough to be a "Teen-ager." The adolescent is now the only totally disfranchised minority group in the country. In America, no minority has ever gotten any respect or consistently decent treatment until it began to acquire political power. The vote comes before anything else. This is obviously true of the Negro at the present time; his recent advances have all been made under—sometimes reluctant—Federal auspices because, nationally, Negroes vote, and Northern Negroes are able to cast a ballot on which their buffeted Southern rural fellows may be pulled to firmer political ground. This is what makes it impossible to stop Freedom Rides; just as the comparative militance of the Catholic Church in proceeding toward integration in Louisiana may have less to do with Louisiana than Nigeria, which is in grave danger of falling into the hands of Black Muslims. People generally sympathetic with adolescents sometimes say, "Well, it really isn't fair; if they're old enough to be drafted, they're old enough to vote," which is about as naive as it is possible to get.

Can the status of the "teen-ager" be improved? Only, presumably, through increased political effectiveness. Yet, it is precisely here that a crucial dilemma arises. For the aspirations of the adolescent minority are completely different from those of other minorities. All the others are struggling to obtain what the adolescent is struggling to avoid. They seek and welcome the conventional American middle-class status that has been partially or totally barred to them. But this is what the adolescent is left with if he gives in and goes along.

In the recent and very moving CORE film, *Freedom Ride,* one of the heroic group who suffered beatings and imprisonment for their efforts to end segregation says, as nearly as I can recall, "If the road to freedom leads through the jails of the South, then that's the road I'll take." It may be the road to freedom; but it is the road to suburbia too. You can't tell which the people are headed for until they are nearly there; but all our past ethnic groups have settled for suburbia, and the people who live there bear witness that freedom is somewhere else.

I am not sure there *is* a road to freedom in America. Not enough people want to go there; the last I can recall was H. D. Thoreau, and he went on foot, through the woods, alone. This still may be the only way to get there. For those with plenty of guts, compassion, and dedication to social justice, who nevertheless dislike walking alone through the woods, or feel it to be a Quixotic extravagance, a freedom ride is a noble enterprise. Compared to them, the individual boy or girl on a solitary journey must seem an anachronism. Such a youngster has very little place in our way of life. And of all the criticisms that might be directed against that way of life, this is the harshest.

1963

1. Two were finally hanged this past June, five years later.

2. A very bad—indeed, vicious—but remarkably ambivalent reenactment of the entire fantasy on which the minority-status of the teen-ager is based can be seen in the recent movie *13 West St.* Here, the legal impotence of the "teen-ager" is taken absolutely for granted, and sadistic hostility of adults against him, though deplored, is condoned and accepted as natural. Occasional efforts are made to counterbalance the, in my judgment, pornographic picture of a brutal teen-age gang by presenting "good" teen-agers unjustly suspected, and decent police trying to resist sadistic pressure from the gang's victim, who drives one of its members to suicide. But despite this, the picture ends with a scene of the gang's victim—a virile-type rocket scientist—beating the leader of the gang with his cane and attempting to drown the boy in a swimming pool—which the police dismiss as excusable under the circumstances. A Honolulu paper, at least, described this scene of attempted murder as "an old-fashioned caning that had the audience cheering in its seats."

3. Cf. Abraham Kardiner and Lionel Ovesey's classic, *The Mark of Oppression* (New York: Norton, 1951), for a fascinating study of these dynamics among American Negroes.

4. Daniel Boorstin, *The Image,* New York: Atheneum, 1962; Leslie Fiedler, "The Fear of the Impulsive Life." *WFMT Perspective,* October, 1961, pp. 4-9; Paul Goodman, *Growing Up Absurd.* New York: Random House, 1960, p. 38; Ernest Schachtel, "On Memory and Childhood Amnesia." Widely anthologized, cf. the author's *Metamorphosis.* New York: Basic Books, 1959, pp. 279-322. A more systematic and profound treatment, I have since learned, is to be found in Norman Brown, *Life Against Death* (Middletown, Wesleyan University Press, 1959).

5. In "Adolescence and the Conflict of Generations," *Daedalus,* Winter, 1962, p. 68.

The Modern High School: A Profile

Not far from Los Angeles, though rather nearer to Boston, may be located the town of Milgrim, in which Milgrim High School is clearly the most costly and impressive structure. Milgrim is not a suburb. Although it is only fifty miles from a large and dishonorable city and a part of its conurbation, comparatively few Milgrimites commute to the city for work. Milgrim is an agricultural village which has outgrown its nervous system; its accustomed modes of social integration have not yet even begun to relate its present, recently acquired inhabitants to one another. So, though it is not a suburb, Milgrim is not a community either.

Milgrim's recent, fulminating growth is largely attributable to the rapid development of light industry in the outer suburbs, with a resulting demand for skilled labor. But within the past few years, further economic development has created a steady demand for labor that is not so skilled. In an area that is by no means known for its racial tolerance or political liberalism, Milgrim has acquired, through no wish of its own, a sizable Negro and Puerto Rican minority. On the shabby outskirts of town, a number of groceries label themselves Spanish-American. The advanced class in Spanish at Milgrim High School makes a joyful noise—about the only one to be heard.

Estimates of the proportion of the student body at Milgrim who are, in the ethnocentric language of demography, non-white, vary enormously. Some students who are clearly middle-class and of pinkish-gray color sometimes speak as if they themselves were a besieged minority. More responsible staff members produce estimates of from twelve to thirty per cent. Observations in the corridors and lunchrooms favor the lower figure. They also establish clearly that the non-whites are orderly and well behaved, though somewhat more forceful in their movements and manner of speech than their light-skinned colleagues.

What is Milgrim High like? It is a big, expensive building, on spacious but barren grounds. Every door is at the end of a corridor; there is no reception area, no public space in which one can adjust to the transition from the outside world. Between class periods the corridors are tumultuously crowded; during them they are empty. But at both times they are guarded by teachers and students on patrol duty. Patrol duty does not consist primarily in the policing of congested throngs of moving students, or the guarding of property from damage. Its principal function is the checking of corridor passes. Between classes, no student may walk down the corridor without a form, signed by a teacher, telling where he is coming from, where he is going, and the time, to the minute, during which the pass is valid. A student caught in the corridor without such a pass is sent or taken to the office; there a detention slip is made out against him, and he is required to remain after school for two or three hours. He may do his homework during this time, but he may not leave his seat or talk.

There is no physical freedom whatever at Milgrim. During class breaks, the lavatories are kept locked, so that a student must not only obtain a pass but find the custodian and induce him to open the facility. Indeed Milgrim High's most memorable arrangements are its corridor passes and its johns; they dominate social interaction. "Good morning, Mr. Smith," an attractive girl will say pleasantly to one of her teachers in the corridor. "Linda, do you have a pass to be in your locker after the bell rings?" is his greeting in reply. There are more classifications of washrooms than there must have been in the Confederate Navy. The common sort, marked just "Boys" and "Girls," are generally locked. Then there are some marked, "Teachers, Men" and "Teachers, Women," unlocked. Near the auditorium are two others marked simply, "Men" and "Women," which are intended primarily for the public when the auditorium is being used for some function. During the school day cardboard signs saying "Adults Only" are placed on these doors. Girding up my maturity, I used this men's room during my stay at Milgrim. Usually it was empty; but once, as soon as the door clicked behind me, a teacher who had been concealed in the cubicle began jumping up and down to peer over his partition and verify my adulthood.

He was not a voyeur; he was checking on smoking. At most public high schools, students are forbidden to smoke, and this is probably the most common source of friction with authorities. It focuses, naturally, on the washrooms which are the only place students can go where teachers are not supposed to be. Milgrim, for a time, was more liberal than most; last year its administration designated an area behind the school where seniors might smoke during their lunch period. But, as a number of students explained to me during interviews, some of these seniors had "abused the privilege" by lighting up before they got into the area, and the privilege had been withdrawn. No student, however, questioned that smoking was a privilege rather than a right.

The concept of privilege is important at Milgrim. Teachers go to the head of the chow line at lunch; whenever I would attempt quietly to stand in line the teacher on hall duty would remonstrate with me. He was right, probably; I was fouling up an entire informal social system by my ostentation. Students on hall patrol also were allowed to come to the head of the line; so were seniors. Much of the behavior that Milgrim depends on to keep it going is motivated by the reward of getting a government-surplus peanut butter or tuna fish sandwich without standing in line.

The luncheon itself is a major learning experience, which must make quite an impression over four years' time. There are two large cafeterias which are used as study halls during the periods before and after the middle of the day. The food, by and large, is good, and more tempting than the menu. The atmosphere is not quite that of a prison, because the students are permitted to talk quietly, under the frowning scrutiny of teachers standing around on duty, during their meal—they are not supposed to talk while standing in line, though this rule is only sporadically enforced. Standing in line takes about a third of their lunch period, and leaves plenty of time for them to eat what is provided them. They may not, in any case, leave the room when they have finished, any more than they could leave a class. Toward the end of the period a steel gate is swung down across the corridor, dividing the wing holding the cafeterias, guidance offices, administrative offices, and auditorium from the rest of the building. Then the first buzzer sounds, and the students sweep out of the cafeteria and press silently forward to the gate. A few minutes later a second buzzer sounds, the gate is opened, and the students file out to their classrooms.

During the meal itself the atmosphere varies in response to chance events and the personality of the teachers assigned supervisory duty; this is especially true in the corridor where the next sitting is waiting in line. The norm is a not unpleasant chatter; but about one teacher in four is an embittered martinet, snarling, whining, continually ordering the students to stand closer to the wall and threatening them with detention or suspension for real or fancied insolence. On other occasions, verbal altercations break out between students in the cafeteria or in line and the *student* hall patrolmen. In one of these that I witnessed, the accused student, a handsome, aggressive-looking young man, defended himself in the informal but explicit language of working-class hostility. This roused the teacher on duty from his former passivity. He walked over toward the boy, and silently but with a glare of contempt, beckoned him from the room with a crooked finger and led him along the corridor to the administrative office: the tall boy rigid in silent protest, the teacher, balding and stoop-shouldered in a wrinkled suit, shambling ahead of him. The youth, I later learned, was suspended for a day. At some lunch periods all this is drowned out by Mantovani-type pop records played over the public address system.

What adults generally, I think, fail to grasp even though they may actually know it, is that there is no refuge or respite from this: no coffee break, no taking ten for a smoke, no room like the teachers' room, however poor, where the youngsters can get away from adults. High schools don't have club rooms;

they have organized gym and recreation. A student cannot go to the library when he wants a book; on certain days his schedule provides a forty-five minute library period. "Don't let anybody leave early," a guidance counselor urged during a group-testing session at Hartsburgh, an apparently more permissive school that I also visited. "There really isn't any place for them to go." Most of us are as nervous by the age of five as we will ever be, and adolescence adds to the strain; but one thing a high-school student learns is that he can expect no provision for his need to give in to his feelings, or swing out in his own style, or creep off and pull himself together.

The little things shock most. High-school students—and not just, or even particularly, at Milgrim—have a prisoner's sense of time. They don't know what time it is outside. The research which occasioned my presence at Milgrim, Hartsburgh, and the other schools in my study required me to interview each of twenty-five to thirty students at each school three times. My first appointment with each student was set up by his guidance counselor; I would make the next appointment directly with the student and issue him the passes he needed to keep it. The student has no *open* time at his own disposal; he has to select the period he can miss with least loss to himself. Students well-adapted to the school usually pick study halls; poorer or more troublesome students pick the times of their most disagreeable classes; both avoid cutting classes in which the teacher is likely to respond vindictively to their absence. Most students, when asked when they would like to come for their next interview, replied, "I can come any time." When I pointed out to them that there must, after all, be some times that would be more convenient for them than others, they would say, "Well tomorrow, fourth period" or whatever. But hardly any of them knew when this would be in clock time. High-school classes emphasize the importance of punctuality by beginning at regular but uneven times like 10:43 and 11:27, which are, indeed, hard to remember; and the students did not know when this was.

How typical is all this? The elements of the composition—the passes, the tight scheduling, the reliance on threats of detention or suspension as modes of social control are nearly universal. The usurpation of any possible *area* of student initiative, physical or mental, is about as universal. Milgrim forbids boys to wear trousers that end more than six inches above the floor, and has personnel fully capable of measuring them. But most high schools have some kind of dress regulation; I know of none that accepts and relies on the tastes of students.

There are differences, to be sure, in tone; and these matter. They greatly affect the impact of the place on students. Take, for comparison and contrast, Hartsburgh High. Not fifteen miles from Milgrim, Hartsburgh is an utterly different community. It is larger, more compact, and more suburban; more of a place. Hartsburgh High is much more dominantly middle class and there are few Negroes in the high school there.

First impressions of Hartsburgh High are almost bound to be favorable. The building, like Milgrim, is new; unlike Milgrim's, it is handsome. External walls are mostly glass, which gives a feeling of light, air, and space. At Hartsburgh there is none of the snarling, overt hostility that taints the atmosphere at Milgrim. There are no raucous buzzers; no bells of any kind. Instead, there are little blinker lights arranged like the Mexican flag. The green light blinks and the period is over; the white light signals a warning; when the red light blinks it is time to be in your classroom. Dress regulations exist but are less rigorous than at Milgrim. Every Wednesday, however, is dress-up day; boys are expected to wear ties and jackets or jacket-sweaters, the girls wear dresses rather than skirts and sweaters. The reason is that on Wednesday the school day ends with an extra hour of required assembly and, as the students explain, there are often outside visitors for whom they are expected to look their best.

Students at Hartsburgh seem much more relaxed than at Milgrim. In the grounds outside the main entrance, during lunch period, there is occasional horseplay. For ten minutes during one noon hour I watched three boys enacting a mutual fantasy. One was the audience who only sat and laughed, one the aggressor, and the third—a pleasant, inarticulate varsity basketball player named Paul—was the self-appointed victim.

The two protagonists were portraying in pantomime old, silent-movie type fights in slow motion. The boy I did not know would slowly swing at Paul, who would sink twisting to the ground with grimaces of anguish; then the whole sequence would be repeated with variations, though the two boys never switched roles. In my interviews with Paul I had never solved the problems arising from the fact that he was eloquent only with his arms and torso movements, which were lost on the tape recorder, and it was a real pleasure to watch him in his own medium. This was a pleasure Milgrim would never have afforded me. Similarly, in the corridors at Hartsburgh I would occasionally come upon couples holding hands or occasionally rather more, though it distressed me that they always broke guiltily apart as soon as they saw me or any adult. One of my subjects, who was waiting for his interview, was dancing a little jig by himself in the corridor when I got to him. This was all rather reassuring.

It was also contrary to policy. There is a regulation against couples holding hands and they are punished if caught by the kind of teacher who hates sexuality in the young. The air and space also, subtly, turn out to be illusions if you try to use them. Hartsburgh High is built around a large, landscaped courtyard with little walks and benches. I made the mistake of trying to conduct an interview on one of these benches. When it was over we could not get back into the building except by disturbing a class, for the doors onto this inviting oasis can only be opened from inside, and nobody ever goes there. Since the courtyard is completely enclosed by the high-school building, this arrangement affords no additional protection from intruders; it merely shuts off a possible place for relaxation. The beautiful glass windows do not open enough to permit a body to squirm through and, consequently, do not open enough to ventilate the rooms, in which there are no individual controls for the fiercely effective radiators. Room temperature at Hartsburgh is a matter of high policy.

Teachers do not hide in the washrooms at Hartsburgh; but the principal recently issued a letter warning that any student caught in the vicinity of the school with "tobacco products" would be subject to suspension; students were directed to have their parents sign the letter as written acknowledgment that they were aware of the regulation and return it to school. Staff, of course, are permitted to smoke. At Hartsburgh a former teacher, promoted to assistant principal, serves as a full-time disciplinarian, but students are not dragged to his office by infuriated teachers, as sometimes happens at Milgrim. Instead, during the first period, two students from the school Citizenship Corps go quietly from classroom to classroom with a list, handing out summonses.

Along with having a less rancorous and choleric atmosphere than Milgrim, Hartsburgh seems to have more teachers who like teaching and like kids. But the fundamental pattern is still one of control, distrust, and punishment. The observable differences—and they are striking—are the result almost entirely, I believe, of *structural* and demographic factors and occur despite very similar administrative purposes. Neither principal respects adolescents at all or his staff very much. Both are preoccupied with good public relations as they understand them. Both are inflexible, highly authoritarian men. But their situations are different.

At Milgrim there is a strong and imaginative district superintendent, who is oriented toward the national educational scene. He likes to have projects, particularly in research and guidance. Guidance officers report through their chairman directly to him, not to the building principal; and the guidance staff is competent, tough, and completely professional. When wrangles occur over the welfare of a student they are likely to be open, with the principal and the guidance director as antagonists; both avoid such encounters if possible, and neither can count on the support of the district office; but when an outside force—like an outraged parent—precipitates a conflict, it is fought out. At Hartsburgh, the district superintendent is primarily interested in running a tight ship with no problems. To this end, he backs the authority of the principal whenever this might be challenged. The guidance office is vestigial and concerned primarily with college placement and public relations in the sense of inducing students to behave in socially acceptable ways with a minimum of fuss.

In these quite different contexts, demographic differences in the student bodies have crucial consequences. At Milgrim, the working-class students are not dominant—they have not got quite enough self-confidence or nearly enough social savvy to be—but they are close enough to it to be a real threat to the nice, college-bound youngsters who set the tone in their elementary and junior high school and who expect to go on dominating the high school. These view the rapid influx of lower-status students as a rising wave that can engulf them, while the newcomers, many of whom are recent migrants or high-school transfers from the city, can remember schools in which they felt more at home.

The result is both to split and to polarize student feeling about the school, its administration, and other students. Nobody likes Milgrim High. But the middle-class students feel that what has ruined it is the lower-class students, and that the punitive constraint with which the school is run is necessary to keep them in line. In some cases these students approach paranoia: one girl—commenting on a mythical high school described in one of our semi-projective research instruments—said, "Well, it says here that the majority of the students are Negro—about a third" (the actual statement is "about a fifth").

The working-class students are hard-pressed; but being hard-pressed they are often fairly realistic about their position. If the Citizenship Corps that functions so smoothly and smugly at Hartsburgh were to be installed at Milgrim, those who actually turned people in and got them in trouble would pretty certainly receive some after-school instruction in the way social classes differ in values and in the propensity for non-verbal self-expression. At Milgrim, the working-class kids know where they stand and stand there. They are exceptionally easy to interview because the interviewer need not be compulsively non-directive. Once they sense that they are respected, they respond enthusiastically and with great courtesy. But they do not alter their position to give the interviewer what they think he wants, or become notably anxious at disagreeing with him. They are very concrete in handling experience and are not given to generalization. Most of them seem to have liked their elementary school, and they share the general American respect for education down to the last cliché—but then one will add, as an afterthought, not bothering even to be contemptuous, "Of course, you can't respect *this* school." They deal with their situation there in correspondingly concrete terms. Both schools had student courts last year, for example, and Hartsburgh still does, though few students not in the Citizenship Corps pay much attention to it. Student traffic corpsmen give out tickets for corridor offenses, and these culprits are brought before an elected student judge with an administrative official of the school present as adviser. But Milgrim had a student court last year that quickly became notorious. The "hoody element" got control of it, and since most of the defendants were their buddies, they were either acquitted or discharged on pleas of insanity. The court was disbanded.

The struggle at Milgrim is therefore pretty open, though none of the protagonists see it as a struggle for freedom or could define its issues in terms of principles. The upper-status students merely assent to the way the school is run, much as middle-class white Southerners assent to what the sheriff's office does, while the lower-status students move, or get pushed, from one embroilment to the next without ever quite realizing that what is happening to them is part of a general social pattern. At Hartsburgh the few lower-status students can easily be ignored rather than feared by their middle-class compeers who set the tone. They are not sufficiently numerous or aggressive to threaten the middle-class youngsters or their folkways; but, for the same reason, they do not force the middle-class youngsters to make common cause with the administration. The administration, like forces of law and order generally in the United States, is accepted without deference as a part of the way things are and work. Americans rarely expect authority to be either intelligent or forthright; it looks out for its own interests as best it can. Reformers and troublemakers only make it nervous and therefore worse; the best thing is to take advantage of it when it can help you and at other times to go on living your own life and let it try to stop you.

This is what the Hartsburgh students usually do, and, on the whole, the results are pleasant. The youngsters, being to some degree ivy, do not constantly remind the teachers, as the Milgrim students do, that their jobs have no connection with academic scholarship. Many of the teachers, for their part, act and sound like college instructors, do as competent a job, and enjoy some of the same satisfactions. The whole operation moves smoothly. Both Milgrim and Hartsburgh are valid examples—though of very different aspects—of American democracy in action. And in neither could a student learn as much about civil liberty as a Missouri mule knows at birth.

What is learned in high school, or for that matter anywhere at all, depends far less on what is taught than on what one actually experiences in the place. The quality of instruction in high school varies from sheer rot to imaginative and highly skilled teaching. But classroom content is often handled at a creditable level and is not in itself the source of the major difficulty. Both at Milgrim and Hartsburgh, for example, the students felt that they were receiving competent instruction and that this was an undertaking the school tried seriously to handle. I doubt, however, that this makes up for much of the damage to which high-school students are systematically subjected. What is formally taught is just not that important, compared to the constraint and petty humiliation to which the youngsters with few exceptions must submit in order to survive.

The fact that some of the instruction is excellent and a lot of it pretty good *is* important for another reason; it makes the whole process of compulsory schooling less insulting than it otherwise would be by lending it a superficial validity. Society tells the adolescent that he is sent to school in order to learn what he is taught in the classroom. No anthropologist and very few high-school students would accept this as more than a rationalization; but rationalizations, to be at all effective, must be fairly plausible. Just as the draft would be intolerable if the cold war were wholly a piece of power politics or merely an effort to sustain the economy, so compulsory school attendance would be intolerable if what went on in the classrooms were totally inadequate to students' needs and irrelevant to their real intellectual concerns. Much of it is, but enough is not, to provide middle-class students, at least, with an answer when their heart cries out "For Christ's sake, what am I doing here?"

But far more of what is deeply and thoroughly learned in the school is designed to keep the heart from raising awkward, heartfelt issues—if design govern in a thing so subtle. It is learned so thoroughly by attendance at schools like Milgrim or even Hartsburgh that most Americans by the time they are adult cannot really imagine that life could be organized in any other way.

First of all, they learn to assume that the state has the right to compel adolescents to spend six or seven hours a day, five days a week, thirty-six or so weeks a year, in a specific place, in charge of a particular group of persons in whose selection they have no voice, performing tasks about which they have no choice, without remuneration and subject to specialized regulations and sanctions that are applicable to no one else in the community nor to them except in this place. Whether this law is a service or a burden to the young—and, indeed, it is both, in varying degrees—is another issue altogether. As I have noted elsewhere,[1] compulsory school attendance functions as a bill of attainder against a particular age group. The student's position is that of a conscript, who is protected by certain regulations but in no case permitted to use their breach as a cause for terminating his obligation. So the first thing the young learn in school is that there are certain sanctions and restrictions that apply only to them; that they do not participate fully in the freedoms guaranteed by the state, and that *therefore, these freedoms do not really partake of the character of inalienable rights.*

Of course not. The school, as schools continually stress, acts *in loco parentis;* and children may not leave home because their parents are unsatisfactory. What I have pointed out is no more than a special consequence of the fact that students are minors, and minors do not, indeed, share all the rights and privileges—and responsibilities—of citizenship. Very well.

However one puts it, we are still discussing the same issue. The high school, then, is where you really learn what it means to be a minor.

For a high school is not a parent. Parents may love their children, hate them, or like most parents, do both in a complex mixture. But they must nevertheless permit a certain intimacy and respond to their children as persons. Homes are not run by regulations, though the parents may think they are, but by a process of continuous and almost entirely unconscious emotional homeostasis, in which each member affects and accommodates to the needs, feelings, fantasy life, and character structure of the others. This may be, and often is, a terribly destructive process; I intend no defense of the family as a social institution. But children grow up in homes or the remnants of homes, are in physical fact dependent on parents, and too intimately related to them to permit their area of freedom to be precisely defined. This is not because they have no rights or are entitled to less respect than adults, but because intimacy conditions freedom and growth in ways too subtle and continuous to be defined as overt acts.

Free societies depend on their members to learn early and thoroughly that public authority is not like that of the family; that it cannot be expected—or trusted—to respond with sensitivity and intimate perception to the needs of individuals but must rely basically, though as humanely as possible, on the impartial application of general formulae. This means that it must be kept functional, specialized, and limited to matters of public policy; the meshes of the law are too coarse to be worn close to the skin. Especially in an open society, where people of very different backgrounds and value systems must function together, it would seem obvious that each must understand that he may not push others further than their common undertaking demands, or impose upon them a manner of life that they feel to be alien.

After the family, the school is the first social institution an individual must deal with—the first place in which he learns to handle himself with strangers. The school establishes the pattern of his subsequent assumptions as to what relations between the individual and society are appropriate and which constitute invasions of privacy and constraints on his spirit—what the British, with exquisite precision, call "taking a liberty." But the American public school evolved as a melting pot, under the assumption that it had not merely the right but the duty to impose a common standard of genteel decency on a polyglot body of immigrants' children and thus insure their assimilation into the better life of the American dream. It accepted, also, the tacit assumption that genteel decency was as far as it could go. If America has generally been governed by the practical man's impatience with other individuals' rights, it has also accepted the practical man's determination to preserve his property by discouraging public extravagance. With its neglect of personal privacy and individual autonomy the school incorporates a considerable measure of Galbraith's "public squalor." The plant may be expensive—for this is capital goods; but little is provided graciously, liberally, simply as an amenity, either to teachers or students, though administrative offices have begun to assume an executive look.

The first thing the student learns, then, is that as a minor, he is subject to peculiar restraints; the second is that these restraints are general, not limited either by custom or by the schools' presumed commitment to the curriculum. High-school administrators are not professional educators in the sense that a physician, an attorney, or a tax accountant are professionals. They do not, that is, think of themselves as practitioners of a specialized instructional craft, who derive their authority from its requirements. They are specialists in keeping an essentially political enterprise from being strangled by conflicting community attitudes and pressures. They are problem-oriented, and the feelings and needs for growth of their captive and unenfranchised clientele are the least of their problems; for the status of the "teen-ager" in the community is so low that even if he rebels, the school is not blamed for the conditions against which he is rebelling. He is simply a truant or a juvenile delinquent; at worst the school has "failed to reach him." What high-school personnel become specialists in, ultimately, is the *control* of large groups of students even at catastrophic expense to their opportunity to learn. These controls are not exercised primarily to facilitate instruction, and particularly, they are in no way limited to matters bearing on instruction. At several schools in our sample boys had been ordered—sometimes on the complaint of teachers—to shave off beards. One of these boys had played football for the school; he was told that, although the school had no legal authority to require him to shave, he would be barred from the banquet honoring the team unless he complied. Dress regulations are another case in point.

Of course these are petty restrictions, enforced by petty penalties. American high schools are not concentration camps. But I am not complaining about their severity; what disturbs me is what they teach their students concerning the proper relationship of the individual to society, and in this respect the fact that the restrictions and penalties are unimportant in themselves makes matters worse. Gross invasions are more easily recognized for what they are; petty restrictions are only resisted by "troublemakers." What matters in the end is that the school does not take its own business of education seriously enough to mind it.

The effects on the students are manifold. The concepts of dignity and privacy, notably deficient in American adult folkways, are not permitted to develop here. The school's assumption of custodial control of students implies that power and authority are indistinguishable. If the school's authority is not limited to matters pertaining to education, it cannot be derived from its educational responsibilities. It is a naked, empirical fact, to be accepted or contraverted according to the possibilities of the moment. In such a world, power counts more than legitimacy; if you don't have power, it is naïve to think you have rights that must be respected. . . . Wise up. High school students experience regulation only as control, not as protection; they know, for example, that the principal will generally uphold the teacher in any conflict with a student, regardless of the merits of the case. Translated into the high-school idiom, *suaviter in modo, fortiter in re* becomes "If you get caught, it's just your ass."

Students do not often resent this; that is the tragedy. All weakness tends to corrupt, and impotence corrupts absolutely. Identifying, as the weak must, with the more powerful and frustrating of the forces that impinge upon them, they accept the school as the way life is and close their minds against the anxiety of perceiving alternatives. Many students like high school; others loathe and fear it. But even the latter do not object to it on principle; the school effectively obstructs their learning of the principles on which objection might be based; though these are among the principles that, we boast, distinguish us from totalitarian societies.

Yet, finally, the consequence of continuing through adolescence to submit to diffuse authority that is not derived from the task at hand—as a doctor's orders or the training regulations of an athletic coach, for example, usually are—is more serious than political incompetence or weakness of character. There is a general arrest of development. An essential part of growing up is learning that, though differences of power among men lead to brutal consequences, all men are peers; none is omnipotent, none derives his potency from magic, but only from his specific competence and function. The policeman represents the majesty of the state, but this does not mean that he can put you in jail; it means, precisely, that he cannot—at least not for long. Any person or agency responsible for handling throngs of young people—especially if he does not like them or is afraid of them—is tempted to claim diffuse authority and snare the youngster in the trailing remnants of childhood emotion which always remain to trip him. Schools succumb to this temptation, and control pupils by reinvoking the sensations of childhood punishment, which remain effective because they were originally selected, with great unconscious guile, to dramatize the child's weakness in the face of authority. "If you act like a bunch of spoiled brats, we'll treat you like a bunch of spoiled brats," is a favorite dictum of sergeants, and school personnel, when their charges begin to show an awkward capacity for independence.

Thus the high school is permitted to infantilize adolescence; in fact, it is encouraged to by the widespread hostility to "teen-agers" and the anxiety about their conduct found throughout our society. It does not allow much maturation to occur during the years when most maturation would naturally occur. Maturity, to be sure, is not conspicuously characteristic of American adult life, and would almost certainly be a threat to the economy. So perhaps in this, as in much else, the high school is simply the faithful servant of the community.

There are two important ways in which it can render such service. The first of these is through its impact on individuals: on their values, their conception of their personal worth, their patterns of anxiety, and on their mastery and ease in the world —which determine so much of what they think of as their fate. The second function of the school is Darwinian; its biases, though their impact is always on individual youngsters, operate systematically to mold entire social groups. These biases endorse and support the values and patterns of behavior of certain segments of the population, providing their members with the credentials and shibboleths needed for the next stages of their journey, while they instill in others a sense of inferiority and warn the rest of society against them as troublesome and untrustworthy. In this way the school contributes simultaneously to social mobility and to social stratification. It helps see to it that the kind of people who get ahead are the kind who will support the social system it represents, while those who might, through intent or merely by their being, subvert it, are left behind as a salutary moral lesson.

1963

---

1. See p. 137, *infra.*

Why Students Leave Science

I

Why do many American students drop the scientific careers which they have spent several years training for with reasonable success? This question is likely to seem more patriotic than scholarly to anyone who is a respecter of science both as an area of inquiry and as a method of scholarship. The missile race, with the values it expresses, has tended to put off any serious and disinterested study of what has been happening to competent youngsters who set out to become scientists in our society. Yet, quite apart from any imputation that students ought to have stayed in science either for their own sake or that of the nation, the self-image of the scientist and the relationship of his culture to that of the humanities, both in the academy and in daily life, is now a crucial issue in itself. The choice of a profession is the one commitment our culture really takes seriously: this is for keeps; it is not a matter, like love or loyalty, to be continually altered to fit new circumstances. Conflicts in this area, if they are serious enough to make youngsters change their plans dramatically and follow any discernible common pattern, are social phenomena worth studying.

At Brooklyn College during the academic year 1958-59, together with my colleague, economist Carl Nordstrom, I set about investigating whether such a pattern existed. The study is a small one as social science research goes in the mid-twentieth century. After a pilot operation confined to a group of twenty Brooklyn College students, we applied to and received from the Cooperative Research Division of the U. S. Office of Education support to extend the study to Ohio State and Stanford Universities during the year 1959-60.[1]

At these schools, we examined the student records, and asked those students who had switched from a major in one of the natural sciences (physical or biological) or in engineering —after having firmly established a satisfactory record in their major fields—to come in for a one-hour research session. For comparative purposes, we secured a sample of excellent students who were continuing in their scientific work.

The total number finally included in the study was 121: 20 from Brooklyn, 60 from Ohio State, and 41 from Stanford. Seventy-five of these had changed from science or engineering to another field; 46 formed our "control group," students who were continuing in science.

Our procedure was as follows: every student was given a deck of thirty-two cards, each of which contained a statement critical of science. These thirty-two critical estimates were meant to be pieces of cautionary advice that might be given to a younger person trying to make up his mind whether or not to become a scientist. The student read all the cards, then sorted them into seven piles (containing, respectively, 1; 3; 7; 10; 7; 3; 1 cards) from the soundest to the most misleading or silliest statement. In other words, the first pile—of one card—contained the subject's estimate of the best advice that could be given to a potential science student; the last pile—again of one card—contained the worst advice.

Immediately after this sorting, an interview with the student was recorded. It began with a question as to whether there were any important things the student might have wanted to advise his imaginary young friend that the cards did not cover. After discussing the subject's answer to this question—it was usually, but not always, negative—he was asked to discuss why he had placed the cards he had chosen in the four extreme piles.

There is no basis for inferring that our 121 subjects are representative of all science students in the country. In fact, they could not be, if only because only about half of those invited took part in the research; and science students who are willing to participate in an unfamiliar research project clearly have a different attitude toward science than those who ignored such a request. Even though our 121 may be atypical in various ways, however, they are still of interest for what they are in themselves. A fact is still a fact, whether or not it can be generalized. The story of Marat and Charlotte Corday is of itself enough to disprove the canard that 18th-century Frenchmen never took baths.

Of the thirty-two cards, seven elicited sharply different responses from the students who had left science or engineering and from those who were continuing in these fields. Three of the seven cards deal with whether scientists get enough money to justify the time and trouble they spend on their training. The texts of these cards read:

> *2.* Scientists' salaries may seem high enough usually, but since they usually work for a company or university on a pure annual basis, they have much less chance than doctors, say, or lawyers, to do well for themselves.
>
> *3.* Over a lifetime, perhaps, a person with a Ph.D. in one of the sciences will earn about as much as other professionals; but it takes him so long to get up there with the others that he and his family have quite a struggle.
>
> *4.* As professional people, scientists have to expect to move socially among people who earn just enough more than they do to keep them in a state of mild but unpleasant tension.

Students who had *left* science tended to reject these cards as containing unimportant or misleading advice more severely than did the students who were continuing. The members of the control group were more willing to admit that these items might be legitimate complaints against a career that nevertheless appealed to them on balance. (When control subjects *did* reject these cards, they were likely to do so on the grounds that their information was misleading, out of date, while students who had abandoned science usually stressed that the money was just not that important to them.)

A fourth card which resulted in sharp differences discussed an unfavorable public image of the scientist. It was extremely unpopular with the students who had abandoned careers in science, but the control group distributed it almost by chance. It reads:

> 5. People are really pretty ambivalent toward scientists. Officially, they are highly respected, but the stereotype of the mad scientist is seldom wholly absent from the mind of the man in the street.

As one Brooklyn College student who had changed from physics to English put it: "I felt that a scientist should just have a love for his work if he goes into it at all, and so, even if there was such a stereotype—I don't know that there is—this should not concern him in the least." Hardly anyone who rejected this card did so because he thought it was a false statement. Generally, they *did* think so, but just did not much care whether it was or not.[2]

The remaining three card choices that distinguish the students who have left science from the control group are all cards that the former science students *favor* as important pieces of advice. And all deal with different aspects of the same issue—the training, method, and approach of scientists. The control group both *dislikes* and rejects the first of these cards, which discusses scientific training. Three of them pick it as the worst card—and none pick it as the best, while two of the ex-science group pick it as the best card and none pick it as the worst.

> 23. Contrary to what one usually expects, scientific training actually seems to offer little encouragement to independence of thought. There is more lecturing and less discussion than in other disciplines; the examinations tend to be rather petty and factual. Even the lecturer's jokes are listed in the syllabus.

Mr. Perry, a bright, personable Ohio State senior who switched from engineering to business management, explained why he picked this card as his first choice.

> PERRY: If this guy was going into engineering with the idea of gaining indepen . . . of being independent and having a broad concept of things . . . the subjects he's going to be taking are very limited and I don't think they encouraged really independent thinking. What they encouraged was the ability to, well, deal with specific mechanical processes in solving problems. . . . In most of the examinations in engineering, if you forgot the formula, well, you just don't solve the problem. Which puts

a premium on memorizing certain mechanical things. . . . It doesn't really lend itself to general discussion because, well, there's not much question about it.

By contrast, Mr. Wheeler, one of the most successful engineering students at Ohio State, rates the same card as the worst. Yet, in his comments, he agrees fairly well with Mr. Perry as to how things are. The contrast is largely between Mr. Perry's short-term irritation and Mr. Wheeler's long-range identification with his vocational goal:

WHEELER: I think actually lecturing, discussing a topic, the more familiar the scientist's professor becomes with his subject, as far as I can see, the more prepared he is to do basic research. It has to get to be, so that he knows these facts and principles upside down, backwards, in his sleep.

. . . .

Possibly there is more opportunity for discussion in the arts, but that probably stems from the fact that so many of the arts questions are not, actually, don't have one answer, while such things as two and two is always four. There's not too much discussion you can carry on about it.

The second of these three cards, on scientific method, is also rejected by members of the control group, though not as sharply. It reads:

25. The scientific method, as it is taught in the classroom and thought of by the general run of scientists, actually hampers efforts to understand many problems. Insight into the way things develop, and their unique, particular meaning, are sacrificed to rigid experimental control and statistical generality in order to keep the research scientifically respectable.

And the control group scatters the last card in a chance pattern; most of the ex-scientists, however, are solidly behind it. It reads:

26. The scientist's commitment to place objectivity first, while it has made science the instrument of empirical mastery of the environment, ultimately limits his power to penetrate to fundamental meanings. With so much of human experience tending toward depersonalization, it is just those perceptions that cannot be "consensually validated" that are often of crucial importance.

The subjects who leave science and engineering, then, insist that their feelings are the source of their integrity; and consider them more important than their economic or social aspirations. They must, therefore, demand respect for them and act them out at once. The students who remain may be equally critical of the limitations of scientific truth and of the society in which they must function—though they generally are not as critical. But they are either less confident of their ability to find any spot outside the system in which they would be any freer than they would be in science, or more confident that if they accept the system they will ultimately find themselves within it. Some seem to combine these two feelings, like Mr. Byron, a Stanford electrical engineer: young, married, cool; bright and sharp as a hound's tooth.

BYRON: I don't think it's the best use of me, but I'm in it now—up to the hilt. I mean, you know, after you get two years of school. I'm perfectly satisfied. I enjoy myself in electrical engineering; it's just that I would have enjoyed myself more in other fields. . . . I do like the technical side of engineering. It's just that I wish there were more of a creative aspect to it than there is. I won't be unhappy in engineering. . . . I don't enjoy being with purely intellectuals, either. . . . People that are for Adlai . . . madly for Adlai and join political causes. . . . I'm for Adlai myself, but not madly.

. . . .

There was the funniest headline: "Nixon will try to run as an individual if nominated." He's not going to run as an elephant, he's going to run as an individual, if he possibly can.

INTERVIEWER: *Card 23* ["scientific training actually seems to offer little encouragement to independence of thought"]?

BYRON: Well, it's true. What's there to discuss?

INTERVIEWER: Then, your most extreme negative card: *Card 5* ["mad scientist" public image]?

BYRON: Yes, I think it's silly. So what? Who is the man on the street? You just don't go fiddling around with the man on the street if you're a scientist.

INTERVIEWER: Any other comments you'd care to add?

BYRON: No. I think I've discussed my reasons for being slightly down on scientists. Definitely an interesting profession; it's just that these people get a slight case of narrow brain. That's just about it.

In Mr. Byron's manner there was nothing at all supercilious or snide. A wiry, bronzed, clean-shaven young man, clad in a sport shirt, jeans, and a pair of *zori* sandals; he broke the toe-strap on one of these by the ardor of his gestures during the interview. "May I?" he inquired politely at the end; and, dropping the *zori* into the wastebasket, strode out of the research office and into the Western world, barefoot.

II

Analyzing the card-sorts of these young men and women by another statistical procedure yields, not a set of individual numerical scores, but clusters of individuals who tend to see things in similar ways.[3] (It produces as well isolated individuals whose card-sorts are different from all others.) There is no magic in this; how many clusters are produced, if any, is as much a consequence of the particular levels of significance the research worker selects as it is of the way the subjects sort the cards. One selects levels of significance that yield the fineness or coarseness of discrimination warranted by the character of the data. *Our* choices yielded us eight clusters of from five to nineteen students, amounting to a total of 64 of the 121 subjects. Thus, 57 of our subjects were not assigned to any group on the basis of their card-sort.

The largest cluster contains nineteen members. They include students from Brooklyn, Ohio, and Stanford, and from both pure science and engineering curricula. Eleven of the nineteen have abandoned science or engineering; eight are continuing. We call this group our *eclectic* cluster.

The favorite cards of the *eclectic* cluster are *17* and *31* which read:

17. The work of the laboratory scientist is less varied and engrossing than the image of the pioneer serving mankind in his laboratory would lead you to expect. Most scientists spend most of their time in rather dull, routine activity.

31. The costs of scientific research today have tied science so closely to the purposes of elite groups in society that it has abandoned most of its critical and skeptical function. When you are dependent on tax exemptions and foundation grants in order to get your work done, you get to be pretty careful never to catch Truth in embarrassing commerce with Mars or Mammon.

Two cards that most of our subjects reject but that the members of the *eclectic* cluster dislike with special intensity are:

8. Scientists don't seem to live like other upper-middle-class people, even when they are quite successful. They tend to have fewer interests outside their work in things like the arts, or even in other people, so that life can get pretty dreary.

and:

21. While there are many exceptions, groups of scientists are generally not as pleasant to be among as other intellectuals. On the whole they tend to be stiffer and somewhat less broad-minded and sophisticated; they hardly seem to know how to enjoy themselves.

Mr. Rabinow, a Brooklyn College senior recommended to our study as one of the most promising young chemists in the graduating class of 1959, illustrates very vividly, though with a manner and volubility that are purely Brooklyn, and a sensitivity that is purely his own, some of the characteristic attitudes of the *eclectic* cluster. On the one hand, there is a compelling —almost a compulsive—identification that leads the subject to insist that he likes science and scientists (whether or not he himself is going on in it). On the other hand, there is a nagging preoccupation with the daily annoyances of scientific work under the conditions in which it must actually be done. Mr. Rabinow explains his choice of *Card 17:*

RABINOW: Well, I've had opportunities, see. I work after school. I work for a big chemical company, and I see what most research chemists are expected to do. . . . Only Ph.D. chemists do actual research. The way they set it up, most of it is dull routine activity. . . . I mean, once in a while you come up with an idea, I mean, that's the fascinating part; but then to go through the synthesis and the library work, I mean, that's actually a big part of science, really, and that is dull and routine. . . . I suppose everybody says Hollywood-type scientists are something glorious, and that's not really true.

. . . .

It's dull and routine, the work, *but it leads to something* [italics are ours]. . . . I mean, you know you're going . . . the work itself is dull and routine, then you get satisfaction after it's all over and accomplished.

. . . .

I know I like a certain kind of recognition when I do a certain type of work. See, the work I do is nothing really, I mean, to be recognized, but on my level, naturally, there isn't any. But even on higher levels, it's always emphasized—one man never gets the credit, it's always four or five men have done it. Usually the —I know this would bother me—I mean the—usually the research director gets his name on it even though he had nothing to do with it, and then other people, you know, sometimes the vice-president, they might stick his name on there too, to show, you know, like a dedication to a symphony or something to your patron sort of kind of thing, and I just don't feel that this is right. . . . In other words, you know, apple-polishing is very prevalent; if you want to get somewhere, you've got to be able to toe the line and show them that, you know, you're with them —very little dissension. Everybody's smooth and calm. No arguments, no fights.

. . . .

Let's say that I'm not particularly satisfied with my work now, but . . . well, after I get out of graduate school, if I go back into industry, I don't feel that it'll be, I don't expect—let's say, I *hope* it will be different, but I don't expect it to be much different from now. . . . This is the way it is.

. . . .

It's really hard for me to say exactly why, the general question, why I chose science. I never had a chemistry set. When I

> wanted to do some things, I couldn't do it at my house. I mean, my parents couldn't see it, you know. I did fool around a little bit; but right away they were on my back for fooling around. Once, I even developed some pictures, and this annoyed my father because of the acetic acid smell; he didn't like it, so that was the end of that. . . . I don't know, I was just curious about different things, and I thought that in science you have opportunity, really, to see a lot of different things . . . really, you need extensive training. . . . I try to tell myself, from the way I talk, I try to tell myself that the thing that I'm looking after in life is not a lot of money. That's the way I feel. [Pause] I feel that I just want to make, naturally, a comfortable living and then devote myself to, oh, reading and learning and things. . . . I also enjoy, well, working with my hands. I enjoy that, and not as a hobby, but more as a career. I rather enjoy that. And science lends itself most to that. . . . I rather like to work with my hands; it fascinates me and I get pleasure out of it.
>
> . . . .
>
> Anyway, it's remarkable the way things fit in. . . . Through high school I got the job where I work now, and when I started to work, well, I mean, they had students working there who were working nights and going to full-time day school and they said, "Well, why don't you do this?" . . . and I started to day school. And everything worked out for the best . . . [*sotto voce*] in the best of all possible worlds.

Though mundane in their attitudes and concerned with the realities of the scientist's or engineer's working life, the members of the eclectic cluster are not happy about those realities as they see them; too modest or not confident enough to make large claims for the authority of their inner life, they nevertheless display that life vividly in their reactions to conditions they hardly hope to transcend. They may continue, as Mr. Rabinow is continuing, in science. But if they do so, their level of aspiration is appreciably low; they haven't much hope of attaining distinction.

An Ohio State member of this cluster, continuing in geology and doing extremely well in it, speaks in this way of his burgeoning career: "I like to study geology, but I'm not sure yet exactly what field of geology. And I don't know, I'm afraid that if I'm married soon and have a family, I might just have to drop geology just to work, so I could make some money." The "experimental" members of the *eclectic* cluster, though perhaps more sensitive to petty details of their experience as science students than to larger value or epistemological issues, at least have the ego-strength and detachment to make a break. Mr. Eero, a stalwart, roughly handsome ex-engineer of Finnish stock, falls into this group. Commenting on *Card 17*, which is his first choice among the thirty-two, Mr. Eero says:

> EERO: I think everybody, when thinking of a profession, tends to glamorize it There is a lot of routine to any kind of job. . . . I think of people like Madame Curie, for instance, and her husband, who worked for I don't know how many years shoveling pitchblende around. . . . All my experience has been that science requires a great deal of precision, and precision sometimes for precision's sake. And, thus, there is a certain going over of things. I think there is a certain amount of scientific work that is dull no matter what level you reach. Even a guy like Einstein has to sit down and work out mathematical formulas, go through a lot of pages and pages of work, and I imagine there are times when they wish they could skip that part. . . . This is to tell someone who you're talking with who's thinking of choosing science. Now if a person is . . . there are people happy doing things that I couldn't do for two minutes, and this is something that a person has to look into and not glorify science as standing in a white coat and "Eureka—" because very little of it is that.

The *eclectic* cluster is not only the largest cluster yielded by the methodology of the study; it is statistically the most central. Its characteristics do not contrast with those of the total group of subjects so much as they emphasize certain of them. The popular cards that warn against the tendency of science to deny subjective truth are distributed within the *eclectic* cluster very much as they are by the total group of subjects. But the *eclectic* cluster is especially troubled about the daily ennui in a scientist's life, and especially reluctant to imagine that ennui transcended by noble vision or purpose, or by heroic individual capacity. No man is a hero to the *eclectic* cluster. Which is, after all, the way we live now.

There is, however, a subsidiary and somewhat less clearly delineated focus of central tendency in the total group which produces a cluster of twelve individuals. We call this the *adolescent* cluster, because its members share a common preoccupation with their own identity and their peculiar perception of the meaning of life. They talk about what it means to be *them* endlessly, enthusiastically, and also refreshingly and well.

The *adolescent* cluster emphasizes cards 23, 25, 26, and 27 far more than most of our subjects do. The first three of these have been quoted; *Card 27* reads:

> 27. An interest in science is, to some extent, something many people in this culture need to grow *through*. An American adolescent, if he has any spontaneous curiosity about the world he lives in at all, almost has to couch his interest in scientific terms, for these are the terms available. But when he gets far enough, he may well find that the questions science can answer are no longer the questions he must ask.

All four of these cards warn against various ways in which scientific rigidity may exclude or impose upon elements of intuition or poetic vision.

The archetype of our *adolescent* cluster is Mr. Hughes, a big, attractive, highly articulate Stanford junior whose interview, rather to his own astonishment, went on for well over an hour. Here is a part of it:

> HUGHES: If you're going to do something you're interested in, you might as well base your education on your interests at the same time. I consider this rather a valid argument.
>
> . . . .
>
> INTERVIEWER: Your mother [Hughes's father is deceased] was anxious for you to enter engineering, or what?
>
> HUGHES: No, she was just worried that philosophy was highly out of date as a paying profession. This is the question I get from everyone: "Well, what in the world are you going to do?" and I smile and answer "I don't know, and it really doesn't matter at the moment," because it doesn't. I'm considering teaching as a profession, and I have a summer job as a teacher in prep school which I will find out just how I like it. . . . I feel profoundly happier. . . . I find that everything I do, from every

discussion I have over coffee on a casual date, or every book I read, every magazine, everything I hear, do, and see is somehow related to everything I'm doing.

. . . .

[Of engineering] I, as I said, was profoundly disappointed in all my classes. Math has been one of my best subjects all my life. It was quite easy for me. I had no trouble in the math courses; the same with the engineering courses. It just came easy, but it wasn't anything there—like sand in soup. . . . A lot of this comes from just realization—it's just one awakening after another, and a lot of these interests I didn't know I had. I didn't know how much I was interested in literature or religion or philosophy because I'd not had an introduction to these, and my life had been full of engineering. I hadn't read but about one or two books in *four years* [emphasis Hughes's].

. . . .

I like engineering. I like math. Math, to me, is art. I like it. I like the way things work out and I like engineering. I will still fiddle with it. I still have junk, electronics stuff in my garage at home and, off and on, kick around with all the time. But the big thing is there's nothing there, nothing I can get my hands on. . . . It's just things that are not covered and I feel that engineering is . . . would limit me too much.

. . . .

I still don't know exactly what I want to go into and this sometimes worries me. . . . But, no; the inner struggle has been pretty much settled. It was rough turmoil for a while but, once I accepted it—accepted the fact that I wasn't an engineer . . . I mean, it's just round; it's nice, inner calm, peace and perfectly satisfied. I know, in general, where I'm going, and how I'm going to get there. I know what I like and, in general, of course this is always changing; it's expanding. . . . It's not because I did not like engineering. I have an awful lot of respect for the guys who can just, in a sense, throw away their lives and settle for just having things cut out for them, and that's—what time is it getting to be?

Another Stanford member of the *adolescent* cluster, Mr. Grant, comments on the reasons for his change from engineering to political science. Mr. Grant's style is less effulgent than

Mr. Hughes's; he broods along like the young adult Westerner that he is. But similar feelings have been stirring the two boys:

GRANT: As far as a career is based, when I changed, I threw away virtually a set career and a job in companies I could have gone to work for, knowing that what I was going to study now was what I wanted to study. I'd just take a chance on what I'd find. I figured I'd find my place.

. . . .

These friends of mine, they were also engineers, they just took this [training in engineering theory] in a way that was just foreign to my nature, because I've seen too many people—young engineers in jobs, I've worked with them—who come out and know it right out of the books but don't have the slightest idea how to get a job done. And I turned away from this, and I knew that I could never be that way and I began to kind of re-examine what I really wanted; I found that engineering wasn't what I really wanted. . . . So, finally I decided it was time to get out. . . . I'd rather get the kind of education that would do me . . . that I'd feel would do me the most good in the long run, and that is a broader, liberal education.

INTERVIEWER: Yes. Do you what sort of good?

GRANT: Just being more [pause]—this is the question, because the things that I figure are . . . least important is the economic angle, because I figure that if I can get the liberal education, why I can make a living anyway; if you've got a college degree you stand a reasonably good chance of making a living. I'm not out to get rich in this world, because there's so much of this world that I don't understand and want to find out about; and I don't think you find it in math books or engineering books. And I know I'll probably never find it, and I know it's very, very easy to think about these things. . . . It's very easy to be all involved with these ideas while you're in school; but I can sit around in a discussion and talk about these ideas and philosophies and different things; and you can walk right out and never think about them again. I'm just more interested in the ideas of politics and political action and theories of government and the way men are, the way men work, why men do things, than I am in building roads for men to drive on. That's it. . . . I don't have any false illusions about going out on any big campaign of any ideal, and that's just it: I'd like to try and sell these ideas [earlier in the interview Mr. Grant had expressed a specific, rather conservative social ideology] or try and influence a few people; but yet, I really don't know whether my ideas are as yet that important or that good. And if I should come to the conclusion that I did have some ideas that could be of some use, I really don't know how I could go about trying to spread them. . . . This way, I don't . . . at the present time have the same connections and ins, but I think I'll find what I'm more interested in here. I don't know where it'll lead me; lead me along the lines I'm more interested in following.

From Mr. Hughes's and Mr. Grant's comments one would infer that the *adolescent* cluster must be composed of youngsters who are lost to science; and it is. Only one member of it —Mr. Bond, of Ohio State—is still in a scientific field. Mr. Bond is a healthy-looking, jolly, crew-cut young man. But he is not exactly a conventional type scientist.

BOND: In my mind, to really do something, you've got to have a skill. It takes more than just aspirations. And you've got to have a certain amount of specific skill that you can offer. I'm talking in terms of humanitarian endeavor, if you want. . . . I'd like to be the organizational type in WHO [World Health Organization] or something like that, if you want. A man in WHO working, I think, can accomplish more than Schweitzer. . . . Schweitzer has become quite a symbol. He has, there's no doubt about it. A young man, you like to think—at least I do— "What can I do with my life, which I consider to be really valuable?" . . . And to me, service is the biggest concept. It really is. Along with, of course, in the end, I'm trying to achieve personal happiness. Let's not get away from that.

. . . .

Science is not an end in itself to me. It's merely, once you go far enough in science, I think that you do have to jump again to other questions, because I think science stops and, if you want, philosophy and a lot of other questions begin to pick up a little bit. And I couldn't. I think you could say that I'm a scientifically trained person with goals which are strictly not scientific research, but an application of science to man. So I guess you would call me, well, a humanist.

. . . .

So, independence of thought; if one just took science courses, I'd feel like he was just regurgitating. Until you reach the state, now . . . that might take me toward research eventually way further on, that you know science so well there's no more regurgitating. From there, it's newness; and if I could find newness in science, there'd be a real challenge.

. . . .

It's been very interesting to be able to sit and analyze. I've thought about this . . . *or else I would have switched out of the curriculum of science which I'm now in* [our emphasis]. And I couldn't go ahead and be a doctor. I'd become a philosopher; but, to me, being a philosopher all of your life isn't achieving what I'd like to achieve very generally. There is a temptation for a young man, I think, once you begin to be exposed to thinking and to new thoughts and to philosophy and to more general readings, and Tillich and a few other gentlemen, to want to do more thinking and less learning of facts. Original thought. And I'd like with science to lead an original life . . . and it's not a life that's so set up that it's rigid to begin with. It's very general. I can't tell exactly what fate is going to take me into, but I can only define things as I clearly see them now. They may change in the future.

The cards the *adolescent* cluster rejects, as might be expected, are the money and status cards (*1* through *5*, and *8*).[4]

Mr. Bond, with his interest in service and in having an impact on the society in which he lives, and his willingness to function within a group like WHO, illustrates rather clearly the characteristics of another cluster to which our procedure assigns him; and he shows how it is related to the *adolescent* one. This ancillary cluster, which we call the *societal* cluster, has eight members, all of whom, except Mr. Bond, have given up on science. (Three of these—including Mr. Bond and Mr. Hughes—also fall into our *adolescent* cluster.[5]) The same cards which the *adolescent* cluster tends to interpret as warnings that scientific training may stifle a student's inner flame and deafen him to the unverifiable comments of his inner voice, the *societal* cluster tends to interpret as warnings against ignoring matters of personal concern in their external lives. The *adolescent* members can thus take the reference (on *Card 27*) to the possibility that "The questions science can answer are no longer the questions he must ask" as an allusion to their deeper subjective interests; while members of the *societal* are reminded of the broader social and political commitments that they might have made. Mr. Bond illustrates the juxtaposition of these two kinds of concern; Mr. Hughes much less so.

Just as the *adolescent* cluster has the *societal* cluster overlapping it from the general direction, ideologically speaking, of the left, the *eclectic* cluster has an ancillary cluster of eleven subjects, overlapping it from the right.[6] What is exaggerated in these eleven subjects is the "conventionality" of the *eclectic* cluster. Among them, the control group members seem almost to parody conventionality in their acceptance by their world and in their reduction of every fundamental conflict to the most stereotyped terms.[7] The students who have abandoned science, on the other hand, seem to have failed to establish their identity.

The qualities of conventionality are revealed by the subjects' slight tendency to accept *Card 1*, "Scientists make too little money . . ." as sound advice, while most other subjects reject it; and by the tendency to reject as nonsensical the cards which emphasize the conflict between science and subjective aspects of experience. These subjects emphasize even more than those of the *eclectic* cluster that science is full of "dull, routine, activity"—Mr. Rabinow is one of the overlapping members—but like the *eclectics*, the *conventionals* also insist that scientists have just as much fun as anybody. "They're people," an Ohio State student continuing in engineering school reported, "scientists are people, educated people. Enjoy getting together, enjoy parties. I don't think I could exist without my golf in the summertime." Another commented: "Many of my friends are engineers or pure scientists or mathematicians and I find that they tend to like music, art; they believe very well in girls—and outside of working hours they're . . . you couldn't stereotype them as scientists at all." Miss Larinn, an attractive and very bright young chemist, who is one of the European subjects in the *conventional* cluster, clearly illustrates the sometimes illogical positivism of this group:

> LARINN: Well, well science doesn't deal with philosophical understanding of problems. It's true that you cannot gain a philosophical understanding of the problem through the scientific method. On the other hand, I think it's impossible to solve any scientific problem through a philosophical approach.

Finally, a last comment by a Stanford economics major (who has not been able to "pin down" why engineering "didn't agree with me"):

> I think that the empirical method will make a lot of things that are now important to people in philosophy, make dead issues out of an awful lot of things. . . . Where now the lot is conjecture, there'll be empirical bases for conclusions later on, and that's going to limit such fields as philosophy quite a bit, and religion. It's going to be a little bit rough on these people.

III

The four clusters so far described comprise the core of our sample and include slightly over a third of its members. We take these clusters, and the common attitudes that generated them, then, to lie at the heart of our problem. Arranging the clusters in terms of the social attitudes they represent, one can order them, moving from left to right, as follows: *societal, adolescent, eclectic,* and *conventional.*

One very unsettling point emerges from this classification. *There are no more science students in our left field.* Our method identifies and groups together youngsters who share a noble and sensitive vision of themselves and their place in the universe, and who *once* planned to become scientists or engineers. They do not plan to do so now. They have been repelled either by what they regard as excessive limitations on their chance to respond and to take account of their own feelings, or by an equally distasteful limitation on their chance to do anything that is both original and useful. Similarly, our method also identifies and groups together youngsters who seem willing to accept, on the whole, the world they live in and who come to the usual terms with it. One group, indeed, the *conventional,* seems unable even to imagine any real alternatives to the values and assumptions of that world: these students defend science and scientists (even though some have left the field in response to various comparatively disorganized feelings of personal dissatisfaction with the way science works today). Others in these two clusters are going ahead as planned.

But have they such stuff as science is made of? In a sense, yes, for it will be made of what they have. Meanwhile, however, the poets and philosophers have packed up, packed it in, and left. An occasional original like Mr. Byron remains as an individual or as a member of a small cluster distinct from the core group. But we have no cluster of brilliant, creative youngsters who expect to fulfill their destiny and their inner vision *within science.* There are many such youngsters; there are enough just at Stanford to lead an immodest visitor to wonder whether he may not have died and passed on to his reward without noticing it. Science and engineering, though, do not hold them.

By way of contrast, we do have a small, five-man cluster composed entirely of highly successful, continuing Ohio State science and engineering students, which in its card choices and comments, treats science as would a group of comfortable "old pros." Its members see *Card 17*—"dull, routine"—simply as trivial, leaving it in the middle of the distribution; and like most of the controls, they vigorously reject *23* and *25,* which deal with the deleterious effects of scientific training and method. But they never seem defensive in the quality of their responses. As one subject said: "I do not feel that science is against religion or religion is against science. I feel that they are perfectly compatible. . . . I think that the scientist and the theologians are coming closer together in their attitudes in working together, and I think that in the future this controversy will die out." To this cluster, both science and religion are against sin and ignorance, and, therefore, are bound to triumph; they are quite intelligent enough to be able to agree afterward on a satisfactory division of their proper spheres of influence.

These are nice guys (one of them is a nice girl) and, as they say, "no sweat." They are committed, though not dedicated, to science or engineering, and they will make good, solid, contributions that will get bigger and better as they learn their way around. They are conventional—their cluster lies closer to the *conventional* cluster than to any other—in their own way, but they are not twitchy. They'll do just fine. In the idiom of fifty years ago, one might have said of them that they would never set the world on fire. Today—well, these are the kind of competent young men and women who get their job done.[8]

The "old pros" are more mature and better adjusted than the *adolescents*. But it seems to me that this means merely that as late adolescents continue to grow up in the United States they find life easier, and are granted more opportunities with fewer conflicts, if the "old pro" values are the ones that come naturally to them. They are more mature in the sense that they are more like successful adults already, and therefore less threatening. But they are not more mature in the sense of being more nearly ready to bear the rich harvest of which the human species, under favorable conditions, is capable,

I am not enough of a nationalist to wish to keep in science the ardent and promising youngsters who leave it, nor even convinced that it would be in the national interest, whatever that may be, to do so. But it does seem to me that the experiences that drive them out have far less to do with science as either a method or an epistemological system than they do with science as a social institution. Those of our best subjects who left did so because of the way scientists are taught and the way they are used; not because of what science essentially is. After all, it is our respondents who believe that science deals with deep and fundamental issues of being, who are correct. But undergraduates do not get much chance to get down to fundamentals.

It would seem that the sensible way for a nation to retain such youngsters as future scientists and engineers would be to try to improve the way they are taught and to modify the opportunities open to them in their later employment so as to provide a legitimate expectation of personal autonomy in work. But this is not the way our culture is actually going about it. Instead, subject after subject in our study complains that the *way* the high school led him into science confused him and made it much harder for him to see just how his career choice was going to affect his life and his image of himself. From an adolescent, considering what it is he has to do to grow up, this is a very serious charge against secondary education.

Mr. Perry, the first subject quoted in this article, and an ex-engineering member of the *adolescent* cluster in excellent standing, is rather sardonic about his high-school experience:

> PERRY: Well, I think it's just because all through my high school that we had sort of the idea that the, you know, the engineer was the person that was—actually, it was just a bunch of propaganda—that the engineer was the person who was going to be successful . . . which I fully believe now is entirely a fallacy. . . . I don't—nobody actually told me this, but it just seemed to be the general consensus of opinion . . . that if you were a boy and did well in math and had a natural adaption [*sic*] for mechanical drawing, well, that "you just come over here and be in engineering." . . . [Then, in college] I just began to think, well now, if doing twenty calculus problems every night, that it's just sort of busy work, really, and, well, I just didn't like it *at all.* I began to think "Well, now, is this what I'm preparing for?" and if I'm going to be using this after I graduate, I don't even *want* to be using it after I graduate. And so, if I'm not going to use it, why am I doing it now?

Mr. Hughes, at the opening of his interview, in response to the "Is there anything that has been left out that you would care to add" probe of the interviewer, stated flatly:

> HUGHES: Now, my decision was made on the grounds that I didn't want to be an engineer—that I *wasn't* an engineer—and my reasons for being in engineering lie, inherently, in the California state public school system,[9] it being that for the person of above average ability and interest there are only two outlets in the curricula of the California high schools which allow for any expansion, any room to vent any extra ability and interest

—and these are the math and physical science fields. . . . And my last two years in high school were spent preparing for an engineering career. Everyone said, "You'll make a *great* engineer!" . . . It's a very easy process. . . . Now, in our graduating class, we had 77 people, and of the about 30 boys in that class that went through the last two years with me in math and science classes—same group went all the way through—there are two left in engineering. . . . But so many go in; it's easy, it's nice, "Oh, you're going to be an engineer, scientist!"

Of course, sometimes the process works, and when it does, the experience may take the form described by Mr. Valcic, esteemed at Ohio State as one of its best young chemical engineers. Explaining his career choice, he says:

VALCIC: Well, in high school, I took an examination with an employment bureau in which our skills were investigated. I was told that I had the ability and understanding of knowledge to do just about anything. And so, well, I had been interested in the scientific field, engineering and so on. I took a scholarship test and received a scholarship to go into chemical engineering. Well, since I'm in it, and I am having all my education paid for, it would be somewhat foolish to go out of engineering, considering that I have the ability to understand engineering as such; and to me, it doesn't make too much difference in what field I actually make my living. Personally, if I hadn't gotten this scholarship, I would have gone into agriculture. Not to have come to college and studied, but just started farming. Try to run farming as a business rather than just a way of life.

Mr. Valcic, I think, may be allowed to have the last word. It figures.

1961

1. Both these institutions most generously provided us with every resource we requested, though neither was a party to our research contract or received any compensation whatever for what they gave us. I mention this simply as evidence that the academic community is still as much a reality as the more conspicuous academic market place.

2. Margaret Mead and Rhoda Metraux, however, in their milestone study of the "Image of the Scientists Among High School Students" (*Science*, 126, August 30, 1957) found the "mad scientist" image one of the most widespread and influential components of the students' image of the scientist.

3. Readers familiar with research

methodology in the behavioral sciences will recognize what is described here as an application of William Stephenson's Q-technic. See *The Study of Behavior* (University of Chicago Press, 1953).

4. *Card 1*, which has not yet been quoted, reads simply: "Scientists make too little money in the course of a lifetime, compared to people in other professions, to justify the costs of getting a doctor's degree." It is the most general of the money cards; and also the most generally rejected by all subjects. For convenience in analyzing, cards dealing with related issues were numbered consecutively, but were presented in random order.

5. Two members of the twelve-person *adolescent* cluster are also grouped, through other portions of their card-choice pattern, into the central *eclectic* cluster; but no member of the *societal* cluster is.

6. Three members overlap—a smaller proportion in this case—and the cluster represents an exaggeration of some of the characteristics of *eclectic* cluster in a comparable way. This cluster also includes former science students or engineers and controls. Its members are drawn from all three schools.

7. Two of these, however, recent arrivals from Northern Europe—one is returning to Norway as soon as he has finished his degree—thus have less reason to be concerned with subtler aspects of the American way of life.

8. C. P. Snow's Minister of Production, Thomas Bevill, is a little blunter about them. " 'It's funny about those chaps,' he reflected, 'I used to think scientists were supermen. But they're not supermen, are they? Some of them are brilliant, I grant you that. But between you and me, Eliot, a good many of them are like garage hands. Those are the chaps who are going to blow us all up.' " *The New Men*, pp. 67-68.

9. Technically, Mr. Hughes should have referred to the Monterey County School System; California schools are not organized into a state system.

The Gifted Student and His Enemies

One of the most heavily emphasized themes in current discussions of education in the United States is the search for potential excellence. In the past we have tended to equate academic promise with high intelligence, and to infer that the most serious wastage of young people in school resulted from the school's failure to recognize and reward high academic aptitude in lower-status youngsters. The search for excellence, on these terms, became an extension of the traditional American quest for equality of opportunity, which served as its moral justification. But this defines the issue far too narrowly. Of perhaps more fundamental importance is the effect of the school on kinds of giftedness that may be useless or even disadvantageous in earning good grades and high recommendations in a typical high school milieu. High IQ and diligence do not exhaust the possibilities of superior capacity. Originality and insight, disciplined but impassioned sensitivity, and a highly personal and unique quality of mind contribute as indispensably to human achievement.

In the school, as in much of our society, creative youngsters seem usually to arouse a specific animus. Teachers dislike them, and the students learn quite early that the spontaneity and subjectivity they prize in themselves cannot be expected to lead to success in school or in later life.

What is the source of the animus, and why is the creative student so likely to encounter it? Particularly useful in answering these questions is a concept which, though explicitly introduced by Friedrich Nietzsche, has only recently had much impact on American social thought. This is the concept of *Ressentiment*.[1] The word sounds like a French translation of "resentment," and this does approximate the meaning. But only imprecisely. *Ressentiment* is less completely conscious than resentment, and less focused on the particular real experiences that are its actual causes. In contrast, it is usually rationalized, covert, diffuse, and largely unconscious. Just as one may legitimately refer to "free-floating anxiety" as a decisive element in certain kinds of personality, *ressentiment* is a kind of free-floating ill-temper. It is the syndrome produced by intense hostility intensely repressed over long periods of time. As such, it is familiar enough. Why then is it worth discussing as a *social,* rather than a psychological, disorder? Because of the peculiar and devastating ways in which *ressentiment* has become institutionalized in twentieth-century mass culture.

The conditions of contemporary life have reified *ressentiment* into a massive social and political reality. The operation of democratic political institutions—and especially their underlying egalitarian value assumptions—has greatly increased the political influence of the most *ressentient* social groups while weakening the will of more affirmative individuals to resist them.

Public education is one of the social institutions most strongly affected by *ressentiment.* The public schools attract, as teachers, administrators, and counselors, individuals from groups in the population that are particularly subject to it, and for reasons which are likely to influence the selection of the more *ressentient* from among such groups. The school is the traditional avenue—and arena—for social mobility, which many of its clientele appear to conceive as its sole *raison d'être*; one goes to school in order to get ahead, or one drops out; few youngsters are held in school by any real commitment to the cultural values represented by education, and few public schools in fact represent those values adequately. But those who are most anxious about social mobility are also most likely to be *ressentient.*

Those social groups are most prone to *ressentiment* whose members are especially subjected to frustration in their position in life, but who feel so impotent that they do not dare to get consciously angry and rebel and hit back, or strike out for themselves against the actual source of their frustration. Generally, they dare not even recognize it. Instead they identify with and accommodate to the very individuals or social forces undermining their position, and whose strength they tend to admire and exaggerate. By thus exercising their impotence, they increase it; what a less threatened individual would have felt as rage becomes resentment, then a kind of small-shopkeeper's fearful and self-pitying distrust, and finally, perhaps, merely an unconscious predisposition to sanctimonious spitefulness.

Ressentiment therefore ravages most seriously the rootless lower-middle or white-collar classes who give up most in order to be respectable and get least real deference and security in return. The threat to them is much more serious now that Western life permits its lower-level personnel to develop so few real skills. Yet, they cannot attack the system that has made their lives meaningless, for they are in collusion with it and want to rise within it.

It is not merely the economic threat that leads to *ressentiment,* for *ressentiment* is not simply anxiety. The *ressentient,* rather, are those who have given up important human potentialities in making deals with the system, and are now faced with mounting evidence that this is not going to pay off. Thus the German inflation of the twenties, wiping out the savings of millions of petty bourgeois who for a lifetime had slaved to confuse thrift and order with decency, helped pave the way to Nazism, which epitomized *ressentiment* in its Eichmannesque combination of sadism and alienation. The essence of the Nazi position, after all, is that its motives were worthy of the highest traditions of the civil service; one likes to think that the executioners of Joan of Arc, by comparison, at least felt that there was something cheerful about a nice fire. Even hatred is too strong an emotion for the highly authoritarian, who can handle feeling only by bureaucratizing it, so that it emerges as prejudice against classes of individuals rather than open hostility. Good authoritarians never get personal.

But the rigidity, hostility, and alienation that reveal the authoritarian personality in face-to-face relationships are not peculiar to adherents of the political far right. In the presence of the doctrinaire young liberal, the professional Negro or Zionist, the militant opponent of atomic warfare, one often senses the existence of the same animus however strongly one may agree with their views. It does not seem to matter very much—it does matter somewhat—whether humanitarian issues are themselves a central part of the ideology. The aggressively poor young college instructor, flaunting his radical views, minority status, and undisciplined children as explanations of his lack of recognition and status, is no fascist. But he does seem to run on the same fuel. Such a person, feeling helpless to begin with, becomes frightened lest his resentment provoke further punishment, and rationalizes it as a more positive emotion: Christian love, the desire to protect the weak, or to secure social justice. All these are perfectly real emotions that may and do arise as spontaneous responses to real human experiences. It is perfectly possible to wish, through love or compassion, to help a suffering fellow being, whether the cause of his misery be poverty, disease, sheer misfortune, or any combination of evils. It is likewise possible to be moved by his plight to genuine and fierce anger at the persons or circumstances that have brought it about, and to commit oneself wholeheartedly to fight the good fight on his behalf. But this is a very different attitude, and expresses a very different character, from that represented by *ressentiment*—which prizes the victim *because* he is a victim, and loves the suffering while covertly exploiting the sufferer.

No one has expressed this difference more clearly, or evaluated it more precisely, than Thoreau in the following passage from *Walden:*

> I would not subtract anything from the praise that is due to philanthropy, but merely demand justice for all who by their lives and works are a blessing to mankind . . . I want the flower and fruit of a man; that some fragrance be wafted over from him to me, and some ripeness flavour our intercourse. His goodness must not be a partial and transitory act, but a constant superfluity, which costs him nothing and of which he is unconscious. This is a charity that hides a multitude of sins. The phi-

lanthropist too often surrounds mankind with the remembrance of his own castoff griefs as an atmosphere, and calls it sympathy. We should impart our courage, and not our despair, our health and ease, and not our disease, and take care that this does not spread by contagion. From what southern plains comes up the voice of wailing? Under what latitudes reside the heathen to whom we would send light? Who is that intemperate and brutal man whom we would redeem? . . .

I believe that what so saddens the reformer is not his sympathy with his fellows in distress, but, though he be the holiest son of God, his private ail. Let this be righted, let the spring come to him, the morning rise over his couch, and he will forsake his generous companions without apology. . . . There is nowhere recorded a simple and irrepressible satisfaction with the gift of life, any memorable praise of God. . . . All health and success does me good, however far off and withdrawn it may appear; all disease and failure helps to make me sad and does me evil, however much sympathy it may have with me or I with it. . . . Do not stay to be an overseer of the poor, but endeavour to become one of the worthies of the world.

In the contemporary American high school, *ressentiment* is much more effectively institutionalized in its "philanthropic" than in its authoritarian form. Individual teachers and administrators representing either tendency are common, but one way of expressing a major change in the climate of American education over the past half-century is by saying that authoritarianism has been placed in a thoroughly defensive position, while the "philanthropic" attitude has become dominant.[2]

Teachers and administrative officials of schools come primarily from lower-middle-class backgrounds. Many come from families of somewhat higher status, but the folkways of the schools are lower-middle-class folkways: the official language, the customs and regulations governing dress—even the food in the school cafeteria. All these tend to be shabby-genteel. They are not forthright expressions of the actual limitations of the schools' financial, intellectual, and social resources, such as peasant life and art express, but cheap reproductions of corporate or academic life, as imperfectly conceived. Schoolteachers by and large have likewise notably resisted, even more than most white-collar workers, identifying with the working class in their own financial interests, as by unionization. One may, of course, dislike joining a union and refuse to do so on a variety of grounds from social ideology to personal taste. But the actual circumstances of the public school teacher's background and vocational life make union membership a promising device for achieving his legitimate economic aspirations. The difficulty seems to be that teachers' economic aspirations are regularly subordinated by their middle-class identifications. Unionization is inconsistent with their insistence that they practice a profession. Fully established professions, like medicine and law, have of course evolved militant organizations to advance and safeguard their economic interests, though these are not called unions. But teachers have not so far created any organization suited to the purpose of direct economic action on their behalf.[3] The life-style of the public high-school teacher remains, characteristically, that of the dutiful subordinate awaiting preferment in a niggardly bureaucratic structure.

Such a life is the very breeding ground of *ressentiment*. The teacher is linked to his principal, his superintendent, and his peers by a pretense of professional equality that prevents him from either demanding the perquisites of status or the liberty to scoff at it. Within a bureaucratic structure in which one depends not merely for advancement but for personal gratification as well on the endorsement of one's peers and subordinates, open conflict generates intolerable anxiety. Frustration and anger degenerate into malicious gossip, and are absorbed into the general ambience of wariness and cynicism. Ultimately, the consequence is alienation; in such people there is no longer direct connection between their actual experiences, their feelings, and their actions.

Nothing about this is peculiar to the career of teachers in contemporary America; this is rather the familiar catalogue of complaint about life in the organized system. *Ressentiment* probably is less prominent among teachers than among many social groups like waiters or cab drivers, whose work keeps them in constant cantact with people visibly enjoying a higher standard of life than they can achieve in a culture that makes it impossible to take pride in performing personal service well—or like social workers, whose "philanthropic" enterprise puts them in a position of unparalleled opportunity to intervene in the lives of other people whose poverty and tendency to act out conflicts make them both particularly tempting and particularly vulnerable to the *ressentient.* And there are many other social groups in which *ressentiment* has become institutionalized under somewhat different conditions: yellow journalism and the pornography of violence, for example. But there are further reasons that are peculiar to the education establishment why the public high school should be the locus of strong *ressentiment.*

The official function of the schoolteacher is still defined in academic and intellectual terms, however irrelevant the definition may be to the daily work a teacher in a slum school actually does. And in academic and intellectual terms, the public secondary school teacher is inferior. This, moreover, is a fact he must consciously face. The elementary school teacher can avoid facing it—if indeed it is a relevant judgment to apply to her—because she is not graded in her professional training in direct competition with people who are going into other work. In other words, she is likely to be—in many states she virtually has to be—an "ed major." High school teachers are not; they are math majors or English majors or history majors and, generally speaking, they are the ones who made poorer grades than those who head into industry, the professions, or higher education on the basis of their specialized study. In graduate school such direct comparisons are again inapplicable, but the norms for graduate students in education on standardized intelligence tests (like the Miller Analogies) are substantially lower than those for graduate students in other academic disciplines.

Students are forced into secondary school teaching because they are not able to make the grade in a specialized or scholarly discipline. Finding themselves comparatively impotent academically, they are unwilling to relinquish respectable intellectual pretensions altogether, and settle for something that, in their own view, is decidedly second-rate. It is perfectly possible, of course, to define the function of a high school teacher as an honorable and extremely significant specialty in its own right; and it is also perfectly possible that, if it were so defined, it would have a rather low correlation with conventional academic and intellectual achievement. If high school teaching *were* so defined, the people who go into it would not have a sense of partial failure, and there would be no reason for their academic situation to lead to *ressentiment*. Certainly, neither the early-childhood nor the primary grade school teacher seems so prone to it. The public image of such a teacher as a constricted and punitive spinster has disappeared—though, as usual, more slowly than the reality—to be replaced by the image of the young woman who thinks of herself as, and very often really is, a professional emissary to the private world of childhood. She may not be especially scholarly or analytical-minded, but she knows her job and does it well. The children know that she does; and there is a good deal of mutual respect and affection. Jules Henry's observations in *Culture Against Man*[4] suggest I may be a little fatuous about this.

In the later grades and in junior high and high schools the situation is much worse.[5] Subject matter has begun to matter, and so has the fact that the teacher is often incompetent to handle it. There is more to this incompetence than relative ignorance or stupidity. There is also the fact that the school has begun to deal with controversial content and controversial purposes. High school civics, social studies, and biology courses are no place for people who do not know their history, economics, or biology. But they are also not the place for timid or insecure people, for people who are especially anxious to make a good impression on the community or to keep out of trouble. These are, of course, exactly the kinds of people that a principal or superintendent who is timid or insecure himself will try to keep there.

Again, in this context, the feeble persistence of identification with academic norms contributes to the high school teacher's *ressentiment*. The identification is not strong enough to make him a hero.[6] But it is strong enough to make him ashamed of himself, and to add to his feeling of impotence. His impotence is real enough; he generally just does not *know* enough to defend an unpopular position on scholarly grounds even if he had the courage. But until he abandons the professional stance, or ceases to link it to academic competence, he cannot accept himself as a part of the local propaganda apparatus either. The statement "You shall know the truth, and the truth shall make you free" is quite false; knowledge can be a dreadful burden. But like pregnancy, knowledge to a teacher is a form of commitment no longer subject to voluntary abridgment without a sense of catastrophic guilt, and to have only a little is no help at all.

I have stated that the most serious consequence of *ressentiment* is alienation. The *ressentient* individual loses the connection between his feelings and the situation in which he is actually living. His emotions, and even his perceptions of reality, are channelled in the directions that cause least anxiety rather than toward the experiences that actually arouse them, either in the past or in the immediate present. All neurosis, of course, has this effect, but *ressentiment* is especially effective because it is the emotion itself—anger, rage, impotence, and fear of retribution—that is the source of anxiety and that must be repressed. So *ressentient* individuals are especially clumsy and insensitive, in contrast to those with other sorts of neurotic difficulty, in using their feelings to help them understand the meaning of their lives and to discipline their moral conduct. This is why they become sentimental; they prefer fake experiences that decorate the actual situation to symbolic evocations of its actuality. This kind of sentimentality has become a negative status symbol, evoking the atmosphere of lower-middle-class life as surely as a whiff of H_2S brings back freshman chemistry: the plastic flowers in the apartment house lobby, which insist that this is a place in the sun; the conventional cuteness of the mass-produced mock-hostile office signs and mock-boastful chef's aprons. The worst thing that could happen, obviously, is that a genius really should be at work.

What happens when one is—even an embryonic one? The essential quality of the creative student, as he is beginning to be defined in the literature, is that his thought is divergent. He doesn't arrive at right answers by deducing them from established premises, but by an intuitive understanding of how the problem he is dealing with really works, of what actually goes into it, and the right answers he arrives at may not be right in the textbook; they will not be, if the textbook has been carefully edited to make it as widely acceptable as possible. He works hard when the problem requires it, and respects facts as a part of reality. But for the creative student, facts are not right answers but tools and components for building original solutions.

How will the high school teacher react to this? If he is a high school teacher because the job gives him joy, and is competent intellectually, he will react with astonished delight. But to the degree that he is *ressentient,* with defensive hostility. Consider the poor mathematician, who manages to salvage enough math to become a high school teacher, or the ninth-grade teacher who hates mathematics and never meant to have any traffic with it at all. Such teachers manage by knowing a set of answers, and a conventional procedure for arriving at them. They maintain their self-esteem by convincing themselves that this is really enough; and the student who really understands mathematics puts them in a dilemma. On the one hand, he may show them up as incompetent. On the other, they don't know but that he may be cheating somehow, and laughing at them for being taken in. They dare not commit themselves either way. If they are authoritarian, they bully him into solving the problems "the way I show you as long as you are in my class." If they are "philanthropic," they respond with studied tolerance and amusement to Johnny's "attention-getting behavior." But in either case they try to make sure that he doesn't embarrass them again by actually getting up and doing mathematics in front of the whole class.

In the humanities the creative student is both more threatening and more vulnerable. He is more vulnerable because there aren't any right answers to support him. He is more threatening because the humanities, if truthfully handled, are themselves threatening to the *ressentient.* It is the job of the humanities to get to the root of human experience, which at best means hewing austere beauty out of some very ugly blocks in such a way that their real character is revealed. This is just what the alienated cannot tolerate. What happens to the adolescent boy or girl who writes a theme about an experience that had deep meaning for him—at this age it will probably be in part a sexual experience—as it really was? For that matter, how does the well-indoctrinated professional educator, suffused with the benign values underlying his course in child development and his belief in the wholesomeness of family living, handle either Medea or Salome?

The position of the social science teacher is more ambiguous. *Ressentiment* is not always such a handicap in the social sciences, which provide a superb eminence from which to look down on one's neighbors while discharging one's scholarly obligations. The convention of objectivity keeps the *ressentient* social scientist from having to face the full responsibility for his hostility and destructiveness; after all, he is just doing his job. The creative student in social studies may therefore get an additional chance. Besides the possibility common to all fields of encountering a superior, *ressentiment*-free instructor, there is the possibility in social studies of finding an instructor who does not clobber the creative even though he is *ressentient,* but identifies with their undisciplined or rebellious disjunctivity and accepts and encourages it as an expression of his own *ressentiment*—taking refuge in academic freedom and his obligation to the truth if detected.

But such teachers are inevitably rare; they are selected out in the process of teacher-training, which requires the candidate to suffer a great deal of nonsense without protest; and administrators get rid of them if they find them out in time as likely to get the school in trouble with intransigent groups in the community. The creative student is far less likely to encounter a social critic on the high school staff than he is teachers with whom he will quickly establish a mutual loathing and who are continually reminded by his freshness of perception that they have consented to devote their lives to teaching what they know to be false or irrelevant; to denying in class that the fundamental experiences of his life can even have occurred.

Hundreds of high school teachers can, and do, spend several hours a day trying to teach slum children in civics courses the official syllabus on the American Way of Life. If the children are creative, the questions they raise are difficult to answer, especially after they have given up trying to ask them verbally, and express them directly through their attitudes and behavior in class. One gets used to it, in time, and learns to maintain order. But the job of an assistant warden in a custodial institution is a long step down from earlier expectations.

Overlying the special influence of *ressentiment* on instruction in the separate fields of knowledge and reinforcing its effects is the "philanthropic" ideology of the school. Students, by definition, are subordinate in status to their schoolmasters; they are in a partially dependent position, and the function of the school is to nurture them. It is appropriate that the school devote itself to their needs and attend to and utilize their interests. Its primary purpose is to serve them.

But an institution designed to nurture the relatively weak and dependent presumably does so because it cherishes their potential strength and autonomy. There would be good reason for it to value most highly those youngsters who show most intellectual vigor and originality in the disciplined handling of ideas; as, in some cultures, a father will love his strongest and most virile sons even though he fears them a little. The *ressentient,* identifying with impotence and resentful of strength, respond very differently. The school, strongly influenced by *ressentiment,* is rather inclined to cherish the weakness of the weak.

Thus one notion that even very poor students of educational sociology grasp eagerly is that schools are generally biased against lower-class students. They certainly are, and this is an important truth. But when the proposition is explored, what it seems to mean in the professional curriculum of education is that middle-class students "have advantages" which they ought to be forced to share more generously. The remedy is to insure that the lower-status students get their share of good grades, scholarships, opportunity for social leadership, and so on.

But these are still conceived almost wholly in middle-class terms. There is no corresponding respect for the lower-status child's own experience of life, his language, and the forms of social organization he spontaneously adopts. It is true enough that the school faces a difficult dilemma; lower-class behavior creates real difficulties in running a formal social organization like a school, quite apart from any question of bias; yet the bias is real and harmful. But professional education both in its curriculum and in its practice tends to respond to the bias as if the chief objection to it was that it gave the privileged too many privileges, rather than with a real, imaginative concern for the quality of life of lower-status youngsters.

This is a major reason why the bias is hard to eliminate. Its most important consequences do not occur in the schools, but in the long run. Giving the children of Southern Negro migrants more high grades even if they don't read or do arithmetic very well is not really going to help them much in getting into medical school. What is needed is something like the original conception of progressive education, which combined an extremely flexible conception of both educational content and instructional technique with a rather rigid adherence to standards of achievement. This is *genuine* acceptance of the meaning of underprivileged life, and real help in mobilizing the youngster's real strengths to either pull himself out of it or learn to live it more richly, at his own choice. Pushed to extremes, this might mean letting the younger brother of the leader of a "retreatist" gang use the backyard marijuana plot as his project in arithmetic and biology, thus utilizing his need for status in the peer group. But what is far more important, it also means giving him an "A" if—and only if—he solves his problems of cultivation, processing, and marketing in such a way as to show high competence in arithmetic and biology—and an "F" if he lets his marijuana go to pot.

So tough-minded a philosophy has, in fact, rather less chance than marijuana itself of taking root in the emotional climate of the American public school. "Philanthropically" inverted, the "emergent" attenuation of progressive education abandons the controversial undertaking of dealing realistically with the experiences of lower-class life. Then to make up for not taking these children seriously, the school tries to equalize their position by expecting less of them. Simultaneously, it prevents them from learning what they are missing by inflating its credentials and subtly derogating the quest for distinction.

Higher-status children also are discriminated against in the public school, if they attempt to live in school as they do at home and in their social life. They do not share the lower-status youngster's difficulty in earning high grades and scholarships; and they are usually adept enough socially to dominate the extracurriculum despite the attempts of the school to democratize it, especially if such attempts are enfeebled by the school administration's fear of parents' possible political influence. So the discrimination higher-status youngsters encounter is not comparable in kind to that experienced by the lower-status pupils. But as indications of *ressentiment,* the forms it takes are significant, and are especially likely to stultify creativity. Any mode of expression that is highly individualized, extravagant, or overtly sensual is forbidden or discouraged. It is assumed that it is better for the school dance to be one that everyone can afford than one with an especially good band and refreshments; that boys and girls whom nature has provided, for the time being, with especially splendid bodies ought not to be allowed to dress in such a way as to derive any special advantage from them; that the illumination of the school grounds, if there are any, be such as to discourage courtship rather than to suggest the exquisite delights to which nature may be encouraged.

Adolescence is a time when highly individualized, extravagant, and overtly sensual modes of behavior do crop out, despite the position the school takes toward them. But by its disparagement, the school abandons its opportunity to help youngsters create a style suited to their romantic age. The essential first step in encouraging creativity in secondary school youngsters is surely to link their new sexual energy and their occasionally flamboyant quest for identity to meaningful larger aspects of present and past culture, which is what taste means and disciplined self-expression requires. If the baroque manifestations of adolescence instead elicit an attitude of sulky oppression, the adolescents are thrown back onto resources they have not yet developed. The twist may then be as far as they can get by themselves in the face of official disapproval. Moreover, the ideology of the school grudgingly supports the numerous *ressentiment,* lower-middle-class youth against the more creative within the youth-culture itself. The school thereby tips the balance in favor of the "teen-age" solution to the problem of adolescence, quietly maintaining support for the unassuming, undiscriminating boy or girl who sees things the way other sensible people do and with other "teen-agers" builds a conventional social group, accepting conventional discipline for occasional stereotyped "teen-age" misbehavior within it. The youngster who is most handicapped by this situation is not the delinquent or the rebel, for both of these are conventional adolescent roles in their own way which society endorses by punishment. It is the innovator who sees things freshly and differently. One does not punish this youngster formally; for to do this would be to admit that he was there and that what he had said was intelligible. Instead, one isolates him by denying him the customary sources of status—that is, recognition for his work and point of view. Then one helps him—helps him to become assimilated within the "teen-age" group. In a little while, it is as if he had never been.

The "philanthropic" refusal to allow excellence to get above itself is not limited to areas, like the fine arts, toward which lower-middle-class American culture is generally hostile or suspicious. Within the school even those forms of distinction that are commonly supported within this culture are treated ambiguously. I suspect *ressentiment* is one factor in the continued, and now apparently rising, complaint about overemphasis on athletics in the school. There is a substantial basis for the complaint in many schools, for athletics is sometimes the only activity that is taken seriously at all. But conversely, athletics is sometimes the only activity that is at all serious, and in which any distinction of style or achievement is permitted or recognized. The clue to whether *ressentiment* is at the root of the complaint lies in the terms in which it is couched. Complaints that the emphasis on the preoccupation with athletics interferes with specific aspects of the academic program are serious and legitimate. What are highly suspect, however, are complaints that the emphasis on athletics allows the athletes to become an elite group and gain favor and eminence unavailable to their less glamorous colleagues. Before considering such protests, one would like to be certain that the history teacher encourages a brilliant and resourceful analysis of American foreign policy with as much joy—and technical assistance—as the basketball coach does brilliant and resourceful play-making and back-court work (for these are not inherently glamorous). It is possible that students respect an elite of athletes because good athletes are encouraged to be proud of themselves for being as good as they can, and that these are the only people left on campus with anything in particular to be proud of.

Among the most important educational consequences of *ressentiment,* then, are failure to recognize the gifted, or to nurture their gifts when discovered; differential drop-out rates among students from different social classes; and fundamental difficulties in curriculum construction that vitiate earnest and costly efforts to adapt the curriculum to the needs of divergent individuals or social groups. *Ressentiment* also influences the total experience of education in ways that are so general that they can hardly even be recognized as problems: the flavor of education itself; whether students will come to think of it as opening their understanding to a wider and deeper range of experiences or as constricting and limiting their range of possible emotional and intellectual response; whether, in the long run, the school tends more to liberate than to alienate. The total social function of education is intimately involved with *ressentiment;* for the secondary school has both a cautionary and a mithridatic function. It is here that one learns to avoid the expression of noble or heroic aspirations in noble or heroic terms, so as not to destroy at the outset the chance that they may be realized. Conversely, it is here that one learns to tolerate without surrender the demands of guilt and humility; to retain, in some measure, the power to continue to enjoy privileges and personal achievements without being disconcerted by the envy they arouse. Now that the differences are neither clearly indicated nor morally defended, many Americans devote their lives to an effort to steal into the first-class compartment without awakening the tourist passengers; and the school is where one first learns how numerous and vigilant they are. The school is where you learn to be an American; and an important part of Americanism is to learn the prevailing norms and limits of achievement and self-assertion and how to maintain them against the encroachments of a mass society that the moral support of a strong egalitarian tradition has made extremely aggressive.

1962

---

1. Max Scheler's *Ressentiment* (Lewis A. Coser, Ed., Free Press, 1961) is the authoritative statement and exegesis of the meaning of *ressentiment.*

2. The shift from "traditional" to "emergent" values in the schools discussed by George P. Spindler in his classic paper, "Education in a Transforming American Culture" (*Harvard Educational Review,* Summer 1955) might be expressed with equal validity as a shift from the dominance of authoritarian to "philanthropic" modes of *ressentiment.*

3. See Myron Lieberman, *Education as a Profession* (Prentice-Hall, 1956), especially chapters 9 and 10. A teachers' union, of course, is again very much in controversy.

4. New York, Random House, 1963.

5. See Martin Mayer, *The Schools* (Harper, 1961) for an excellent treatment of observations dealing with this point.

6. Not, to be sure, that college and university people, in the social sciences at least, behaved particularly heroically under pressure. See Paul Lazarsfeld and W. Thielens, *The Academic Mind* (Free Press, 1958) for a canny account of the extent of accommodation, from widespread self-censorship to occasional outright betrayal of colleagues, that occurred during McCarthy's dreadful reign.

An Ideology of School Withdrawal

Compulsory school attendance in the United States has been justified from the beginning as essential to democratic polity. Everyone knows Madison's statement to the effect that popular government without popular education is the prelude to a tragedy, or a farce, or both. We have had both, continuously ever since. I have just finished Theodore White's *The Making of the President, 1960*; and I think this book is the strongest indictment of American public education I have ever seen, though Mr. White does not discuss the issue directly. Still, the laws are on the books. Within a century, with the Kalamazoo decision (1874), the legal basis had been laid for what Madison thought so necessary.

And, be it noted, for the reasons he gave. So far as I know, public support of education in this country has never been justified on the grounds that education was beneficial to the individual student, except to the extent that this pertained to equality of opportunity. It is logical to argue that the individuals who share the responsibilities of citizenship must learn what they have to know in order to discharge them. I wouldn't say the logic was water-tight. In Louisiana, where I was raised, we have never regarded either ignorance or lunacy as a bar to high public office; and this liberalism has permitted us to enjoy unusually creative leadership. But, on the whole, the point is well taken. If public education can be justified on the grounds that it is essential to citizenship, it can also claim, for that reason, to be good for the future citizens themselves.

School attendance laws, however, are a very distorted reflection of the purpose implicit in Madison's phrase. They are not *licensing* laws. They do not require attendance until a specified minimum level of competence deemed essential to the conduct of adult life has been attained; this would mean a life sentence for some. Nor are they *contractual*: they do not assure the student any outcome or even any minimum standard of educational service or decent treatment in exchange for his obligation to attend. Other laws, to be sure, do set up such standards, but the student has no remedy against their breach. Even if he can establish that the school is sub-standard and that he personally is mistreated there, he cannot legally withdraw; he can only try to force the school authorities to make improvements which, usually, they would already have made long ago if they possibly could.

From this point of view, compulsory school attendance appears as a gross violation of civil liberty: a bill of attainder against a specific age group that guarantees no compensation in return. The school may, indeed, benefit the child; but it doesn't have to in order to earn the right to retain him. In talking about the youngsters who drop out, therefore, I am not going to start with the assumption that they ought to be retained. My hunch is that a large proportion of the dropouts may be doing what is best for themselves under the atrocious circumstances that exist. But I do want to analyze those circumstances, and see why the schools have so little to offer these youngsters.

In the small Southern Methodist college I attended, we had chapel services twice a week; and after the opening hymn there was a responsive reading. The Dean—it was a poor school and could only afford one—would read a portion of Scripture aloud; and the students, assembled as a congregation, would read the following portion: his in light-faced type, ours in bold. There was one of these that I liked especially well, and I remember fragments of it distinctly—not accurately, but distinctly. It began:

> DEAN: *Whereof from a young man's fancy shall he wend his way?*
>
> STUDENTS: *By taking heed unto the Lord, and the firmament thereof.*

This responsive reading, in the version in which I recall it, is admirably suited to its purpose. The first line reveals real evidence of poetic influence. It ties in with the culture, showing that we share in its heritage, and it alludes to the necessity for progress and achievement; while the second line asserts the necessity of basing these on a sound moral imperative. By saying it over together we experienced a feeling of mutuality and belonging, of being the same kind. Yet we ran no risk of binding ourselves to too literal an interpretation of its mandate, because it doesn't actually make any sense at all.

For the types of students it is designed for, the public high school and junior high school curriculum serves, I believe, exactly the same purpose as this responsive reading. Its function is liturgical. This is not as true of elementary school, because the basic skills really work. If you read as you are taught there, you will understand at least the words; if you write, your words will be understood; if you follow the rules of arithmetic, your calculations will check out and your books will balance, though you may never have the remotest conception of mathematics.

High school, however, is another matter. What would happen to the businessman, or just citizen, who attempted to apply what he was taught in high-school civics to the actual power structure of his community or his country? Who learns to love reading, or to find the kind of reading he can love among the classics and the bitty anthologies of the high-school English course? High-school history, by and large, is not even propaganda, because nobody is expected to believe it or to be moved by it; it is received as official myth. We tell youngsters that the Pilgrims came to New England searching for religious freedom not in order to give them an understanding of the actual root values of Colonial New England, but in order to provide them with the relevant cliché about the relation of church and state in America, and to let them know that a good middle-class American thinks of "my religious affiliation" or "the faith of my choice." This keeps the youngsters from getting hung up on religion, like an Italian peasant or rural Southerner. As for high-school science, it has, since Sputnik, increased its work load enormously and often tries to duplicate the content of college science courses. But essentially, it serves not as an introduction to science but to legitimate the American middle-class epistemology; science proves that Truth is an aggregate of general principles induced from empirical data that observers can agree on. The function of science is to protect people from odd-balls by setting up the rules so that subjective feeling is discounted. The scientific method, then, becomes a way of separating ends and means. When we want to win an election, or spy on the Soviet Union, or redevelop a slum, we go about it scientifically—i.e., by defining what we are trying to do as a technical problem. Naturally, we care about the feelings of the people affected; people's emotions are a very important factor. That's why we have psychologists on our team.

It is even truer than the progressives have always maintained that there is no valid distinction between the curriculum and the extra-curriculum. What counts is the total experience of the student, and what he learns in both the classroom and the playing field is a posture, a pattern of anxieties and a pattern of responses for dealing with it. There is seldom any pleasure in scholarship or ideas as such; the classroom and the playing field alike are places where you try to make it, and learn the techniques for making it that alienate you least from your peers. The over-all rules are the same in both: learn the ropes; don't get hung up; always be friendly, sincere, and creative. And win!

The important thing about this familiar picture is that it is a picture of a totally instrumental institution. Nothing about the institution is meant to be valuable, here and now, for its own sake. I don't mean that high-school students don't have any fun. Of course they do; in the suburbs, at least, the high school is a "fun place." But this sort of fun is a part of the social pattern to be learned; being "fun" helps you to make it as well or better than anything, and it takes a great deal of social skill which American adolescents, notably, do learn.

We have never had much interest in what education means and feels like to the youngsters who are subjected to it; only in what it might help them to make of themselves. Even the Supreme Court, in its decision against segregation, could not rest on the moral obloquy and insult that segregation imposes on Negro children; that was not enough. It had to support its position further by pointing out that a major reason why separate schools could not be equal even if they were identical was that the Negro students couldn't make the same contacts there that white students could in their school, and that this was what people really go to school for.

So it is: the Court has done our motives no discredit, but merely reaffirmed our tradition. The public school gives poor boys a chance to develop their potentialities, both by formal education and by providing an opportunity to mingle with and learn from their social superordinates. The commonwealth is then the richer for the skills they later contribute, which would otherwise have been forever lost. This is exactly the opportunity our dropouts need, and which they ought presumably to welcome. So what has gone wrong?

What has gone wrong is pretty complicated; but basically I think one might locate it in the schools' perennial assumptions about the nature of what they have had to offer the children of the poor. These assumptions were probably never valid; but both the school and the poor once believed them. Now, only the school continues to assert them, though no longer with much conviction.

The schools assumed that in order to get ahead in America the student had to learn not only a body of skills, but also a set of social conventions, increasingly subtle and refined as he climbed up the ladder. In school he was taught techniques for handling things and manners for getting along with people. The teachers were the transmitters of an alien culture—alien to them, too. Social mobility was a process like preparing to get a job as a rice farmer in China or a coffee-grower in Brazil. There was a strange language to be learned—from instructors who didn't speak it too well themselves; a strange body of techniques to be mastered—from teachers who had never practiced them at first hand. It would all have to be learned over again when he got there; but at the time it seemed relevant, and made the student feel that he was well on his way.

Now, there are three important ways in which this situation differs from the condition in the high school today. In the first place, the problem of dropouts did not then exist. Most of the students who drop out today would never have been in high school fifty years ago; the school-leaving age has risen irregularly over the past decades, and a more rigid and self-confident school policy would not have hesitated to keep students in grade school until they reached it, whatever it was, if they did not pass. A good many of these dropped out, and took unskilled jobs, which existed; and that was the last anyone thought of them till election day six or seven years later. They weren't a dropout problem; they were the working class.

But those who didn't drop out, even though they came from a working-class background, did not feel at the time that they were losing their identity. This happened later, after they had made it, in the classical discovery of the loneliness of the long-distance runner. In school you were still you: *striving* didn't separate you from other poor, immigrant boys; it was exactly what poor, immigrant boys were supposed to do. There was no intimation at the time that you were leaving yourself behind. It wasn't that you were becoming a different person; the old *you* was learning new tricks. Education was instrumental, all right—it has always been that in America—but the instruments were thought to be in the curriculum. The student didn't have to learn to think of *himself* as one.

And finally, nobody doubted what the norms were. It seemed very clear that the people in the next stratum up were the ones who knew what the student had to learn; he had to be able to do what they did. This wouldn't make them accept him willingly; but it would allow him to work his way in even if they didn't.

I don't mean to imply that the school actually delivered the social mobility it promised; sometimes it did, more often it didn't. But this was the way it was supposed to work, and why there was so little controversy over whether compulsory school attendance was good for the individual as well as for the commonwealth. As long as the students who stayed in school believed in education naïvely, it served—much better than religion could have in this heterogeneous country—as the opiate of the people. And opium vendors don't have dropout problems.

Apparently, however—to judge by the present situation—they can: the American poor are getting over their addiction.[1] It takes more and more education every year to invoke the same dream; and reality breaks through too often, leaving them sick, mean, and edgy. The educational establishment, fearful of losing popular support, is naturally much concerned with the possibilities of a *rapprochement*, of which two have already been tried. The simplest of these is an effort to beef up the traditional, but paradoxically faltering, economic appeal of education. Students are reminded over and over that today, more than ever, you need a high school diploma to get any sort of job and a college degree to get a good one. They are given the statistics on the fabulous return education, as an investment, brings in over a lifetime in increments of annual income. The unemployment data on adolescents and unskilled labor are stressed so that the youngsters will understand how hopeless things will be for them if they drop out of school. If they and their teacher are sophisticated enough, the demographic shift in job-type may be explained: how unskilled and blue-collar work has fallen off, while service and white-collar jobs, demanding a higher level of school achievement, have enormously increased in proportion.

All this is true enough; but the implication is false. It does not follow that most of the students now dropping out would have a better chance, even economically, if they stayed in school. As S. M. Miller and Frank Riessman have pointed out in a recent WBAI broadcast, the illusory success of some of these school-retention efforts in leading students to better jobs is based on the fact that they made hardly a dent in the number of school dropouts; if the programs had been successful in reaching the students they would inevitably have failed in delivering the jobs. In our economy, the demonstrable economic value of an education is partly a consequence of its scarcity. The blue-collar-white-collar figures are relative, and one loses sight of how much smaller the white-collar one was to begin with. The absolute increase in white-collar opportunity does not compensate for the absolute loss in blue-collar jobs—a discrepancy which is rapidly increasing in magnitude as automation proceeds. Today's dropouts are, perhaps fortunately, pretty skeptical kids; if they all believed that the school could deliver them to a brighter economic future we would soon have unemployed IBM operators and technicians hanging around the way India and Africa have lawyers.

The other, and more sophisticated, *rapprochement* is represented by the Higher Horizons Program, about which I wish I could bring myself to be less doubtful, for it is a program that seems to me characterized by much intelligence, ingenuity, enthusiasm, and sheer good will. Its appeal, moreover, is not purely economic. I understand it to be an attempt to convey to students that middle-class culture, *in toto,* is not beyond their grasp. It can be theirs, if only they do their work. As the title implies, the Higher Horizons approach seeks to make education appear more worthwhile to the student, and encourages him to remain in school to develop his potentialities, by raising his level of aspiration not just economically but culturally. As the boy lifts himself to gaze beyond the slum there comes into view the Museum of Modern Art.

It is heartening to find the middle class so generously willing to share its resources, and, for once, apparently confident of their value. It is also obvious that if the middle class cannot somehow make public education acceptable to the poor on its terms rather than theirs, middle-class dominance of public education—a long established fact of American life—is doomed. But if the effort is successful, it will remind me of a story that a very intelligent, very British, very working-class hospital orderly used to tell, in a sensitive effort to ease his middle-class patients' embarrassment at the services he was obliged to perform for them. This story concerned a small pharmaceutical firm that was facing bankruptcy. It had an established reputation as Britain's most reputable manufacturer of suppositories. But respect for craftsmanship, as is well known, was declining; their customers, apparently, were turning to other sources for satisfaction. Things looked black. Then the firm consulted one of Madison Avenue's most resourceful advertising agencies. And the agency, after much brainstorming, came up with a slogan that at once opened vast markets to the company by motivating the very segment of the population which had hitherto most successfully resisted its appeal. The slogan was, very simply, "If you don't like our suppositories, you know what you can do with them!"

The dropouts, by and large, don't like middle-class culture; and they know quite well what we can do with it. Dropping out is one way of telling us, and it is about time we turned our attention to the things about the school that are bugging them. The school is the arena in which these youngsters encounter middle-class life; this is where the dropouts fight the ten-year's ideological war that ends in their defeat and rout. In this warfare the core values of their culture and the values the school represents are at issue, and any one that we start by considering will lead to the others. I think the most fruitful might be the familiar question of deferred gratification, or impulse control, which is the source of so much conflict with the school authorities.

We all know the school's side of the question; and know that lower-class youngsters act out their conflicts. Retention programs try to face up to this by helping the youngsters learn more self-control and giving them some valid experience of being rewarded for it, so that they will discover for themselves that certain very desirable goals exist that can only be achieved by people who plan, save, and give a soft answer to wrath-provoking circumstances. In this way the kids learn that there may be more desirable rewards than the immediate pleasure of blowing up and shooting your bolt. "Now, Dionysus, let's think about what we're really trying to get done here," friendly Apollo is always urging; and of course he is right. The difficulty lies in getting Dionysus to listen.

Or does it? Let me return for a moment to Mr. White's account of the 1960 election, and the Apollonian behavior it elicited from the Republican candidate.

> And this, finally, was the only summary one could make of the campaign that Richard M. Nixon had so valiantly waged, under such personal suffering: that there was neither philosophy nor structure to it, no whole picture either of the man or

of the future he offered. One could perceive neither in this last climactic proposal nor in his prepared speeches nor in his personal discourses any shape of history, any sense of the stream of time or flow of forces by which America had come to this point in history and might move on. Nixon's skill in politics was enormous, his courage unquestioned, his endurance substantial. But they were the skills, courage, and endurance of the sailor who knows the winds and can brave the storm and recognize the tide. There was missing in him always the direction of the navigator. . . . Thus, it is impossible to distinguish, from his campaign performance, what Nixon's personal political attitude was to the arrest of Martin Luther King when that hero figure of American Negroes was arrested in the last days of the campaign. . . . On the afternoon of the sentencing of Martin Luther King to four months of hard labor in Georgia, the Department of Justice—at the suggestion of a wise yet shrewd Republican Deputy Attorney-General—composed a draft statement to support the application for release of the imprisoned Negro minister. Two copies of the draft were sent out immediately for approval—one to the White House, one to Mr. Nixon's traveling headquarters. No one has yet revealed who killed this draft statement that was so critically important in the tense politics of civil rights. Either President Eisenhower or Vice-President Nixon could have acted—yet neither did. However obscure Eisenhower's motivations were, Nixon's are more perplexing, for he was the candidate. He had made the political decision at Chicago to court the Negro vote in the North; only now, apparently, he felt it quite possible that Texas, South Carolina, and Louisiana might all be won to him by the white vote and he did not wish to offend that vote. So he did not act—there was no whole philosophy of politics to instruct him.

There could never be any doubt of the Vice-President's pugnacity or innate courage; yet it was a pugnacity and courage committed without a framing strategy to make them effective.

The terms of Mr. White's criticism are as interesting as the incident itself. No philosophy of politics? No framing strategy? On the contrary, he was all strategy. What he lacked was heart and a sense of outrage: the capacity to make moral judgments. Yet, Mr. White cannot say this because his whole book, though very sensitive to moral factors in the contest, shares the assumption that a candidate's first duty is to get elected. Nixon lost, and the figures do indeed show that his expediency on this issue may have cost him the election. But to infer from this fact that the worst thing about Mr. Nixon's behavior was that it didn't work is to share his posture.

Earlier on, Mr. White describes the situations in the campaign that found Mr. Nixon at his best:

> One had to see Nixon entering a small Iowa village—the streets lined with school children, all waving American flags until it seemed as if the cavalcade were entering a defile lined by fluttering, peppermint-striped little banners—then see him stop at a Harvest Festival (in Red Oaks)—where on the festival tables lay the ripened ears of field corn . . . to see him at his best. For in such small towns he found an echo. These people were his natural constituency, his idiom their idiom. . . . He woke in Marietta, Ohio, on Monday, October 25th, to begin his last "peak" effort, and it was clear from his first speech of the day that he was at one with his audience as he had not been since he had passed through the corn fields of Iowa in the first week of the campaign. A sign outside the courthouse of Marietta, Ohio, read: HIGH SCHOOL DEBATERS GREET WORLD DEBATER—the sign was apropos and of the essence of this last trip as he revived. For he *was* a high-school debater, the boy who had some thirty years before won a Los Angeles *Times* prize for his high-school oration on the Constitution. He was seeking not so much to score home a message as to win the hearts of his little audiences; his style was homestyle and during the next two weeks told much about him.

In Red Oaks and Marietta they don't have much of a dropout problem. Good, solid communities, with woodsheds ample to the needs of youth, they turn out clean-cut boys and girls among whom Mr. Nixon is right at home. It was the urban proletariat, and overwhelmingly the Negroes, who refused to take part in his Harvest Festival, though the corn be ripe and the harvest long overdue.

To carry this illustration further would not make my point clearer; in any case, it is simple enough. I think the youngsters who drop out are probably, in many ways, a more promising moral resource than those who stay in, and I think they are driven out in part by moral revulsion from the middle-class life of the school. They could never, themselves, identify their feelings as moral repugnance because they view morality as being on the side of the enemy and therefore square; they imagine they dislike morality and have never been allowed to realize that they have morals of their own. They don't have a complete moral *system,* because they are not systematic; they are unprincipled in their behavior, because principles are too abstract for them to handle. But in a concrete situation they can be trusted more safely than their middle-class peers who are trying to make it.

Mr. Nixon and his silent superior are symbols, too; and I am not naïve enough to attribute the lower-class response to them solely to the revulsion they arouse in the breast of the noble savage. The opposition was well-organized and well-manipulated. But there are natural affinities and polarities in politics that set limits to what manipulation can achieve, and these, among other things, are reflected in the class structure of American society. Officially, American society is, however, middle-class and opportunistic—in the Land of Opportunity these are the values that receive official support and that in fact prevail. It is surely fair enough to take Mr. Eisenhower, and Mr. Nixon at the zenith of his presidential aspirations, as representative of what is most American. But one need not be wholly partisan. President Kennedy has also stated emphatically that we need technical rather than ideological or philosophical approaches to the problems that confront us.[2]

This moral attitude dominates our life. We are caught in it in crisis after crisis: in the U-2 incident, the Cuban invasion, the presence of our observers in Vietnam organizing the forced evacuation of peasants so that their farms can be burned, and helping the government see to it that the Viet Cong guerrillas don't get any antibiotics. Time after time the world finds a nice, friendly American standing in the middle of somebody else's ruins, with no more to say for himself than a rueful "It shoulda worked, but somebody must have goofed!"

I have a name for this boy. I call him Edsel, and I think it is time we withdrew him from production and got out a more responsive and less hazardous model. Even the practical-minded may not have much use for him any more; the locals seem to be getting pretty tired of Edsel and are about ready to get him out of there, with a hammer and sickle if necessary. But if we are to grow anything better, the dropouts are the kids to start with, for they have come part way on their own, against heavy opposition, already. They are ill-disciplined. They have no basic skills. They are so sore that any place you touch them hurts, and when they are hurt they hurt back. They are extremely parochial, limited in their experience of the world to a few city blocks of desolate slum, and therefore both gullible and suspicious about anything beyond it. They are sometimes homeless, and never have any quiet place to study and think. They are inconveniently aware of their own sexuality and inconveniently skilled at bringing it to the attention of others. They live, their teachers sometimes say, like animals; and as they say it, a ghost sobs, harshly. But if these youngsters are trapped, it is not in their apprehensions of pseudo-events. They are not alienated from themselves. They still have access to their sense-data, and, on their own terms, they are accustomed to fidelity.

These are the qualities that, I believe, we hoped to preserve and continually renew by building an open society in which a sensitive, compulsively masculine boy could become an Ernest Hemingway and a poor but beautiful waif a Marilyn Monroe. But at this juncture, less fatal alternatives to mediocrity are needed. Can a school geared to success and social mobility help formulate them? Its traditions are against it, its staff is against it, its relationship to the community power structure is against it.

To reach the dropouts and give them a reason for staying, the school would have to start by accepting their *raison d'être*. It would have to take lower-class life seriously as a condition and a pattern of experience—not just as a contemptible and humiliating set of circumstances that every decent boy or girl is anxious to escape from. It would have to accept their language, and their dress, and their values as a point of departure for disciplined exploration, to be understood, not as a trick for luring them into the middle class, but as a way of helping them to explore the meaning of their own lives. This is the way to encourage and nurture potentialities from *whatever* social class. Talent, and genius, when real, are expressions of individual experience and the inner life. But success and higher status are not the first goals to which talent or genius is devoted—though they are sometimes the last.

I do not mean to imply that I accept Sitwell's Fallacy: that the poor are happier in their station in life and should be left to enjoy it. Most lower-class people of whatever age hate lower-class life, I am sure: the noise, and the filth, and the crowding, and the vulnerability to the police and illness; never feeling quite well or quite rested. Worst of all, perhaps, is the constant din of the mass media—including the school—telling them that if they were any good at all they would be middle-class like everybody else, and live in loveliness in Larchmont. But the fact that they have reason to hate their life of fear and deprivation does not give us the right to force ours on them as the only acceptable alternative to it. This is something they must work out for themselves, and the school's job is to help them understand most fully the meaning and nature of what they have to work with. Basically, the problem of reaching the dropout is analogous to that faced by the Peace Corps in reaching the peoples of underdeveloped countries. Can we—do we even really wish to—help them deal with their situation on their terms with our resources, while leaving our way of life aside till somebody asks for it?

Frankly, I doubt it. This is not how the teachers I know approach lower-status youngsters. They are afraid of them, for one thing. The principal is afraid of disorder which looks bad in his record and in the records of his teachers, and they each have their careers to think of, too. So they learn early to keep the kids in line; this comes first. Order *is* helpful to learning, but it doesn't come first, it grows out of the common task; and teachers who put it first are not enthusiastic allies in keeping disorderly youngsters in school till a basis for order can be created. Order is not, to be sure, the central issue, but it will serve to symbolize the sharpness of the issue between those whose security depends on the suppression of impulse, and those who depend on its expression.

In the urban public school today, the former predominate, and I don't think they can be easily changed, within the limits of personality and bureaucracy that characterize the school. If they can be, there is no fundamental reason why the kinds of youngsters who now drop out may not be well served. But this is a big *if,* for the public school, as it is, is profoundly expressive of our culture. And the fate of the "dropouts" is just one more expression of their actual status in our democracy.

The answer, then, may be "No; this plant makes only Edsels." But if it is, I see no dropout problem. Let them go, let them go, God bless them. They may pop up again. St. James (or Santiago, as this chiliastic figure is known in Spanish) is not merely more merciful than the school system; he is far more flexible and versatile. He can accommodate a wider range of talent; he has a great Court, as well as an Infirmary, and though no familiar avenue bears his name, he has, like James Madison, been thus honored by the inhabitants of certain cities. The nearest, unfortunately, in Cuba.

1963

1. Thus, in her recent study of the schools in Big City, Patricia Sexton reports dropout rates even in *elementary school* of 15.5 per 10,000 children from families earning from $3,000-5,000 annually, falling to 3 children per 10,000 for families earning $5,000-7,000. For families making more than $9,000, the rate was less than 1 child per 10,000. In high schools, of course, the rate is enormously greater, but follows the same pattern. There is no high school in Big City whose median family income is less than $5,000. For schools with median family incomes ranging from $5,000-5,999, Sexton found a dropout rate of 19.2 per cent of the total registration falling to 7.9 per cent for schools whose students had a median family income of $7,000-7,999, and to 3.6 per cent for the school whose students came from families having median incomes above $9,000. (*Education and Income,* Viking, 1961, pp. 97 and 202.)

2. In the 1962 Commencement Address at Yale. See William Lee Miller, "Some Academic Questions About a New Yale Man," *Reporter,* July 5, 1962.

THE SCHOOL AS A SOCIAL ENVIRONMENT

OUR FREE PUBLIC HIGH SCHOOL has from the beginning discharged two paramount social functions, neither of which has burdened secondary education elsewhere to anything like the same extent. The first of these is to build a common pattern of values and responses among adolescents from a diversity of class and ethnic backgrounds; the high school is a very important unit in our traditional system of melting pots. The second has been to help youngsters, as we say, to better themselves. In most industrial countries this second function has by now assumed about as much importance as it has in the United States; but this is recent.

Until World War II secondary education of university preparatory quality in the rest of the world was essentially education for adolescents who had a reasonably high level of ascribed status. They came, as we used to say, from good homes; and, good or not, what they learned in school was culturally continuous with what they were used to at home. The same symbols had roughly the same meanings in both *ambiances*. In the United States, however, this was not true.

The public high school, being locally run, has generally deferred in various ways to the claims of status, devoting a preponderance of its resources and granting a preponderance of its rewards to solidly middle-class boys and girls to the relative neglect of lower-status youngsters, whom it often treats with great hostility. But its *own* folkways and traditions are not solidly middle-class; and if the higher-status youngsters are more favorably treated than their lower-status classmates, it must be recognized that the high school also extracts from them extra service as laboratory specimens for aspiring lower-status youth, and that the favor they receive is to some extent vitiated by the experience of immersion in a shabby-genteel and often envious environment for a period of years.

The melting pot and mobility functions of the high school are complementary. In combination, they are peculiarly potent. The atmosphere of the high school is permeated by the values they generate when combined. The combination is synergistic, and it really works. Taken as the high school directs, public education efficiently produces the kind of individual who can, and does, operate to sustain and augment his own position in a limitless variety of situations; and who does so with a characteristic American style regardless of his antecedents. This is just as true of rich antecedents as poor, and probably truer. The American ideal of equality is nowhere stronger than in public education; and if its administrators tend to be "realistic" about status, they nevertheless keep a school in which an upper-class vocabulary or accent is informally corrected as surely as that of the slum; and the *insouciance* and spontaneity of rich and poor alike is reduced to the guarded good humor of the executive. In metropolitan areas, at least, the high school dropout rates for upper- and lower-status students appear to be roughly comparable. Figures on this are not available to my knowledge, because schools do not directly record the social class of their students, and upper-status youngsters who leave public school for private school are not considered dropouts. But leave they do, in large proportions; and they are not always fleeing from the Negro. Even from the suburbs that have so far excluded Negroes, upper-class white parents manage to send their children to Chaminade or Country Day, and the Negroes they meet there may ask them home to dinner, if they like them.

Upper-class rejection of the public school of course reflects a variety of motives, including sheer snobbery and an often erroneous presumption that the private school selected can get its students into Ivy colleges. But it also reflects a search for what parents call higher standards. On examination these standards often turn out to be no higher than those of the public school, but decidedly different from them. No more and no better work may be demanded of students, but it is slightly different work, and it is demanded for different reasons. This is true, of course, only of those private schools that do, in fact, have a social function different from the public schools. To the extent that the school depends for patronage on the anxiety of ambitious and socially insecure parents, it will compound the defects of the public school and add a few of its own. All private schools in America, no doubt, receive many helpless adolescents from such sources; but there are still some schools in which these students do not set the tone and they may therefore find refuge and real help in working out the meaning of their own lives under the illumination of disciplined study. This is harder for the public school to provide under its twin mandate to serve as a melting pot and a rocket to the moon.

There is something to be learned from etymology. The original meaning of education as a "drawing-out" makes an important point about the process—the same point that John Dewey and the progressive education people, at their best, also made. Education, if it is to have any depth, must start with and be derived from the life-experience of the student, which is in some measure unique for every boy or girl. It must cultivate this experience with a disciplined and demanding use of the best resources offered by the humanities and the sciences—to help the individual understand the meaning of his own experience. The consequence of such education, though it clearly leads the student to share in a universal cultural heritage, is more fundamentally to *sharpen* his individuality, to clarify and emphasize to *him* the ways in which he is unique.

A school that serves as a melting pot must inhibit this process, not facilitate it. Its purpose is to establish a common response to certain key stimuli, regardless of how different the respondents started out to be. Not only the content becomes stereotyped; so do the values underlying it, for the function of the school is to make it unnecessary to take account of the differences that might have resulted from the heterogeneity of life. It often fails, of course, and the student's folder receives a notation that his personality is defective; that he underachieves or is immature or emotionally disturbed—perfectly true, too; regression and ritualized internal conflict are classical responses to unbearably painful pressure on the emerging self.

When, however, the mandate to contribute to social mobility is joined to the melting pot process, the result is far more inhibitory to education. The student now learns that it is no longer sufficient to give the same answer; he must learn to distinguish the *right* answer. And he must learn to do this reliably and, as nearly as possible, automatically while his inner voice continues to shriek that the answer is wrong. Of course, his inner voice gradually gets a lot softer and more plaintive, and may finally show up as nothing more than a symptom. At this juncture, however, it would be a little unfair to say that the student's values are stereotyped; a real value has emerged. It has become important to him to learn to give the right answer quicker and more often than the next boy, who now is seen as a competitor rather than a person. And the inner voice is no longer irrelevant. It becomes, instead, the voice of the betrayer.

Professors Jacob W. Getzels and Philip W. Jackson in their recent work on *Creativity and Intelligence*[1] illustrate this process statistically. They drew their sample from a private, university-affiliated high school which afforded them, I should judge, an unusually abundant supply of the kind of "far-out" youngster that their methodology defines as creative. Their independent variables—that is, the criteria by which they assigned individual youngsters to their "high-creative" group—are essentially measures of "divergent thinking," as Professor J. P. Guilford of the University of Southern California defines this kind of mental activity in contrast to the "convergent thinking" of conventional high IQ students. Getzels and Jackson, in other words, started out by setting up a procedure in which the kind of adolescent who is especially prone to find a wealth of unconventional meanings in familiar material, and to use these meanings to arrive at perfectly workable but sometimes shockingly original solutions to problems, was contrasted with the kind of adolescent who is adept at setting such meanings aside as distractions and marching with power and determination along the path of conventional wisdom.

From a sample of 449 private high school students with a

mean IQ of 129, Getzels and Jackson selected 26 students who were in the top 20 per cent on their Guilford-type measures of creativity, but not in IQ; and 28 who were in the top 20 per cent in IQ, but not in creativity. The two groups were then compared with each other and with the total group of 449 on school performance as measured by standard achievement tests; teachers' preferences for having them, when identified by name, in class; and the quality and manner of their response to a series of pictures like those used in the Thematic Apperception Test.

Both groups did equally well on the subject-matter tests of school achievement, and better than the total group of 449. The teachers, however, preferred the high IQ students to both the "high creatives" and those who had not been included in either group; and though they did prefer the high creatives to the average student, the difference was too small to be statistically significant. It should be borne in mind that this was a private secondary school with an exceptionally intelligent student body, and teachers who, to some extent, had chosen to teach gifted students and were accustomed to them. But they nevertheless preferred school achievement to be expressed in conventional terms, which the creatives were unlikely to do.

Getzels and Jackson quote illustratively the following sample responses to one of their story-pictures. "One picture stimulus was perceived most often as a man in an airplane reclining seat returning from a business trip or conference. A high IQ student gave the following story: 'Mr. Smith is on his way home from a successful business trip. He is very happy and he is thinking about his wonderful family and how glad he will be to see them again. He can picture it, about an hour from now, his plane landing at the airport and Mrs. Smith and their three children all there welcoming him home again.' A high-creative subject wrote this story: 'This man is flying back from Reno, where he has just won a divorce from his wife. He couldn't stand to live with her any more, he told the judge, because she wore so much cold cream on her face at night that her head would skid across the pillow and hit him in the head. He is now contemplating a new skid-proof face cream.'"

This is perhaps sufficient to illustrate the contrasting cognitive styles of Getzels' and Jackson's high creatives and high IQ's; and also to suggest what it is that teachers dislike about the former. The youngsters in their high-creative sample *do* disrupt the social environment. You can lead them to the pot; but they just don't melt, they burn. Intelligent and perceptive critics of Getzels' and Jackson's work have pointed out that the actual power of the creative students to create anything worthwhile remains, at their age, unestablished; but their prickliness, hostility, and aggression show up on nearly every instrument of the study. Getzels and Jackson included among their procedures one of having each subject draw whatever he liked on a sheet of paper captioned "Playing Tag in the School Yard." The drawings of the high IQ subjects are literal and humorless, "stimulus-bound"; the high creatives' drawings are fantastic and comical, with something of the quality of Till Eulenspiegel about them; but they are also gory. Combining Getzels' and Jackson's Tables 10 and 11,[2] we get the following statistics on these drawings as they rate them:

	Type of Student	
	High IQ	*High creative*
Number of students in sample	28	26
Humor present	5	14
Humor absent	23	12
Violence present	1	9
Violence absent	27	17

We do not, of course, know how this spiral of reciprocal hostility starts; whether the youngsters become hostile and sarcastic because they are punished for their originality, even though at first they express it openly, innocently, and warmly; or whether a youngster will only think and feel divergently if he starts with a certain detachment from and distrust of conventional, established attitudes and procedures. Most likely—say, on the basis of such a cogent analysis as that in Ernest G. Schachtel's brilliant and classic paper, "On Memory and Childhood Amnesia," [3] the beginnings of creativity in the exploratory sensuality of childhood are quite free from hostility; they are innocent, though hardly chaste. But exploratory sensuality is punished long before the child gets to school, and certainly before he gets to high school. Among the initially gifted, the high creatives are perhaps those who have received enough affection through the total process that they can afford to respond to insult by getting angry and verbally swatting back. The high IQ's have been treated almost wholly as instruments of parental aspirations, even at home, and become anxious at any sign that they are getting off the track; anger and hostility are beyond their emotional means. The findings of Getzels and Jackson on the home background of their contrasting subjects bear this out.

But their most poignant data were obtained from an instrument that they called the Outstanding Traits Test. This consisted of 13 thumbnail descriptions of such traits as social skill, goal-directedness and good marks, using phrases like "Here is the student who is best at getting along with other people"; "Here is the student who is best able to look at things in a new way and to discover new ideas"; "Here is the outstanding athlete in the school," and so forth. The students in their sample were asked to rank these 13 descriptions in three different ways: as "preferred for oneself," as "favored by teachers," and as "believed predictive of adult success." The rank-order correlations obtained between the high IQ and high creative students as to how these traits contributed to later success was *unity;* as to what teachers preferred, it was 0.98. The high creative and high IQ students, in short, were in absolute agreement as to what traits would make a person succeed in adult life; they were virtually agreed as to what teachers liked in students —though the two ratings were not identical. Nevertheless, the correlation between the two groups' ratings of these traits as "preferred for oneself" was only 0.41. This can only be interpreted to mean that one or both of these groups believed that pleasing teachers and becoming successful was just not worth what it cost, even though they agreed completely as to what that cost would be.

Which group rejected the image of success that both shared? The data clearly permit me to resolve this question and end your suspense. Here, instead of correlations *between* the high IQ's and the high creatives, we need, of course, correlations *within* each group for the three possible bases of sorting. Here they are:

Components of correlation	Students: *High IQ*	Students: *High creative*
Personal traits believed "predictive of success" and "favored by teachers"	0.62	0.59
Personal traits "preferred for oneself" and "believed predictive of adult success"	0.81	0.10
Personal traits "preferred for oneself" and "believed favored by teachers"	0.67	−0.25

I would interpret these statistics to mean that the high creatives cannot bring themselves to be what they believe success requires, and are even more strongly repelled by what the teacher demands. The correlation coefficients on the two "favored by teachers" categories are really very curious and interesting across the board. I find a .6 correlation here astonishingly low for *both* groups—with these N's of 26 and 28 such a correlation has little statistical significance. While, for the high IQ's, the correlation between "preferred for oneself" and "predictive of success" is high, for the high creatives, it is negligible.

Both High IQ's, High Creatives Show a Need to Achieve

All these data could be explained very satisfactorily by the hypothesis that the high creatives, spontaneous and joyful as the happy-go-lucky Negro slave of song and story, just don't give a damn; that this is their way of singing "Hallelujah, I'm a bum." But it won't do. Using two standard measures of the need to achieve, David McClelland's *need: achievement* and Fred L. Strodtbeck's *V-score,* Getzels and Jackson were unable to find any significant differences between the two groups, or between either group and the total population of 449; the figures given for the high creatives are actually slightly higher on both measures. So we must turn for our interpretation to the relationship between the students and the school itself.

Both groups, I infer, see the teacher as on the side of success, but being too naïve and square to be a very reliable guide as to how to go after it. Since the high IQ's are determined to *be* the kind of person who succeeds, this reduces the relevance of the teacher to him, but not the relevance of the school. Or to put it another way, the importance of the school as the monitor of his progress is quite enough to bring the high IQ to terms with it; and the terms are generous enough not to demand that he listen to what it actually says. To the high creative, the whole experience is rather frustrating and annoying, and relevant only because there is no viable alternative to high school for a middle-class adolescent. Lower-class adolescents who are not interested in economic success or who feel the school too suffocating can just drop out, go off on a kick, and let the authorities conceal their relief while they pretend to search for them. But this kind of direct action would cost the middle-class youngster his role, and cause him too much anxiety to be a satisfactory alternative. Generally he stays, and looks for ancillary satisfactions in specialized relationships with his peers, in sports or hobbies or sometimes sex and even love, building up a credential while inwardly rejecting the qualities the credential symbolizes.

For both groups, however, the function of the school becomes essentially liturgical, not epistemological. It isn't supposed to make sense. It is not appropriate to believe, disbelieve, or test what one is taught in school. Instead, one *relates* to it; one tries to figure out why this line has been taken rather than another, to figure out what response is expected, and give it.

The result is a peculiar kind of moral vacuity; a limitation of responsible *perception,* and therefore, of moral behavior, to situations that are wholly concrete and immediate. The public school is not primarily an educational institution. I have forgotten who first said that most Christians would feel equal consternation at hearing Christianity denounced and at seeing it practised; it ought, presumably, to have been Mary. But I am quite sure that this could justly be said of most Americans with respect to public education. In many ways, the relationship of the school to the community is like that of a TV station that carries mostly network programs but that is largely dependent on local advertising for support. Like the TV station, the school has its own technical staff, and such autonomy as it possesses is derived from their custody of the mysteries and the records, rather than from any considerable measure of popular deference to their authority. The entertainment provided is frequently of high quality and shrewdly geared to the public taste. Concessions to the intellect and culture, provided as a public service, tend to be more ponderous, conventional, and unconvincing. Though the staff likes to boast about how much of this sort of thing they program, they are self-conscious about it, and rather fearful. The commercials for the local way of life are interminable, boring, and egregiously dishonest, and the audience knows it. But they are hard to change for they are the real basis for the support the school receives. And they are effective, as good commercials are, not so much in stimulating an active desire for the product as in convincing the audience that only a social misfit would be without it.

Students Prepare for Next Step

What the students learn best in high school is how to function in and utilize a limited power network to achieve limited personal and social objectives. They learn how to get along and make ready for the next onward state. By the time they reach college, they are likely to be thoroughly impatient of anything else; and in our culture, college seldom tries their patience much; the process continues. To me, the most interesting finding in a recent study of medical students[4] is the righteous resentment with which the young medics respond to instruction in medical—to say nothing of social—theory. What they want from medical school is conventional knowledge and practical hints (what they call pearls) and a clear road to the practitioner's license. To get this they are willing to work like dogs;

but they resist any suggestion that they work like a higher primate.

Doctors, of course, have notoriously high IQ's, and it is not astonishing that medical students should resemble Getzels' and Jackson's high IQ's in their characteristic cognitive style. But they are also quite creative, when they feel that circumstances and the American Medical Association permit; as are many high IQ's. Creativity and intelligence, like height and weight, are undoubtedly highly correlated. Getzels and Jackson adopted a classic design for their study to permit them to examine contrasts; just as biologists studying human metabolism might deliberately set out to study the differences between short, fat people and tall, thin ones. But both are exceptional, which is why the sample fell from 449 to 28 in one quadrant and 26 in the other. Had they chosen to study youngsters who were in the top 20 per cent in both creativity and IQ, they would probably have found 60 or so in the sample. How would *they* have fared in school?

Getzels and Jackson tell us nothing about this. My own understanding and observation of public education suggests that they would probably be very successful, indeed, and would be well received by the school and acquire a substantial proportion of positions of leadership. We would accept them as our best young Americans—executive material. And the school would teach them to be discreet: not to let their creativity get the upper hand, not to jeopardize their chances by antagonizing persons more stupid than themselves who might nevertheless turn up later on some committee that was passing on them. The pitch would be made on a high moral plane—usually in terms of keeping their availability so as not to impair their usefulness—but the net effect would be to convince the youngster that he ought not to get out of line or speak out of turn, if he hoped ultimately to put his creativity to use in the service of, say, General Electric or the United States Food and Drug Administration.

A statistic frequently cited in the United States is that we spend a little more on hard liquor than we do on public education. I have just finished reading a book which seems to me more striking in its educational implications than any work directly *about* education since Martin Mayer's *The Schools*.[5] This book is Theodore H. White's *The Making of the President 1960*;[6] and after reading it I find that datum shocking. We ought to be spending a *lot* more on hard liquor. We are going to need it, and besides, it works. But I have introduced Mr. White's book into this discussion, not primarily as a vivid portrait of the failure of public education to instruct a trustworthy electorate—though that, according to James Madison, was its essential function—but to allude to one particular passage as a specific illustration of creativity and what happens to it. Mr. White gives a circumstantial account of Richard Nixon's suspiciousness of the press and ineptness in communicating with it, which made the job of the reporters assigned to cover his campaign—for papers primarily committed to his support—almost impossible. The reporters themselves came to dislike and distrust Mr. Nixon and his program. In their dispatches, no hint of their actual feelings or personal appraisal appeared.

But Mr. White reports:

> "Then having done their duty, they began frivolously to write imaginary dispatches of what they felt would be a more accurate transcription of their private understanding. I reproduce here a few leads of such dispatches as illustrations of what happens when the press feels itself abused.
>
> "Guthrie Center, Iowa [read one]—Vice-President Nixon said today farmers should eat their way out of the surplus problem. . . .
>
> "Guthrie Center, Iowa [another]—Vice-President Nixon admitted today that the farm problem was too big for the Republican Party to handle. He said that if elected President, he would appoint Senator Hubert H. Humphrey as Secretary of Agriculture and let him wrestle with the problem. . . .
>
> "Guthrie Center, Iowa [another]—Vice-President Nixon today called on Pope John XXIII for guidance in finding a solution to the troublesome farm problems which have plagued Catholic, Jew and Protestant alike. . . ." [7]

My point is that Mr. White also illustrates what doesn't happen even when the press feels itself abused. These "imaginary dispatches" may well afford "a more accurate transcription of their private understanding" than what the reporters actually transmitted. Their responsibility as reporters, I should say, included that of letting the public know not only what Mr. Nixon had said but what they thought he was actually like, properly labeled, of course, as a subjective judgment. This they were too canny to release until too late for it to do any good.

It is self-evident, I believe, that the quality of these imaginary dispatches is identical with the quality of the picture stories produced by the high creatives in Getzels' and Jackson's study, but the factually correct dispatches are the kind of response the high IQ's produce. The reporters, then, must have been both; but they had learned better than to be both when the chips were down and people were watching. They were not deliberately taught this in school, but school is a very good place in which to learn it.

Mr. White further writes:

> "One had to see Nixon entering a small Iowa village, the streets lined with schoolchildren, all waving American flags until it seemed as if the cavalcade were entering a defile lined by fluttering, peppermint-striped little banners . . . to see him at his best. . . . These people were his natural constituency, his idiom their idiom . . .[8]
>
> ". . . He woke in Marietta, Ohio, on Monday, October 25th, to begin his last 'peak' effort, and it was clear from his first speech of the day that he was at one with his audience as he had not been since he had passed through the corn fields of Iowa in the first week of the campaign. A sign outside the courthouse of Marietta, Ohio, read: HIGH SCHOOL DEBATERS GREET WORLD DEBATER—the sign was apropos, and of the essence of his last trip as he revived. For he *was* a high-school debater, the boy who had, some thirty years before, won a Los Angeles *Times* prize for his high-school oration on the Constitution. He was seeking not so much to score home a message as to win the hearts of his little audiences. . . ."[9]

It *is* a little like entering a defile. Some of us would prefer to enter a demurrer. On the basis of cognitive style I would infer that this would include a disproportionate number of high creatives. But how, in the present public high school, does one go about it?

One of the traditional forms of demurrer in our society is to get up and slowly walk away. We have always counted on pluralism as our most effective weapon against conformity and, in de Tocqueville's phrase, "the tyranny of the majority"; and I think it is one of the best social instruments that could be devised and inherent in the nature of democracy. For that reason, I am very much in favor of private and parochial schools. As a matter of social policy, I think they should receive some tax support. I am not a constitutional lawyer, and I cannot judge the legal merits of the argument that aid to church schools, granted at their request, would constitute the Congress making a law respecting an establishment of religion. Personally, I think this is a ridiculous interpretation of the First Amendment; but, then, the First Amendment has always been my favorite passage of the Constitution, and I am naturally reluctant to believe that it is against anything that I favor.

I am convinced that private schools—and in this country many of these are church-supported—contribute more to the general welfare even than they do to their own constituency. We so desperately need alternative life-styles and *ethical models that are related to a particular community and to the experience of life within it,* rather than recipes for tearing away from one's roots and learning to function smoothly among successively more affluent groups of strangers. As to the risk of encountering God, well, it is true that He can be very tricky. But I doubt if the encounter can be altogether avoided. It would certainly not harm any youngster—rather in the spirit of the New England gentlewoman who took up the study of Hebrew at the age of eighty-five—to learn how to confront Him and thrash out those issues on which they were in disagreement. Adolescents generally get along very well with God, anyhow. The Creation is exactly the kind of thing they can imagine having done themselves, and they can sympathize with the kind of trouble He got himself into by acting out His creative impulse. It is only in later life, the image having become somewhat tarnished, that the meeting tends to be rather embarrassing to both.

It is difficult to suggest practical ways in which the public school might represent and support a greater diversity of values and a less purely instrumental conception of learning. At present, the public high school lacks dignity. It is often incoherent. Whatever is learned of graciousness and leisure in English or art class—and it isn't likely to be much—is undercut by the food and the noise and standing in line in the cafeteria. The social studies class may discuss civil liberty, but the students still need a pass to walk through the hall and school disciplinary procedures are notably lacking in due process. The students are encouraged to get together in groups to discuss important issues, as long as there is somebody to represent all sides and the criticism doesn't go too deep. But there isn't anyplace to do it that is out of reach of the public address system announcing when you have to go to get your yearbook picture taken or directing Tom Brown to report to the principal's office *at once;* the efficiency of the p.a. system depends on the fact that you can't get away from it.

All these are trivia; what is not trivial is the continuous experience, day after day and year after year, of triviality itself; of being treated like a tiny unit in an administrative problem. So, really, it does add up; this is *how* you are taught not to take yourself too seriously. This is where you learn that whatever may be officially said, actual official decisions are made with the short-run purpose of getting the job done and keeping out of trouble. This is where you learn to keep your conversation brief, friendly, and to the point, instead of getting all hung up on ideas like an egghead or an Oxbridge don.

Of course, these things and worse occur in many private schools which can also be barren and stultifying. But when they are, there is at least the theoretical possibility of appealing to an explicit educational tradition that transcends American middle-class practice to try and change them. These *are* basic American middle-class values, however; so there is not much use appealing there, though a smart public school administrator may develop considerable skill in identifying subgroups in his community that take education and youngsters more seriously. But it is a laborious and dangerous process. Public school administrators who try to give their communities better education than they are used to have a very short life expectancy. If you wish to see a case study of such a situation in detail, *Small Town in Mass Society,*[10] contains a superb one. But you know it already.

There is nothing wrong with the school as a social environment, except what is wrong with America. One of the sailors in my company when I was in the Navy during World War II had a stock proposal that he used to make with reference to any of our mates who was seriously annoying to him. "Let's ostracize him," he said. "You hold him, and I'll do it." Technically, what Coleman proposes is the exact contrary. But I am afraid it comes to the same thing in the end.

It seems to me, then, that I have no choice but to conclude on a note of satisfaction. As a social environment the public high school, by and large, functions very effectively. It is expected to socialize adolescents into the American middle-class, and that is just what it does. You can actually see it doing it. If that isn't what you want, go fight Livingston Street.

1963

1. (New York: John Wiley & Sons, Inc., 1962).
2. *Ibid.*, p. 49. The tables indicate that the statistical probability of a chance difference between high IQ's and high creatives, as great as that shown here, is .02 or less.
3. Included in *Metamorphosis* (New York: Basic Books, Inc., 1959), pp. 279-322.
4. Howard S. Becker, Blanche Geer, Everett S. Hughes, and Anselm L. Strauss, *Boys in White* (Chicago: University of Chicago Press, 1962).
5. (New York: Harper & Brothers, 1960).
6. From *The Making of the President 1960*, by Theodore H. White. Copyright © 1961 by Atheneum House, Inc. Reprinted by permission of the publishers.
7. Theodore H. White, *op. cit.*, pp. 274-275.
8. *Ibid.*, p. 277.
9. *Ibid.*, p. 300.
10. Arthur J. Vidich and Joseph Bensman (Princeton, N. J.: Princeton University Press, 1958).

The Purpose of Liberal Study versus the Purposes of Adult Students

It seems to me that a major source of difficulty that adult educators must face—though we rarely do—is that many of the assumptions that we make about our clientele, and particularly about its reasons for *being* our clientele, are quite simply false. They are not who we think they are; and, what is much more serious, they are not who *they* think they are. Nor are they, or we, fully aware of their purposes in associating themselves with us in study groups.

This is not a particularly serious matter with reference to those who are interested primarily in further technical or vocational study. Whatever purposes and conflicts may underlie their vocational choice, the reality of having made it requires that they pursue it more or less straightforwardly. But it is much more serious with respect to liberal study, *for the significance of liberal education is dominated by the purposes and character of those who undertake it.* Its meanings are derived from the subtly delineated interface where values interact with experience. What one can do with liberal education depends very much, therefore, on what kind of person one is and on what one really wants with it.

The reasons why people interest themselves in liberal education as adults are as varied, to be sure, as the individuals themselves; and that is infinitely varied. Nevertheless, there are norms and central tendencies; for adult education is itself a social institution and is molded and limited by its social context.

Adult education—particularly *liberal* adult education—in the United States is largely a middle-class business. We know, from analyses of the characteristics of American social classes by Lloyd Warner, Robin Williams, and other sociologists, that working class individuals belong to relatively few formally organized groups, and that these are not primarily intellectual in character. And it seems hardly necessary to assert in 1958, as President Hoover's speeches of a quarter-century ago again reveal their timeless quality, that the American upper-class is not characterized by breadth or profundity of intellectual interest. Those who are motivated to formal study in later life come overwhelmingly from life's intermediate walks.

To the seeking of educational goals they bring the attitudes and values of the American middle-class. Again, these are various; again, there are systematic regularities of outlook and purpose that recur frequently enough to color the educative process. To a degree, the middle-class orientation is a limitation on educational aptitude and the dignity of the educative process: to the degree that it *is* such a limitation, our conception of democracy compels us to be blind to its implications. It is these implications—or some of them—that I wish here to examine.

It is no mere historical accident that we define liberal education as the kind of education that helps to make men free and that is worthy of free men. Our conception of democracy, with its accompanying slogans, has led us to confuse the free with the merely enfranchised. Yet only sentimentality can spare us the inference that freedom is what many of the enfranchised most deeply fear and most successfully avoid.

It is quite possible that adult education may do a great deal to increase the proportion of the enfranchised who can accept and even desire freedom. The recent and ongoing research of Stern and others at Syracuse University[1] suggests that this can be done with college students; and there is no intrinsic reason why similiar procedures should not work with adults.

Stern and Cope began by dividing their students into three groups according to their scores on the American Council on Education's *Inventory of Beliefs:* the *stereopaths,* or highly authoritarian students; *anti-authoritarians,* who expressed strongly humane and liberal attitudes with, however, a degree of almost ideological rigidity comparable to that of the stereopaths though precisely opposed to their viewpoint; and *rationalists,* who reject stereotypy of all kinds and try to think for themselves.

The fact, however, that the Syracuse research group have found it necessary to teach their "stereopaths" in very carefully selected and skillfully organized groups, if any relaxation of their rigidity is to result, suggests that this outcome is not likely to be achieved in an ordinary adult class or discussion group; quite the contrary, in fact. Until such methods as theirs can be more widely and fruitfully applied, we must recognize, I think, that many of our clientele are not free men and do not wish to become free men, in the sense that liberal education assumes.

What they are more likely to want is some assurance that the various roles each fills in society are meaningful, and that they are capable of filling them without embarrassment.

This is particularly true if they have attained these roles by striving after more money or more status without really understanding what this would get them into if they succeeded, and without maintaining adequate reserves of self-esteem to protect them if they failed. Adult students who are so motivated are likely to be quite ambivalent in their attitude toward liberal education, and with very good reason, for to them it is certainly a two-edged instrument.

It *can* be their most powerful resource, if they have the strength to use it properly, and their teacher or group leader has the insight and the firmness needed to show them how. For the way in which liberal education liberates is precisely by *examining the meaning of life* in its particular complexity. Liberal education works by using the arts to illuminate the immediate specifics of life as well as its goals, and the sciences—social and natural—to explain its dynamics.

The writings of Gustave Flaubert, C. Wright Mills and Sir Charles Snow can convey to the middle-class man, with some precision and economy of means, just what his position in the world is, and how it has evolved from what it was a century ago; and this gives him something to go on from, in defining the meaning of his life in society for himself; if that is what he wishes to do. But they cannot compel him to accept this responsibility—even though there is actually no way in which he can avoid it—and their message provides no immediate reassurance.

Reassurance, however, is what a large part of our clientele comes to us for. Sometimes they want the *content* of the adult education program to be reassuring; more often they want something much more detrimental to their actual chance of being liberated: they want to read into the *experience* of participating in an adult study group a factitious assurance *that they have already become what they would wish to be.*

They use their conscientious attendance and their eagerness to enter into discussion as evidence with which to convince themselves that, as citizens, they have a significant influence on current political processes; that, as parents, they are open-minded, tolerant, and committed to furthering the growth of their children as independent human beings; that, as consumers of the arts, they combine sound critical judgment with an enlightened sympathy for the experimental approach and the novel point of view.

In each case, these propositions may be valid or they may not; but it is certain that no individual who participates in an adult education program primarily to prove such points, is likely to experience any liberation.

People have always been driven to knowledge by sheer uneasy snobism: Voltaire used to complain bitterly about it. What makes it a matter of special concern for us is that they now usually feel the need to seek it in groups. This almost pathological craving to submit our private sources of self-esteem to the "consensual validation of our peers" is now everywhere recognized as the special affliction of the American urban middle-class; this is "other-direction" in action.

All groups evolve their own dynamics and informal sanctions. A group whose members are gathered primarily for the purpose of validating one another's claims and assuaging one another's anxieties, can provide yet another social arena in which the kind of people actually there can win status and distinction. But it will rather quickly manage to protect itself from liberal education's other and more cutting edge, while using the group itself to put the finishing touches on the flattering self-portrait they are carving out.

Such a group will ensnare itself thoroughly in pompous superficiality unless it receives a great deal of help from its leader. But this help is unlikely to be available because the prevailing *ethos* of adult education in certain respects encourages the devotion of the group to just such illiberal purposes. We are, in the first place, so aware that participation in adult education programs is voluntary that we are very anxious to have everyone enjoy himself.

It seems to me that we ought to be somewhat concerned if they do enjoy themselves, at least at first, because it is almost certain that some members of any adult group that is devoting itself to serious study of the humanities, the sciences, or the relationship between them will have come for adventitious reasons. We know perfectly well that the majority of the community study group must reflect the values and insights prevailing in its total culture, and that there is scarcely any possibility that all of them will have come with the understanding that study requires both courage and self-discipline and the wish to devote these to it. Those who come with the unconscious conviction that adult education can be effectively conducted in the posture of a tired housewife sitting in front of the TV and "noshing" away at her own fantasy life ought not to be encouraged to remain on those terms.

But another part of our *ethos* says that they ought to; that it is undemocratic not to start where they are—no matter where anyone else in the group may be. We tend to conduct our groups as if it were in itself desirable to have every member participate; we adopt devices—like calling on each member of the group going clockwise around the table—to see that they do. We welcome each contribution equally, without much distinction as to its value, and we tend to discourage the person who really knows what he is talking about from dominating the discussion. We call our authorities "resource persons" to make it perfectly clear that they may have authority over our field of study but they don't have it over *us*.

Intellectual authority, however, is a form of rational authority, in Fromm's sense, and is quite real and binding. Students, adult or not, who feel free to reject Freud's ideas on psychodynamics, Keynes' on economic theory, or Parsons' theory of social structure *as personally distasteful to them*—they have, of course, the right and even the duty to check the implications of these and any ideas against their own experience—are talking nonsense. But we seldom seem to feel free to tell them so, although the information might be very useful to them. The *mystique* of group participation has seized us, and we are sometimes powerless against it.

How often have you seen the chairman of a program in which a distinguished authority is presented to an audience of hundreds conclude the meeting by soliciting ten minutes of discussion from the floor, even though the very physical circumstances of the meeting made this ritual obeisance toward the group process quite meaningless?

What seems to be wrong is that we operate from certain serious misconceptions about the nature of the processes of participation and policy-making in a modern democracy. Many of us became interested in adult education because we believe that our democracy must rest in the decisions of a rational electorate that understands the world in which it lives.

Since the clients of adult education *are* the electorate, it must follow that they are either already fit to participate fully in any group consideration of significant issues, or their unfitness must be regarded as a problem and a challenge. In any case, by virtue of their citizenship, they are already responsible, and our duty as adult educators is to give ourselves no rest till we have managed to get them involved in their responsibilities.

Yet, there is something wrong with this argument. There must be, because most of our electorate is profoundly uninformed, intellectually irresponsible and undisciplined, and—so far as the specific consequences of the policies among which its government must choose are concerned—it is largely ignorant. Half of it is of subnormal intelligence; though the other half, by definition, is above average.

Yet, despite these handicaps, our social system—works? No, not exactly: it doesn't always work; it is subject to recessions that resemble depressions, and police actions that are just like wars, though these cannot be called by those names, since if they were the people wouldn't stand for them. Still, we get along; we live till we die; we keep a job, stay out of jail, and feed our family most of the time. If that isn't democracy, what is?

Like other political states, we accomplish these miracles of survival because, regardless of the premises from which we work, the actual social dynamics operate so as to insure that power *is* very unequally distributed, and that those who have most of it usually understand at least in part what they are doing and what some of the results will be. They may be selfish, greedy, and even corrupt; they often are. They may even be cruel, though this is a serious misfortune. But they must not be incompetent to predict the consequences of their policies in the spheres for which they are responsible. And they must not be continually required to justify these policies to a public that cannot, in view of the diversity and complexity of the issues involved, be similarly competent. This is why, jealously as it guards its power, the Congress has been obligated to enact very broad legislation, delegating much of its authority to nearly autonomous agencies and commissions, with the intent that these should maintain staffs qualified to deal with highly specialized technical and social problems.

Indeed, in the view put forth by Ortega y Gasset in *The Revolt of the Masses* 30 years ago, and much more recently by Walter Lippmann in *The Public Philosophy*, a crucial problem of modern democracy is the failure of its citizenry to accept any limitations of competence on its right to intervene directly in complex and delicate matters of public policy. Ortega puts the matter succinctly:

> I believe that the political innovations of recent times signify nothing less than the political domination of the masses. The old democracy was tempered by a generous dose of liberalism

and of enthusiasm for law. By serving these principles the individual bound himself to maintain a severe discipline over himself. Under the shelter of liberal principles and the rule of law, minorities could live and act. Democracy and the law—life in common under the law—were synonymous. Today we are witnessing the triumphs of a hyper-democracy in which the mass acts directly, outside of the law, imposing its aspirations and its desires by means of material pressure.

It is a false interpretation of the new situation to say that the mass has grown tired of politics and handed over the exercise of it to specialized persons. Quite the contrary. That was what happened previously; that was democracy. . . . Now, on the other hand, the mass believes that it has the right to impose and to give force of law to notions born in the cafe. . . . If the individuals who make up the mass believed themselves specially qualified, it would be a case merely of personal error, not of sociological subversion. *The characteristic of the hour is that the commonplace mind, knowing itself to be commonplace, has the assurance to proclaim the rights of the commonplace and to impose them wherever it will.*

The issue raised here has dual, and contrasting, implications for adult education. The most obvious, and the one to which we have usually responded, is that adult education ought to undertake to correct the condition to which Ortega refers by making as many people as possible competent to handle the problems of modern democracy.

It is our responsibility to provide the citizen with the intellectual skills and discipline which will enable him to function fully. This is a tenable position; though when one emerges from the subway at the end of a working day with a vivid image of one's fellow citizen in mind it hardly seems so.

Personally, I find the converse implication more convincing. I do not think any large proportion of our citizenry is going to undertake seriously either to qualify itself for citizenship or to restrain its impulses to intervene. Nor do I think we are going to be so compulsive in our observance of the letter rather than the spirit of democracy as to allow our affairs to fall into disorder.

I would judge then that if we are to survive as a nation

that can at least provide a measure of freedom to those who are not unduly afraid of it, our social institutions must evolve in such a way as to make them less immediately responsive to public pressure than they now are. To some extent, unfortunately, this means that our invocations of democracy will become more ritualized rather than less, but the alternative seems to me to be the total abdication of privacy and dignity in the affairs of our society.

This means, then, that the one thing adult education should *not* do, if it is to be liberal in its effect, is to contribute further to the public conviction that one man's opinion is as good as another's; and that democracy means that you have a right to be heard whether or not you have anything relevant to say.

We should, on the contrary, emphasize through our programs that the function of liberal education for adults is to root dignity and the sense of self firmly in intellectual competence; to make available to adults the documentary, musical, and plastic resources that will help them to make sense of their present position in reality, and to chart with some confidence their course through a world always uncertain, usually indifferent, sometimes breathtakingly significant. This is our purpose, and we can, I believe, do meaningful work only with those adults whose purposes in a measure coincide.

1958

---

1. Stern, George C. and Alfred H. Cope, "Differences in Educability Between Stereopaths, Non-stereopaths, and Rationals," *American Psychologist*, 11, 8, 1956.

INTIMATIONS OF MORTALITY IN THE LITERATURE OF PUBLIC EDUCATION

SINCE WORLD WAR I we have had in successive waves a primarily child-centered literature of professional education; an educational literature urging the use of the school as an instrument of liberal social reconstruction, and a literature of protest and condemnation, excoriating the public schools for their intellectual irresponsibility and alleged sentimental coddling of pupils. Examples of the first of these are the early publications of the Progressive Education Association; of the second, George S. Counts' work prior to World War II; while the third is fairly represented by Arthur Bestor's *Educational Wastelands*[1] and, in a less responsible vein, Albert Lynd's *Quackery in the Public Schools.*[2] Most recently, James Koerner has developed this position further in *The Miseducation of American Teachers.*[3] Rising above these waves, though not very conspicuously, have been occasional works of apology like Paul Woodring's *Let's Talk Sense About Our Schools,*[4] and, more recently, Raymond Harris's *American Education: Facts, Fancies and Folklore.*[5] The waves have, of course, overlapped, and a more refined scrutiny would certainly reveal variations in the stream. But, though they have beaten against and occasionally sought to undermine American educational practice, they have nevertheless invariably accepted it and been channeled by it. Serious books about American education have attacked the public school and defended it; educators have argued that the schools should be devoted to a variety of different social purposes that they felt to be unwarrantably neglected. But none has questioned the American conception of public education in principle.

This omission is, in itself, quite American. We are no

longer much inclined—if, indeed, we ever were—to examine our institutions critically; we prefer instead to waver between complacency, defensiveness, and bouts of self-flagellation like a Peter Arno drunk. We are, however, empiricists in the sense that we work out rather successful alternatives to failing institutions without ever commenting publicly on their failure. The competitive free-enterprise economy, which we have gradually and rather furtively abandoned in favor of an unplanned and inequitable but functional form of corporate organization is the most obvious example.

There are signs that a comparable quiet change in attitude toward public education—especially secondary education—and a corresponding diversion of some of its functions from the school to evolving and as yet unnamed social institutions may be taking place. Public education, in principle, is too deeply involved with our fantasies of equality of opportunity and too useful a part of the apparatus by which the American poor are kept unfit and unready for actual insurgence to be either attacked or abandoned. But the current intense concern over school dropouts—who have not increased in relative proportion to enrollments, but who palpably have no place to go and no alternative means of socialization—is leading for the first time to consideration of large scale alternatives to compulsory school attendance. These alternatives vary in appeal—some may be dangerous to liberty and none shows a very gracious conception of American youth and its character. But regardless of their merit they do indicate, for the first time, that solutions may be sought beyond the jurisdiction of the local school board and its function as agent for the local status system. They also suggest, I think, considerable dissatisfaction with the kind of *place* the high school has become and a certain despair about the kinds of people who run it.

This process is mirrored in some rather interesting developments in the literature of education; the new wave is, for the first time, really sociological, anthropological and, indeed, almost clinical. This is as true of Martin Mayer, a serious journalist who has written about a wide range of aspects of contemporary life and morals before coming to education, as it is of a professional social psychologist like Frank Riessman. In comparison to most earlier work (the classic exception being Willard Waller's *Sociology of Teaching*[6]) these books of the past two or three years differ from their predecessors much as Machiavelli's *Prince* did from earlier hortatory volumes of pious precepts intended to guide the conduct of rulers and generally ignored by them. The best recently published work on education, though calm and even sympathetic in tone, is devastating in its implications—more devasting, surely, than the complaints of a Bestor or Rickover.

Martin Mayer's *The Schools*[7] is written from just such a viewpoint of sympathetic understanding. This, indeed, is the book's most serious defect, giving it a bland, good-humored tone that is sometimes inappropriate to the outrages it recounts. Mr. Mayer states:

> Willy-nilly, all schools must work from the basis of Emile Durkheim's rather grim definition: "Education consists of a methodical socialization of the young generation." . . . American schools are always going to promote middle-class values, because the national community they serve is overwhelmingly middle-class in orientation and even in "self-image." It is more than a little unrealistic to expect teachers who are fighting hard for recognition as "professionals" to cultivate in their classrooms the values of an unprofessional subgroup in their community.

Much of Mr. Mayer's discussion is directed against the view that the school can or should transcend the values of the community.

> School is not really the place for questioning authority. . . . The highly charged words of the culture—"democracy," "Communism," "love," "prejudice" and so forth—cannot be seriously analyzed in school.

The school is the agent of society and to expect it to be anything else is to expect too much.

> Beginning with the fourth grade, the books are full of buncombe, but it is the kind of buncombe that children like and schools must provide. . . . By the time the child finishes sixth

> grade . . . he will have acquired an almost complete stock of "common-sense" knowledge about the world around him—knowledge that is mostly false, but serviceable enough in the adult world.

In a book that provides, as *The Schools* does, a tight analysis of how a curriculum is constructed and discusses this in a context of comparative education, telling exactly what is done in classrooms from California to Finland, that maintains a continuous concern about the different epistemological characters of the various subjects taught, passages like these are damning. They amount to saying, in the kindest possible tone, that education is too important a matter to be left to the schoolteachers, who are not professionals after all.

What distinguishes the professional from a technician, however skilled, is that the professional at work depends for discipline and guidance on his own integrity, on what he is trying to do, and on the properties of what he has to work with. In order to respect these, he resists social demands that impinge on him externally and temptations to sacrifice his professional purpose to short-term gains in wealth or status. The professional accepts responsibility for ends as well as means, and tries, within his specialty, to fit them to each other elegantly. If he is ambitious or greedy, as he well may be, he nevertheless tries to fulfill his ambition through professional achievement, rather than in violation of its inner structure. He may, as physicians working through the AMA, for example, do, try ruthlessly to advance his profession and with it his own status at the expense of the general welfare; but when he is actually practicing medicine he must care for his patient as well as he can, or be guilty of a breach of professional ethics.

This does not mean that the professional functions independently of society; but that society has defined his role as requiring autonomous functionaries if it is to be carried out effectively. The classic conception of democracy as dependent on an informed and independent-minded citizenry, competent and free to inquire, and obligated to deliver informed judgments on public policy obviously implies, as James Madison recognized, universal education in the arts and technics of freedom, and this in turn implies, as the concept of academic freedom expresses, that educators are specialists in the cultivation of human autonomy. Mr. Mayer's rueful observations attest the degree to which this model has become obsolete. His comment that teachers who are fighting for recognition as professionals cannot be expected to sympathize with the values of lower status groups is particularly, though unintentionally, ironical. It is based on sound enough observation: shabby-genteel teachers are threatened by, and generally hostile to, working-class youngsters who are not "trying to better themselves." Since most of the clientele of the school is working class, the result is a very widespread attitude of spiteful denigration. But in a teacher, contempt for students is unprofessional and precludes any possibility of professional status. What Mayer's position finally implies, then, is that a public school serves no truly professional function in our society—it has, that is, no tradition of genuine autonomy and no established respect for its own social function on which to draw. A professional knows that a part of his social obligation is precisely to maintain his craft against changing social pressures; he is the custodian of certain mysteries that society needs and trusts him to protect even from itself. This is just what the school fails to do.

If all this meant was that the school, by and large, has an unrealistically pretentious conception of its social function the matter would hardly be worth discussing; there must be millions of people who think they are professionals when, in fact, they are only executives. But the issue is subtler, and rather more interesting than that. The school enjoys prerogatives that depend on the assumption that something more significant, and more trustworthy, and more beneficial than what Mayer describes is taking place there. Compulsory attendance, the substitution of the concept of *in loco parentis* for any civil rights the student would otherwise enjoy as a protection from the demands of strangers, the discipline and decorum for which the school strives with decreasing success in the larger and more decayed urban centers—all these are predicated on the assumption that the school is not merely a socializing agency, but the socializing agency that is professionally equipped to utilize the maturing ego of the subject, to secure his rational and willing participation in a society whose values and major institutional arrangements he understands and accepts. If this is not even remotely what happens, or could be expected to happen, then the educational system becomes a proper and provocative subject for reappraisal, rather than simply something to be bucked up and supported.

This reappraisal ought appropriately to consider not only what the schools now really are, which Mayer quite brilliantly conveys; but how they got to be that way. Even this, curiously, remains a rather novel task. There have been many histories of education, to be sure, and they have their customary central figures: Rousseau, Pestalozzi, Froebel, Mann, Dewey. It is conventional to note certain administrative and methodological developments that were conspicuous innovations at their time: the monitorial system, for example, or the Winnetka Plan. The difficulty with these works is that they are themselves systems of historical cliché. Education has no history apart from that of the society, and its values and events, that the schools serve. In a sense, to be sure, nothing does; but it is possible, for example, to write a history of science that deals selectively with individual scientists and their contributions aside from the social processes in which they participated, because the scientists were part of an intellectual community that persisted through time; they knew what their colleagues and predecessors had done and built on it; their journals and learned societies performed a genuinely integrative function. Scientists, up until the time of the Manhattan Project, moreover, really did run their own enterprise according to their own method and their own code. So a history of science from Paracelsus to Rutherford or Einstein makes perfectly good, through limited, sense, even if it ignores the underlying mercantile, industrial, and political changes which defined and set limits to the scientist's role.

But the school has never been as independent of the community as the laboratory; and Rousseau and Dewey are about as much a part of the tradition of a contemporary American school principal as Pericles is of a fraternity pledge who learns the Greek alphabet to avoid a paddling. School administrators are often very able men, but their abilities are seldom intellectual and they have no use for—and no place in—a history of ideas or philosophy. They are mediators, organizers, politicians trying to keep a school functioning in a community that depends on it to keep its young out of the way and out of mischief, justifies their confinement in educational terms, and then becomes frightened that they may learn something subversive. One of the most effective ways of reassuring such a community is for the school administrators to present themselves as men who in no way transcend its intellectual limits. A history of education, properly speaking, is then a history of the relationship of school practice to social pressure and demographic change; the sort of thing Raymond Callahan has done so brilliantly for the first quarter of the century in *Education and the Cult of Efficiency.*[8]

Because of its highly specialized character, I shall not discuss Callahan's book further here, except to recommend it as a model of its kind. Lawrence A. Cremin's widely acclaimed *The Transformation of the School,*[9] which deals in detail with the mainstream of recent educational events and ideology, is a better example for the purpose of this essay-review.

The Transformation of the School is essentially a study of the progressive education movement from its earliest ideological roots in the American progressive climate of the eighteen-seventies to the demise of the Progressive Education Association within the past decade. As such, the work is rather a *tour de force.* It is not very well-written. Professor Cremin has a tendency to cliché and popular maxim. But it is exceptionally scholarly both in its use of quite unfamiliar and obscure original sources and, moreover, in the way Cremin establishes linkages between the evolving rationale of education and the fundamental social thought of the time. The book really is a history of education, or of one central aspect of it, rather than a sentimental gallery of the philosophers and philanthropists whom educationists like to regard as their forebears. One difficulty, to be sure, that is more troublesome to a historian of the progressive education movement than to, say, a historian of Elizabethan society is that the topic itself is somewhat less interesting to begin with. But Cremin's book turns out to be more engrossing than its topic might promise.

No other book has yet revealed so consistently the pettiness and timidity of American educational leadership; none has made so clear the remoteness of the great names of pedagogy and the leaders of its councils from other contemporary enterprises of great pith and moment. Professor Cremin is both a perceptive obstetrician and a seismologist of extraordinary delicacy; he detects the virtually imperceptible trembling of the mountain in response to the paroxysms of the mouse within; he conveys, withal, the mouse's extraordinary sense of responsibility for developments in the educational enterprise that an external observer would surely have attributed to other forces. Anyone who participates in the politics of pedagogy, either academic or municipal, will recognize instantly the validity and representative tone of the following description of the reception of the report of the Committee on Social and Economic Problems of the Progressive Education Association by its Board of Directors:

> Following the instructions of the membership the Committee was charged with promoting within the schools and their affiliated agencies "thoughtful and systematic study of the economic and industrial problems confronting us today." The Directors must have known what they would get, for in addition to (George S.) Counts, they appointed Merle E. Curti, John S. Gambs, Sidney Hook, Jesse H. Newlon, Willard Beatty, Charles L. S. Easton, Goodwin Watson, and Frederick L. Redefer to the Committee. Yet there was surprise, and a measure of consternation, when the Committee reported back to the Board in March, 1933, and outlined a contemplated program. To begin, there was a long discussion of the relation of national committees to the larger Association, one of those interminable controversies in which academics revel in the business of hairsplitting. Carleton Washburne questioned the advisability of giving any committee's report the approval of the Association, while Willard Beatty affirmed that no committee had the right to speak on behalf of the Association. A motion was finally passed holding that committees functioned "primarily for the purpose of furnishing to members of the Association channels of thought and

action for the improvement of education" and that "neither the Board of Directors nor the Association is committed officially or as a whole to any philosophy, program, or policy embodied in the report of any national committee." (pp. 261-262)

Then, again:

Late in 1938 the Association appointed yet another Committee on the Philosophy of Education, this one destined to produce the most fundamental statement of principles ever to issue from the PEA . . . The Committee's report, *Progressive Education: its Philosophy and Challenge,* is Deweyan from beginning to end. Insisting that any philosophy of education appropriate to the time needed both a clear view of human nature and a realistic understanding of the industrial crisis inherent in the depression, the Committee envisioned an education that would "make the culture aware of itself in order that its essential values may be made the more effective." The educated individual of this report is Dewey's intelligent man, working cooperatively to solve the problems and reconstruct the values of the community to which he belongs. . . . Based on this general position, the Committee reiterated the usual homilies: "the school should be the exemplification of democratic living at its best"; "there should be greater recognition of and cooperation with other social agencies on the part of educators" . . . "those who teach should capture the dynamic character of individual behavior, not ignore it"; and, finally, "if we are to entertain real hope for the progressive advancement of democratic values, our present practices in the education of teachers must be revised and reconstructed."

The Committee's report was published in mimeographed form in May, 1940, and reprinted as a special supplement to the May, 1941, issue of *Progressive Education.* But, so far as can be determined, it was never formally adopted by the Association. Redefer recalls that on the one occasion when the Report was discussed by the membership in open session even the Committee could not agree on what it really meant. (pp. 266-267)

The Committee's position, which came to be universally accepted as representative of the Association that never achieved the courage or the unanimity required to endorse it, nevertheless prevailed; it became as Cremin points out, the Conventional Wisdom of contemporary education. However little its homilies may have stirred the depths of day-to-day school practice they are accepted as slogans by the administration and the students themselves even in the most benighted public schools and teacher-training institutions. This is the American way with ideas, inherent in our social system. Our public rhetoric at the national level, like our public self-image, is always vaguely liberal, just as our actual policies are overwhelmingly conservative in the sense—and only in the sense—that we adapt to the existing power structure and support it. Ambitious men, in a stratified but open society have always done this, and personal ambition is the heart of our ideology. Educationists do not differ from industrialists in this; they merely race for smaller stakes.

But even the size of the stakes makes a crucial difference. A history of a major corporation or of any central trend in our economy as candid and specific as Professor Cremin's book would be scandalous, no doubt, but it would be scandal of a more impressive order and better suited, I think, to serve as an example to the young.

What is school actually like? How does it feel to go there, and to know that you must go there, day after day for twelve years? In Deweyan terms, what is the nature of this reality that the school and its students generate in their protracted and often mutually antagonistic interaction? More generally, what aspects of school experience make the most difference—that is, make the student most different from what he would have been if he had not been subjected to them? In asking this, I have the advantage of never having attended school myself before college, which makes it easier for me to recognize that schools are not an essential component of the natural order.

When I go into a school to do research that requires me to interview students, about a tenth of my time, and much more of my psychic energy, are spent writing out corridor-passes for them. I had never previously realized that there was any building except a military installation subject to espionage in which people could not go about their legitimate business without let or hindrance. I knew about restricted areas, but not about restricted people. High school students learn for four years that they cannot so much as walk down the hall to the library or the toilet without written permission.

In two schools I have recently studied there have been incidents in the past few months in which boys were required to shave off beards or face suspension, though the school admitted that it had no specific authority to do this. In both, there is a constant punitive furor over smoking in the washrooms; and one keeps the washrooms locked between periods. This particular school has more different classes of washrooms than the Confederate Navy; in one of these marked *Men, Adults Only* (teachers have another category), a teacher sometimes hides in the private compartment, jumping up and down when he hears the outer door open to peer over the sides and see if a student is sneaking in for a smoke. During lunch periods, the corridors resound with snarling and scolding at students who move too slowly, though the regulation against talking in the chow line is only sporadically enforced. At certain times, all this is drowned out by saccharine Mantovani-type music played over the P.A. system. In both schools, and in most others the official punishment for minor offenses, which is liberally awarded, is detention for two hours or so, which of course works a special hardship on students who have to work. In their comments, students distinguish between what the school has taught them to call "public detention," which is entered in their permanent record, and "private detention," which is not.

If all this were resented, it would occupy a very small place in the catalog of twentieth-century injustice. But I am discussing education rather than justice, and the point is that it rarely is. What happens is much worse; the students accept it as the way schools are, the way life is. What really sinks in is that young Americans have no rights that the school, or society, is obligated to respect, and they are entitled to no privacy. They have only privileges, which are either petty status distinctions—like the privilege of seniors to go to the head of the chow line—or relaxations of restrictions that conditionally restore to the privileged individual a right that he and the rest of the youngsters had anyway, until the school took it away.

It is idle to talk about civil liberties to adults who were systematically taught in adolescence that they had none; and it is sheer hypocrisy to call such people freedom-loving. A juror who saw no reason why he should not have to get written permission to use the lavatory until he was seventeen years old, and who put up with the embarrassment and delay of showing his permission to various teachers and students on hall patrol between his study hall and the convenience, is not, in my judgment, very likely to understand why the State Department must not be allowed to withold passports on political grounds. I have just finished informal discussions with the young official at one of these schools who is called an attendance teacher. He certainly is, except on weekends, when he is a parkway policeman. Unlike many moonlighters, this man has profited from the opportunity to apply in each of his jobs the technics learned in the other. He carries the modern, collapsible lead billy on him at school, presumably, like Linus's flannel, only because it gives him happiness and security. And he has a two-way radio installed in his personal automobile with which, he boasts, he can get truants rounded up in an hour or two and sent back to school without the delay and inconvenience of proceeding through social agencies. He has a certain fondness for kids and believes, quite correctly, that he speaks their language; he is a good and even sympathetic interviewer. But though he suffers from role-confusion he is clear on one point: no kid is going to cost the district five bucks a day in state aid just because he thinks he's rocky.

Whether these schools are representative or not, I cannot prove; though they are superior in their interest and participation in affairs of the pedagogical world: research, conferences and the like. But this does not really matter very much. It suffices that they are acceptable within the canon of public education; that no one regards them as outrageous *per se*. It suffices that a pedagogical ideology that regards itself as Deweyan and has reduced Dewey to slogans about teaching the whole child and learning by doing in a democratic community should never have developed enough self-discipline or consistent enough standards to judge what the school in fact *does* to the whole child, and what he learns by the way he is required to live, to become intolerant of such institutions. If these are professional practices, then education has no professional ethics with any authority.

For this reason, even a book as good as Frank Riessman's *The Culturally Deprived Child,*[10] which has foreword by the same Goodwin Watson who served the PEA to so little avail thirty years ago, is in some ways unsatisfactory. The title itself is a clue to the limitations of the book. Riessman shows perfectly clearly that he knows that these children are not culturally deprived; they have a culture of their own. By accepting this title he endorses the standards of the school and society; and his book appears, not as the exploration of the sources of a tragic cultural conflict, but as an effort to clear up a minor misunderstanding among men of good will.

Riessman gives an exceptionally clear and well-documented picture of the way lower-status children learn, their conception of discipline and authority as related to their family life, their rich if, by middle-class standards peculiar, use of language. He gives a wealth of specific suggestions, mostly sound and useful, for improving school practice so as to reach them better. His book, however, is geared more to the problems of the elementary school teacher than to those of the high school; though it is the high school where the most serious conflict and the dropouts occur.

In a way, there are sound reasons for this. It is only in the elementary school that there is much chance that the teacher will see the problem as reaching and teaching these children. If she thinks of them as "culturally deprived" she is likely to defeat herself by being matronizing; but aside from certain neurotic defenses about the children's manners, language, and hygiene she is not likely to be in much conflict. Elementary school teachers mostly like children; they may be sentimental and intellectually sloppy in approaching them, but child-nurture is their specialty and they are not unwilling to learn new approaches to new categories of children, since this adds to their job-satisfaction. The high school is a different matter. Its teachers are not specialists in child-nurture, but usually subject-matter specialists *manques*; and the more they must depart from academic norms in order to reach their students, the more they are likely to despise those students as the very source and symbol of their exclusion from *academe*.

By not calling these *lower-status* students, Professor Riessman plays down the most important thing about them in their relationship to the school. They *are* low in status; in a school run by the local community they can be pushed around without much danger; they are expendable. The school personnel does not respect them at all, and the youngsters have no firm conviction that they ought to be respected; when they are abused they may lose their temper and get into worse trouble by striking back against authority, but they are incapable of a principled, effective, politically astute demand for better treatment. The application of political pressure—though not the formulation of policy—is a middle-class function. It is the middle class that indoctrinates its children—and everybody else's that it can get its schools on—with the importance of the *structure* of government, while discouraging discussion of the actual processes of power that govern it. These are the people who exercise themselves getting out the vote, and who learn in infancy how to function in committees. A dependent public bureaucracy like the school is their natural habitat.

It seems natural, therefore, that they should flourish in it to the detriment of lower-class children. The chief limitation on a work like Patricia Sexton's *Education and Income*[11] is a certain naïveté implicit in its indignation. Surely, no sociologist can be astonished that the American status system is real and brutal; that poverty is more viciously destructive in this country than perhaps in any other; for the poor in America are denied both self-respect and a sense of community with one another by our value system. Professor Sexton's book is a clear, concise, admirably disciplined statistical study of the public schools of Detroit (she calls it Big City), that demonstrates conclusively that every amenity as well as every conceivable educational advantage provided by this school system is distributed in a manner closely correlated to median income received by families with children in each school. This is rather an impersonal criterion, which bars Professor Sexton from the use of the case or illustrative material that would have made the book vivid. But it is certainly a valid one. Professor Sexton does not show us that poorer children are unhappy in the public schools of Detroit, but merely that they are crowded into older buildings with fewer facilities—often without even facilities for feeding them lunch—under the supervision of more poorly prepared teachers; and that they participate less frequently than their peers from higher-income homes in the ancillary activities the school provides, especially the programs for gifted students, from which they are virtually excluded. So if they are not dissatisfied, they ought to be; and she does, indeed, cite other research (James V. Mitchell's study of personality concomitants of status difference) to establish that this means personal misery and low self-esteem.

But the children of the poor are themselves the best witness to their incompatibility with the school; in Big City, as elsewhere, dropout rates are highly and consistently negatively correlated to income. Sexton brings out the much less familiar and very interesting fact that this is equally true of dropouts from *elementary* school. The absolute rate is, of course, far smaller—ranging from less than one student per ten thousand among youngsters from the poorest homes. In high school, *about a fifth* of the youngsters from lowest-income homes drop out during a one-year period. But at both levels, the holding-power of the school rises sharply and steadily with parental income.

The present furor over high school dropouts is not an expression of any deep sense of loss the departure of these youngsters causes school personnel. Nor, and this is more serious, does it reflect in any large measure the professional's guilt and chagrin over a job badly done. It *does* reflect fear of a loss of state support, which is based on average daily attendance, but this is nothing new, and the *relative* rate of dropouts is not, as I have said, rising. It is moreover, generally higher in rural areas and small towns than in cities; though there is much less fuss about it there.

The real source of the anxiety, I believe, is that the present urban-dropout is enough of a troublemaker to call the attention of the public to the failure of the school; and the basic anxiety of school administrators, especially those who have a degree of national responsibility and influence through the NEA, the American Association of School Administrators, and such organizations, is that the school may be left out of our evolving approaches to a final solution of the juvenile question. Youth camps, domestic peace corps, urban planning programs and the like transcend the local school district; they reflect aspects of national policy. Institutionalized professional education is still, I think, trying to make up its mind whether to oppose these as usurpations of the school's function or to try to get some of its own men on the bandwagon before it is too late. The present tendency, in any case, is to greet the putative invaders as colleagues and assume that institutionalized education is going to be expected to contribute. Though the less sophisticated local school superintendents and principals are a little slow to get with it, they tend to respond by calling the newcomers, with their entourage of social science consultants, impractical theorists. As if any New Frontiersman had ever been that.

In this plight, the school people are partly the victims of their own past complicity in the American social order. The American public school and its leadership have, by and large, reflected the anti-intellectualism of their local constituency and have regarded it as their pleasure as well as their clear duty to give the community what those of its members who were in a position to express their wishes in politically effective terms wanted. What they wanted, by and large, was economic advancement and job security; the school was expected to get some youngsters into college and others into jobs, certifying them as loyal, competent, and trouble-free. It also served willingly as the community's trusted and ubiquitous Sitter, and altered its conception of the Sitter's role to suit the community's attitudes toward youngsters of different ages. The elementary school sits with children and the high school sits on "teen-agers." If this all adds up to a rather limited professional function, the community has seldom demanded more and the profession has seldom challenged it by insisting on specifically educational goals of its own.

So it is now too late for the school to point to any function and say "This, uniquely, is our *job*. This is what we have trained ourselves to do, better than anyone else. These youngsters whom we trust and respect are our clientele, because they come to us with certain purposes that we are qualified to help them achieve. They can trust us, as a lawyer or doctor can be trusted, to know our own business, and to mind our own business. There are some for whom we can do nothing, because they have literally no business here; their interests and their goals are beyond our competence. We wish them well, but we do not wish to detain them; we cannot abandon our profession in order to serve as policemen, or propagandists, or custodians, physical or moral." If educationists had been secure enough in their professional self-conception to defend and maintain such a position the public school would undoubtedly be a much smaller and in every sense a less popular institution than it is now. But it would also have known what it was doing. Since, instead, it has been willing to do almost anything to keep the young from troubling their elders, it can now only be judged by its success or failure on these terms.

Some of the expedients now proposed for dealing with our "youth problem" seem to me dubious and more than dubious. They may well prove worse than the schools. But it will at least be healthy, I believe, to break the school's monopoly; to get it through the minds of school administrators that unless they and their staffs manage to find a modicum of respect for youngsters and convey it to them in practice; to find some common cause with them, they must let them depart in peace and dignity. I would vastly prefer alternative *educational* solutions to work camps and paramilitary organizations, which are sore temptations to a people who have never disliked Fascism quite as ardently as they like to believe. It seems to me particularly unfortunate that state support of private or parochial education should have become identified in this country as a wholly conservative and even reactionary position. I would like to see financial arrangements rather similar to those envisaged in President Kennedy's ill-fated Medicare bill, by which payment could be made to any school, public or private, the student chose to attend and for which he was qualified—a kind of GI bill for youngsters without the prerequisite of war. There would have to be minimum standards set up, as there were under the GI bill, to prevent exploitation of the youngsters and the public treasury by worthless institutions; and special provisions like anti-discrimination clauses in government contracts to prevent use of the measure to maintain school segregation. But these safeguards have presented no insuperable legal difficulties in other contexts. And it would give me great satisfaction to hear my friend, the attendance teacher, using his two-way radio for singing commercials on behalf of his school. It would develop his character and, certainly, his imagination.

1964

1. Urbana, University of Illinois Press, 1953.
2. Boston, Little Brown, 1953.
3. Boston, Houghton Mifflin, 1963.
4. New York, McGraw Hill, 1953.
5. New York, Random House, 1961.
6. New York, Wiley, 1932.
7. New York, Harpers, 1961.
8. Chicago, University of Chicago Press, 1962.
9. New York, Knopf, 1961.
10. New York, Harpers, 1962.
11. New York, The Viking Press, 1961.

The Uses of the University

By Clark Kerr

This short book contains the text of the Godkin Lectures for 1963 which were given at Harvard by the President of the University of California, an institution which, according to the dust jacket, had "more than 58,000 students on seven campuses." President Kerr's subject is the operation and support of such protean institutions whose social functions, various though they are, barely include and surely do not emphasize, the traditional purposes of a university: that is, liberal study, the cultivation of a socially responsible intellectual elite, and a sense of continuity with the culture of the past.

The acquisition and organization of knowledge through research are more recent and certainly more conspicuous functions, and the most interesting part of President Kerr's book is devoted to explaining just how their function changed, as individual scholarship, self-generated within the faculties, has been swamped by federally supported projects. Federal funds may now account for more than four-fifths of a university's total expenditure; the classic definition of a college as Mark Hopkins on one end of a log and a student on the other no longer quite fits—unless these same gentlemen are pictured as rolling the log instead of sitting on it.

Dr. Kerr is sensitive to these changes, and he is articulate about them. But he does not deplore them. Social psychology has by now established that executives tend to be happier in their work than other men, but even among them, President Kerr is distinguished by his exceptional felicity. *The Uses of the University* is the work of a deeply satisfied man. So many first-rate creative minds are dismayed by the conditions of modern life that it is a rare pleasure to observe one of them basking in the light of continued social progress. Dr. Kerr rather resembles Dr. Pangloss with the difference that he is attuned, not to the best of all possible worlds, but to the world as it is. Thus, his reply to David Riesman's complaint that leading American universities have become "directionless . . . as far as major innovations are concerned," is:

> The fact is they are not directionless; they have been moving in clear directions and with considerable speed . . . But these directions have not been set as much by the university's visions of its destiny as by the external environment, including the federal government, the foundations, the surrounding and sometimes engulfing industry.

This passage appears toward the end of the book where, I might add, his tone becomes somewhat regretful. But his regret is unconvincing, because it contradicts the Social Darwinist position which Dr. Kerr maintains with such complacence throughout this book:

> The really new problems of today and tomorrow may lend themselves less to solutions by external authority; they may be inherently problems for internal resolution. The university may now again need to find out whether it has a brain as well as a body.

If, like Father William, the university could be perfectly sure it had none, it could continue to stand on its head, again and again, in response to the social pressures upon it. This, Dr. Kerr suggests, is in effect what it always has done; its traditional activities were merely responses—now obsolescent—to earlier social pressures and opportunities. He traces these changes in the university through Newman, Flexner, Hutchins, and others, whose ideas of what a university should be reflect, like Kerr's own, the social necessities of their time. These men became commanding figures in the history of higher education because, at the time, command was needed; but today, skilled and flexible negotiators are more useful in expressing "The Idea of a Multiversity" (as the initial lecture in the series is called). Margaret Fuller's record has been broken; Dr. Kerr accepts the multiverse. And Carlyle's famous reply still holds—in his position, he'd better.

Dr. Kerr attaches considerable importance to the University's increasing dependence, since World War II, on Federal support—which he feels results not only in the diversion of scholarship and research into areas which will attract government support, but also a shift in the making of policy, away from the University administration and self-governing faculty groups. President Kerr is, of course, too sophisticated to fear that the government will try to dominate university policy directly—this would seldom serve their interests anyway, and it is a rare form of intrusion. What does concern him is that the coordination of the faculty will be destroyed by the efforts of its individual members to compete for government grants, that professors will seize the opportunity to build empires of their own. He fears that the university will be unable to control them, and that promotion and planning and the allocation of the university's funds will be subverted by the arrangements with government agencies that favorably situated instructors will be able to make on their own. Dr. Kerr notes that this catch-as-catch-can situation has some desirable features—it can, for example, help to provide recognition to the kind of brilliant work that is often obscured because of antagonism within the university.

But Kerr's very conception of the multiversity as a structure designed to accommodate itself to social pressures and opportunities only increases his fear that it will disintegrate if exposed to the temptation of government support. Its members are committed to no common undertaking and the center will not hold. The President of the University of California, as eclectic an aggregation of Institutes as ever flourished under a university charter, certainly has reason to think that these risks are real. Dr. Kerr speaks from too much experience to exaggerate the dangers. But these dangers are implicit in his own definition of the university as a complex invertebrate, having an evolutionary history, a nervous system, an elaborate apparatus for ingestion—and no backbone. If the organism itself has no unifying conception to govern it, it has no way to control the actions of its members, whether or not, as Dr. Kerr recommends, it may try to do so by altering the bureaucratic balance toward more "institutional grants," and fewer individual projects.

Nor can it chart its own future—and Dr. Kerr's concluding lecture, on "The Future of the City of Intellect," is particularly unconvincing. A City of Intellect would have very little use for a multiversity, and the uses Dr. Kerr conceives of seem to me servile in their readiness to accommodate to immediate social demand.

> The real question, it seems to me, is not one of balance in any historical or monetary sense, but rather what is most appropriate to each field in each period . . . Each should receive support in accordance with its current potentialities, and potentialities vary. There are no timeless priorities. . . .
>
> The major test of the modern American university is how widely and how quickly it adjusts to the important new possibilities. The great universities of the future will be those which have adjusted rapidly and effectively . . . Knowledge is exploding along with population. There is also an explosion in the need for certain skills. The university is responding to all these explosions. . . .
>
> The vastly increased need for engineers, scientists, and doctors will draw great resources to these areas of the university. Also, some new professions are being born. Others are becoming more formally professional—for example, business administration and social work. The university becomes the chief port of entry for these professions. In fact, a profession gains its identity by making the university a port of entry. . . . The life of the university for a thousand years has been tied into the recognized professions in the surrounding society, and the universities will continue to respond as new professions arise.

Of course it is true that the university, like every social institution, is always influenced by the economic needs and structure of the society. But it does not always respond to social influence by simply training up students to the skills and values the society demands. Whatever its contribution to vocational education, the university should be the society's specialized organ of critical self-scrutiny. It is only when the university functions primarily as a port of entry for aspirants to the higher reaches of the social system that it loses its critical function; for aspirants do not criticize, they accommodate.

I am not saying that true universities and colleges are wholly impossible in this country. But if we accept Kerr's view of the multiversity's role, it hardly matters which channels society uses to make its pressures felt: the federal bureaucracies are at least responsible public institutions which set reasonably high technical standards for the work they support. Dr. Kerr establishes convincingly enough that "The Realities of the Federal Grant University," (as he calls his second lecture), include a substantial loss of autonomy to the granting agencies. But does this matter? He makes it clear that the university would have used that autonomy only to mediate among the conflicting demands upon it. In his concern for the "realities" he sounds like a vice-president for production considering how the new demands of the personnel office will affect output. He does not sound like the head of the largest university in the world discussing the ends of education.

> The university has become a prime instrument of national purpose. This is new. This is the essence of the transformation now engulfing our universities. Basic to this transformation is the growth of the "knowledge industry," which is coming to permeate government and business and to draw into it more and more people raised to higher and higher levels of skill. The production, distribution, and consumption of "knowledge" in all its forms is said to account for 29 per cent of the gross national product, according to Fritz Machlup's calculations; and "knowledge production" is growing at about twice the rate of the rest of the economy. Knowledge has certainly never in history been so central to the conduct of an entire society. What the railroads did for the second half of the nineteenth century and the automobile for the first half of this century, the knowledge industry may do for the second half of this century: that is, to serve as the focal point for national growth. And the university is at the center of the knowledge process.

And California, surely, is the ideal case in point. The railroads gave it Stanford, which is a positive item on the balance sheet. The automobile has transformed it, physically and culturally. President Kerr, at ease among the freeways, has convinced me that the multiversity, in its turn, is indeed likely to wreak a comparable transformation in our intellectual life. The City of Intellect, as he conceives it, does finally emerge from the smog enshrouding its Future, visible and oddly familiar. Its features are not those of Berkeley, nor even quite of Westwood. This, as we approach it more closely, can only be downtown Los Angeles.

1963

The Schools
By Martin Mayer

Martin Mayer's *The Schools* is the best book about education I have ever read. This is rather an embarrassing admission for a professor of education, who has necessarily read a great many books in his own field; yet I make this assessment on detached, professional grounds, judging Mr. Mayer's work as a piece of scholarship on a specialized subject. While the general standard of American educational writing is not high, it is not as low as popularly supposed. The mode is undoubtedly *la mode de Caen*; but as usual, half is above average, and the best is very good. *The Schools* is better than that.

Embodied in the text are exceptionally clear and precise discussions of the history of education, learning theory, and evaluation—that is, tests and measurements and their relationship to the purposes of education. Most astonishing of all is Mr. Mayer's preoccupation with the distinct epistemological character of different subjects, which he quite rightly maintains to be a crucial issue in their presentation, however elementary. When he discusses the teaching of arithmetic, or of a foreign language, Mr. Mayer immediately answers the question of what mathematics, or communication, is, and why, therefore, the procedures used to teach either are almost certain to fail in some ways and to succeed in others. Again, when he discusses "social studies," he first makes clear what it is—usually a big nothing—then argues why it almost has to be.

On this point I am in sharp disagreement with Mr. Mayer and for reasons that I believe challenge him on a basic element of values; but I will return to this difference after noting a few more of *The Schools*' extraordinary qualities. Exceedingly comprehensive, it maintains the same level of competence in each of the many areas it discusses (departments of education treat them as the bases of specialized careers); and it includes one of the best and clearest discussions of teaching methods to be found anywhere, illustrated by examples of resourceful, dedicated classroom teaching that are indeed exceptional. The construction is masterly, alternating throughout passages of lucid theoretical or historical analysis with vivid and well-selected examples drawn from specific classrooms. The book is also a pleasure to read, terse and humorous—not witty, perhaps, but still sharp: "From fourth grade on," Mr. Mayer writes, "the readers have the form of anthologies with the individual pieces 'altered' the way one alters a tomcat." When one finishes this book, he will have a rather profound, detailed, and well-organized understanding of American public education. He will also know enough about British, French, and Danish public education to have a pretty clear idea of both the actual alternatives and the limits set by the always formidable nature of the enterprise.

But I hope he will not agree with Mr. Mayer as to what these limits are. *The Schools* has already been hailed as an unusually even-tempered, well-balanced presentation of a topic that usually provokes acrimonious and ill-informed special pleading. So it is, and perhaps the more effective for that: scolding is a poor educational technique. But Mr. Mayer, though never bland, is too calm for me. Much American education is outrageous; so many of his examples are outrageous, and it seems to me perfectly realistic to be outraged by them. Mr. Mayer does a superb job of showing why the public schools are as bad as they sometimes are, and why one is likely to be disappointed if he expects them to be better. But to explain is not to justify: "*tout comprendre, c'est tout pardonner*"? No. Not at all.

"Willy-nilly," Mr. Mayer says, "all schools must work from the basis of Emile Durkheim's rather grim definition: 'Education consists of a methodical socialization of the young generation' "; and while ours is a pluralistic society, Mr. Mayer argues, the schools are dominated by and transmit a narrowly selected range of social values: "American schools are always going to promote middle-class values, because the national community they serve is overwhelmingly middle-class in orientation and even in 'self-image.' It is more than a little unrealistic to expect teachers who are fighting hard for recognition as 'professionals' to cultivate in their classrooms the values of an unprofessional sub-group in their community." Much of Mr. Mayer's reiterated argument is directed against the view that the school can or should transcend the values of the community. Only the individual himself—if he has the guts and the inclination—can undertake that. "School is not really the place for questioning authority—somebody has to be marking those exams, and the marker has to be right. The highly-charged words of the culture —'democracy,' 'Communism,' 'love,' 'prejudice' and so forth—cannot be seriously analyzed in school." The school is the agent of society and to expect it to be anything else is to expect too much. "Beginning with the fourth grade, the books are full of buncombe, but it is the kind of patriotic buncombe that children like and schools must provide." Or, finally: "By the time the child finishes sixth grade . . . he will have acquired an almost complete stock of 'common-sense' knowledge about the world around him—knowledge that is mostly false, but serviceable enough in the adult world." It is hard to understand, then, how—in a society from which the horse has all but vanished—the school gets it material. Mayer examines alternative sources in detail; and he shows very clearly why most textbooks are stupefying, and many teachers are petty, timid, and vulgar-minded.[1]

I agree, of course, that the schools are middle class: they have to be, as Mayer says, if they are to make the children run on time. But it still matters that this should be true. The difficulty is not that the schools have a middle-class bias, but that the middle class—and especially the lower middle class, from which, Mayer tells us, most teachers come—provides a peculiarly unpleasant model for human life. It is what being middle class does to the potentially free, spontaneous mind and heart that matters, as the author of *Madison Avenue, USA* knows.

From Mayer's reasoning, it is clear that *all* U. S. public agencies are and must be dominated by the values of the society they serve; and it is just this domination that at certain times becomes intolerable. Basically what is wrong with the schools is, I suspect, identical with what is wrong with the Central Intelligence Agency, another very middle-class organization: both have become and are functioning as agencies of self-delusion. They perpetuate reassuring folk-myths, while the total society depends on their functioning in the service of—well, intelligence. It is not relevant to say that the schools (or the CIA) cannot be much better than their society; they have a specialized function to perform in that society. Durkheim's "grim definition" does not limit the school to the uncritical transmission of anxiety-free social residues, and any society that permits the "methodical socialization of the young generation" on so limited a basis runs a grave risk of falling within the scope of Durkheim's more widely known—and even grimmer—masterwork on suicide.

But Mayer accepts these limits. Improving disgracefully low efficiency to perform more effectively the job that society actually expects and will support, with the kind of personnel actually available—this, the book implies, is really the schools' business. And to this end Mayer makes many valuable and practical suggestions. But he is then logically obliged to discuss education problems largely in terms of improved teaching methods.

An earlier reviewer—I think in the *New York Times*—particularly approved of this passage:

> There are a million and a quarter classroom teachers, and by the normal curve of distribution most of them are not especially talented. It was observed some years ago that most steelworkers are not especially talented, either—but they all turn out pretty good steel. The steel industry has developed a technology that enables routine operatives to perform satisfactory work. The schools appear to be trapped in a technology that can be employed successfully only by good teachers.

It seems to me that the most obvious inference to be drawn from this illuminating analogy is that we need more good teachers. But if we cannot get them, I am not sure the analogy helps much. Teaching youngsters really isn't much like making steel—I am willing to grant an exception in the case of the educative experience shared by Shadrach, Meshach, and Abednego—and essential as good technique is, I don't think education is basically a technological problem. It is a problem of drawing out of each youngster the best he has to give and of helping him to see the world he is involved in clearly enough to become himself—among other people—in it, while teaching him the skills he will need in the process. This is a custom operation, not for the assembly line; and Mr. Mayer has not shown, or tried to show, that any series of technical improvements can supplant it, though they may certainly facilitate it. Instead, he has come very close to showing that public education in a democracy is impossible. But, as the best of his illustrations reveal, the schools do not know it and teach anyway.

1961

---

1. He does leave out of his account, however, even though some of his illustrations mildly suggest this point, the small but impressive and growing body of literature that reveals how often teachers are also compulsive, controlling, and punitive, with no love to lose on any youngster. Cf. Egon G. Guba, Phillip W. Jackson, and Charles Bidwell, "Occupational Choice and the Teaching Career," *Educational Research Bull.*, 38, 1, 1959.

The Education of American Teachers

By James B. Conant

Dr. Conant's new book sets a high stylistic standard for administrative documents. It is bland, slightly tart, and absolutely clear; at times lightly personal, never contentious, often convincing. Its calm and precision are surgical; the surgery proposed, however, is not radical, but extensive and superficial.

This superficiality is a consequence of Dr. Conant's conception of the subject as an administrative problem, rather than a moral and social one. Indeed, within this framework he could not have done more, nor done it more scrupulously. He and his collaborators spent a year of a two-year study visiting seventy-seven colleges and universities in twenty-two states. These schools graduated in 1962 twenty-seven per cent of the teachers granted degrees in those states, or about one-fifth of all the teachers graduated in the country. Dr. Conant himself visited fifty-two of these institutions, including the one in whose Department of Education I was teaching at the time. I remember very clearly the care with which those of my colleagues who were to confer with him were selected, and the satisfaction with which they later reported their encounter. What Dr. Conant knows about the preparation of teachers he learned at the horse's mouth. It was probably the safest place to stand.

This is, above all, a practical book devoted to shrewd observation of the structure and content of the teacher-training process and pragmatic recommendations for improving it. Dr. Conant manages to avoid both theoretical insight and social controversy with traditional American good-humored disdain. By focusing sharply on teacher training, to the exclusion of any consideration of the way students, schools, and society are related to one another, he manages to avoid scholarship: he cites none of the significant social, anthropological, psychological, or economic studies bearing on the schools and their function, but uses only descriptive and demographic data.

This is paradoxical, because Dr. Conant's book is much more than just a survey. Its neglect of *social* dynamics is matched by a contrasting perception of, and sensitivity to, the *political* dynamics of American education. Thus, one of the best things in the book is the clarity with which it describes the complex relations among the various self-appointed accrediting agencies linked to the National Education Association, which compose the American educational establishment. Conant traces the precise pattern of their influence on state educational policy. This is a very important matter: Those who protest most against NCATE [1] and TEPS [2] seldom say exactly what they do and how they do it. Dr. Conant, who protests too little, completely dissects the power structure which controls the accreditation of teacher-training programs, in about three strokes. Similarly, his analysis of the consequences of the "approved program" approach, by which state departments of education grant or withhold approval to an institution for teacher-training without stipulating its program in terms of credits and hours, is masterly. The "approved program" approach is generally accepted as giving the institution more freedom than do licence requirements that specify particular courses. Conant shows that in fact it often does not:

> The problem is inherent in the structure and composition of State Departments of Education. Even the best of the Departments include few persons with significant amounts of experience in college teaching or administration. Most of the Department staff is made up of experts in public school administration, curriculum design, or the teaching of some subject—music, mathematics, foreign language, physical education, etc.—on the elementry or secondary school level. Rarely is an experienced college teacher of educational psychology, educational history, or philosophy of education included; and it is even more unusual to find a college teacher of English, history, mathematics or science. . . . After a brief visit, the Committee makes its report and recommendations. . . . Ironically enough, the reasons

given for withholding approval are never those I would consider most important. A college is never told that a careful evaluation of the actual standards of teaching and grading on the college campus proves them to be of very low quality; that careful testing of the college's graduates showed them to be still too ignorant to teach; or that in observing its candidates actually teach, the state Department found them incompetent. This type of question is never asked, not only for political reasons, but also because of difficulty of measurement.

This passage illustrates Conant at his best; but also, I should say, at his most profound. His strength lies in understanding how things work, and on that basis he makes crisp and decisive policy. He meets the situation just described with an eleven-point recommendation, the core of which is stated in its first item:

For certification purposes the state should require only (a) that a candidate hold a baccalaureate degree from a legitimate college or university, (b) that he submit evidence of having successfully performed as a student teacher under the direction of college and school personnel in whom the state Department has confidence and in a practice-teaching situation of which the state Department approves, and (c) that he hold a specially endorsed teaching certificate from a college or university which, in issuing the official document, attests that the institution as a whole considers the person adequately prepared to teach in a designated field and grade level.

In the succeeding chapters of the book, Conant develops in detail his recommendations for the college teacher-training program, the basic principle of which is to make available what, in his judgment, would be most useful to the teacher as technician. Practice teaching, certainly; and Conant recommends the establishment of a new kind of clinical professorship of teaching in particular fields, to serve as supervisory liaison between the school of education and the public school in which practice teaching is done. Subject matter, emphatically; Conant goes through this field by field for both elementary and secondary teachers, and stresses as a general proposition that *"we should endeavor to recruit our teachers from the upper third of the graduating high school class on a national basis.*" [Italics his.] This, however, would make less difference than Conant seems to think. A very large proportion of college graduates, and hence of those who become teachers, are already drawn from the upper third of their high school class; and teachers, being mostly lower-middle class in social origin, make their high school records in mediocre high schools, which are quite numerous enough to lower any possible "national basis" for comparative evaluation of high school records. This is what happens now. The young people who become teachers do well enough in high school; later, they help to make the high school the kind of school they did well in, and in which students with their constrictive lower-middle-class patterns of value and behavior most easily succeed.

Education courses? Conant goes to great lengths to defend colleges and college departments of education against the general and bitter condemnation with which other critics—most notably and recently James D. Koerner in *The Miseducation of American Teachers*—have approached us. While, as a member of this target group, I am grateful for Dr. Conant's courtesy, it seems to me that it not only softens his criticism, it deflects it. Koerner's intemperate and biased book gets closer to the issues than Conant's does. Koerner deals specifically with the pretentious and self-righteous vulgarity that so frequently colors the practice of public education in this country; and with the hostility to intellectual distinction implicit in the way the public school defines its commitment to equality. These dismal and grievous faults are indeed reinforced by the "Educationist" (as Koerner calls us) ideology, though they do not have their source there. Conant simply does not raise such offensive questions. Yet the recommendations of both men would have strikingly similar consequences. Both would sharply curtail the influence of the NEA and its counterparts at state level, eliminate prescriptive licensing requirements, and restore substantial autonomy to colleges and universities in teacher preparation. Both would retain and emphasize practice teaching; and both would eliminate most of the present course offerings in education—especially those at the graduate level, as they are now conducted—or transfer them to the hands of persons trained in academic disciplines, such as psychology or sociology. Conant's proposals appear less drastic than Koerner's, because they are made without anger by a man almost over-anxious to give to us Educationists credit where due. Koerner sounds like Herakles trying to clean the Augean Stables, while Conant sounds like a Wildlife and Conservation official who recommends that a few valves be opened and others closed, so that the waters will be redirected to encourage trout and eliminate the breeding places of what conservationists call "coarse fish." But he does not dislike coarse fish personally; Koerner does.

As one of the coarse fish, I find my enthusiasm for both books tempered by a combination of critical judgment and enlightened self-interest. But I prefer Koerner; there really is a coarse fish problem, and he faces it. Conant avoids it by a curious maneuver:

> In our own society . . . the education of a leisure class is no longer an issue; and now the use of the adjective "liberal" to denote the content of an educational program can only add to confusion. One of my friends . . . has pointed up the issue as follows: ". . . A liberal education, one might say, is a process begun in childhood, carried on through a varying number of years of schooling, and best tested by the momentum it sustains in adult life. It is characterized by what it aspires to, rather than what it embraces. . . . Accordingly, the process of educating liberally is not confined to the classroom and is not circumscribed by the subjects of study or the experiences which may contribute to it."
>
> In accordance with this view, I should like to urge that "liberal education," if the term be used at all should be used in reference to a person rather than a program of study . . .

And with the completion of this paragraph, Dr. Conant dismisses liberal education as a useful concept in planning the preparation of teachers. But its clear implication, surely, is that *no* formal program of collegiate education can affect the performance of teachers as strongly as their upbringing and general background; and subsequent criteria for selecting the more competent among them must still make do with what is available. In short, one of the things Dr. Conant should have been considering all along is what kind of people become teachers and where—in the old illiberal sense—they come from.

Liberal education is not the education of a leisure class, but of free men. From our grubby, Protestant-ethic viewpoint, the most striking thing about an aristocracy is that it does not have to compete for status and a living. But the social function of an elite is to preserve and express the values in a culture that are constantly threatened by petty social and economic pressures; and liberal education is designed to teach it what those values are and how to protect them. It seems very risky for a mass society to vest this crushing responsibility entirely in the hands of nine elderly attorneys.

Teachers ought to be our first line of defense—indeed of attack—in the maintenance of dignity and freedom; and preparing them to be so is a fundamental function of teacher education—assuming that it is not too late by the time they get to college. As the schools now function, teachers are too often a profoundly illiberal force: easily threatened by exuberant intellectual activity, so hostile to sexuality that they punish youngsters for wearing form-fitting clothes or walking down the hall holding hands, and terrified of a public opinion that a liberally educated individual would take to be impertinent. Conant himself calls the first "component of the intellectual equipment that would be a prerequisite to the development of teaching skill" the "democratic social component"; and asserts that "Public schools and the teachers in those schools are charged with the responsibility for developing certain attitudes." But he never considers what, in the public schools of today, those attitudes have become; though E. P. Torrance, Patricia Sexton, Jules Henry, and other competent social scientists who study the way schools function, see this as crucial in assessing their role in society.

Perhaps the best way of discussing a book like this—as valuable for what it includes as it is distressing for what it ignores—is to supplement it. The heart of what Conant omits is conveyed in a single essay by Herbert Gold "A Dog in Brooklyn, A Girl in Detroit, A Life Among the Humanities,"[3] an account of the experience which led him to renounce college teaching in a lower-status metropolitan university. In this short piece he shows the consequences of entrusting the humanities to a clientele more interested in using them to qualify for a teaching position than in understanding what they mean. The piece might have been called, but fortunately wasn't, "The Education of American Teachers."

1963

---

1. National Council for the Accreditation of Teacher Education.

2. National Commission on Teacher Education and Professional Standards.

3. Included in Gold's *The Age of Happy Problems* (New York, Dial Press, 1962).

An Introduction to the Sociology of Education
By Karl Mannheim and W. A. C. Stewart

This is the sixth and last of the volumes attributed to Karl Mannheim that has been prepared and published since his death fifteen years ago. His friend and student, Professor W. A. C. Stewart, observes in the introduction:

> There were few relatively complete manuscripts on which any section of this book could be based. Many, many fragments and notes, a very small number of complete lectures, with the usual pause and accent markings, sheets of bibliographies, schemes for lecture courses, diagrams for ideas, characteristically bold and handsome doodlings—these constituted the materials from which the book has been constructed. . . . While it is true that I have been more than an editor, it is clear that the basic ideas of the book are Karl Mannheim's.

Technically, Professor Stewart has done an excellent job. Presented in the first person throughout, the material is well-organized, readable, and very clear. The reader receives the impression than Mannheim is addressing him directly in a well-prepared and thoughtful presentation.

For this very reason, unfortunately, Professor Stewart has done Mannheim's memory no service; and he has done very little for the serious contemporary student of educational sociology. The material in this book raises grave questions as to why Mannheim should have accepted appointment as Professor in the University of London Institute of Education just a year before his death. Readers familiar with the subtlety, depth, and originality of Mannheim's social thought can only be distressed by the simplistic and ethically neutral character of these discussions. He was incapable of talking down to his students, and the tone of the book is not itself patronizing. But it is a very elementary summary, and it makes clear that he thought of these students as "ed majors," grossly inferior in scholarship and breadth of culture to his usual audiences.

What value the book has, paradoxically, derives from the fact that it *is* dated. Mannheim was so able a scholar and so much at home in the social thought of his era that his judgment as to which psychologists and sociologists were significant was unfailing. None of the materials he cites have become obsolete; instead, they have emerged from the underbrush of compulsive publication as a series of landmarks. The book is nostalgic, however, in a way that the material it summarizes is not. For a specialist in the critical analysis of Marxist thought, Mannheim seems curiously willing to assume that the school, as a social instrument, can be trusted to respect the individual and meet his needs once teachers are given the necessary background instruction to permit them to understand the student's inner dynamics and relationship to society. No sense of tension between the individual and the society of which the school is the agent is conveyed in the book. Its ideological position is "liberal," in the invidious sense in which the late C. Wright Mills used the term. In Professor Stewart's hands, Mannheim may well have become the last distinguished sociologist to treat public education in a democracy without irony.

1962

The Educational Decision-Makers

By Aaron V. Cicourel and John I. Kitsuse

This short paperback is a thoroughly penetrating and highly significant study of a new aspect of American educational practice, the values underlying it, and its long-range social implications. *The Educational Decision-Makers* is a case study of the function and activities of counselors in a 3600-student high school in a mainly upper-middle-class high school in Chicago's North Shore suburbs. Median family income for the community in 1960 was $9193; the median male had completed half a year of college. Eighty per cent of the parents expect their children to go on to college, and 75 per cent of Lakeshore's graduates do, in fact, go.

This is what makes the counselor's function in the school decisively important. At Lakeshore, their decisions and the dossier they compile determine what, if any, college will admit a graduate. Moreover, their placement of entering freshmen determines whether the student will finish high school with or without the courses required for college admission. Parents, Cicourel and Kitsuse find, know little or nothing about the details of college entrance requirements and make no substantial effort to learn; 97 per cent of the parents from the top three social classes in their sample simply assumed that their children would go to college; and this assumption was independent of their children's entering grade-average from elementary school and their tested scholastic aptitude.

The result is to leave the high school student's future educational career almost entirely to the discretion of Lakeshore's counselors, and to make their perception of him paramount in determining his opportunities. Lakeshore, apparently, does not offer separate general, commercial, and academic tracks. But it does have what are called, in the language of 1984, "opportunity courses" for students deemed less able and "honors courses" for more able students, as well as regular sections for well-rounded students. High grades in "opportunity" sections, and low grades in "honors" sections are both discounted in determining grade averages for recommendations to college; and the "opportunity courses" do not as a rule meet specific college entrance requirements in any case. At Lakeshore, then, a student whom counselors assign on entrance to a program of primarily college-preparatory courses virtually has it made from the beginning; those whom they bar from or counsel out of such courses may find it impossible to get into college at all, however well they do in the program.

Cicourel and Kitsuse demonstrate that counselors' assignment of students cannot be accounted for on the basis of entering grades or SCAT scores alone; there are important residual factors. They never succeed in quite identifying these, though they are nothing so simple as social class attributes alone. The authors' extensive quotations from interviews with counselors suggest that no greater precision is possible; the counselors themselves are not that clear about what they are doing.

What is frightening about this new bureaucracy is not prejudice or ill-will, but the zeal with which it assigns students to categories designed to justify its own *raison d'etre*. "Underachievers" and—surely a remarkable concept in itself—"overachievers" are canvassed and disposed of in order to give substance to the counselor's function. As the authors state (pp. 81-82):

> In their attempts to define a professional domain, therefore, school counselors have been concerned with establishing a claim to what we may term "surface" problems that students may encounter in their day-to-day school and extracurricular activities. It sould be noted, however, that in a highly bureaucratized school system the counselor occupies a position in which he coordinates the referral of students to the various special services, including those of the psychologists and social workers. . . . In this position of interprofessional rivalry, the

counselor seeks to develop his own definitions of problem types that will not conflict with or overlap those used by social workers, psychologists, and psychiatrists.

The expansion of the counseling function in American schools is a consequence both of our extreme emphasis on the school as the instrument of social mobility and of our recently increased concern for developing talent that might be overlooked by less formal processes of search and seizure. But, as Cicourel and Kitsuse rather drily observe (p. 136):

> The advances and setbacks in the process of mobility in such a system are governed less by the folk norms of the larger society than by the doctrines and practices of a professionalized bureaucracy. Insofar as the rationalization and bureaucratization of procedures imply greater "objectivity" in the evaluation of performance and distribution of rewards, it might be argued that the application of such organizational techniques represents an institutionalization of the folk norm of contest mobility. Our materials do not support such an argument.

And the danger resulting from these doctrines and practices cannot be stated better than they state it (p. 147):

> It would not be an exaggeration to state that the high school as a "talent farm" produces its own problems, and that it has developed a "clinic" to deal with them. . . . Suspending the question of the validity of interpretations of student problems made by the counseling personnel and the modes of treatment that are prescribed and practiced, the issue which must be addressed is whether or not the school is or should be authorized to engage in such activities. We do not doubt that from a psychiatric point of view the behavior of some students may be diagnosed as serious problems that call for specialized treatment. . . . We do question, however, the propriety of a procedure that routinely assigns students to counselors who not only monitor their progress but actively seek and probe for "problems." This is an invasion of privacy, however disguised it may be by an ideology of service and "help," and an invasion during a period when maintaining the privacy of unique personal experience may be critical for the adolescent's awareness of his own individuality. What is even more disturbing is the

prospect that this solicitous treatment will produce a new generation of youth socialized to the practice of easy confessions and receptive to "professional" explanations of who they are and what they aspire to become.

Indeed, Cicourel and Kitsuse do not exaggerate the peril. In collaboration with Carl Nordstrom, I have recently completed an intensive study of nine secondary schools in their observable effect on student values, dealing specifically with the issue these authors raise. Nearly all our student subjects accept as legitimate any invasion of their private life the school may undertake in the name of "helping" and declare that it is very important for their parents to co-operate with the school when this occurs. What these youngsters have lost in freedom, sad as it is, may be less than what they have renounced in dignity. Unfortunately, the record of our life as a people since Tocqueville's time and before hardly suggests that we have ever been greatly devoted to either.

1964

The Adolescent Society
By James S. Coleman

Values and Ideals of American Youth
Edited by Eli Ginzberg

These two works are further evidence of the intense concern that behavioral scientists and makers of public policy have been showing for several years about the values of American youth. They continue the trend that became conspicuous in 1957 with the publication of the Jacobs report, *Changing Values in College,* and that has produced as its high point so far Paul Goodman's *Growing Up Absurd.* This is all that these two books have in common. Coleman's work is a large-scale empirical study; Ginzberg's is a set of twenty-two unrelated papers either prepared as background for or presented at last year's White House Conference on Children and Youth.

Yet perhaps there is one more, subtle common quality. Both books show more concern about youth than interest in it. There is no manifest delight in youngsters and in the workings of their lives in society—the sort of thing that makes it so clear that C. P. Snow, say, is *interested* in administration even when he is appalled by it. This quality of being "with it" is certainly not inconsistent with scientific rigor and detachment; it is one of the distinguishing marks of great scientific work. And it has nothing to do with whether one is writing for a technical audience or a general readership: Coleman's style, as such, is exceptionally lucid and clear, though his book is completely a formal research report. But in spite of this, it is difficult to follow because it is difficult to keep in mind what it is *about.* What it is about has got into his hot-rod and driven away with his girl-friend, smelling so strongly of athlete's rub-down that she will never again think of wintergreen as a flavoring for children's candy. Indeed, we do not follow.

The Adolescent Society is solid, substantial sociology. Coleman enlisted the cooperation of nine public high schools in suburbs and towns around Chicago, and a Catholic boys' high school in the city itself. The schools were carefully selected to represent the various kinds of communities one finds throughout the country, so that a variety of possible social climates could be studied. This yields him a sample of about four thousand boys and four thousand girls, which is huge for a study of this kind.

His staff spent about a fortnight at each school administering a 175-item questionnaire and taking data about each student from school records in the fall of 1957 and again in the spring of 1958. There were "informal interviews with a number of students in each school," but these were not treated systematically, though they are occasionally quoted illustratively in the book.

The Adolescent Society, then, is essentially an intricate analysis of what these questionnaires—along with school data as to grades, IQ, attendance, and such—reveal about the values and patterns of social interaction characteristic of the students in these ten schools. In short, Coleman finds:

> Our adolescents today are cut off, probably more than ever before, from the adult society. They are still oriented toward fulfilling their parents' desires, but they look very much to their peers for approval as well. Consequently, our society has within its midst a set of small teen-age societies, which focus teen-age interests and attitudes on things far removed from adult responsibilities, and which may develop standards that lead away from those goals established by the larger society.
>
> . . . efforts can be made to redirect the whole society of adolescence itself, so that *it* comes to motivate the child in directions sought by the adult society.

This is partly an inference from his data, and partly a recommendation based on them. The recommendation is practical enough; disc-jockeys and dope pushers make a living by following it. Coleman believes that the adolescent societies *selectively* adopt the trashier and more superficial components of American adult life because they work these into a pattern of living that is their own, while they reject more mature patterns of behavior that find no social basis in their irresponsible community.

This is to be remedied by organizing the more mature values which the adult society officially supports in such a way that they become sources of status within the adolescent society instead of being forced to compete from the outside with the values the youngsters have endorsed for themselves. Coleman recommends, for example, that externally-judged regional competitions be held in the various academic fields so that the youngsters would feel that they were winning for the school—that is, their own group—rather than taking time off from it to study. He recommends the use of computer games to stimulate the problems of adult life in classroom instruction: "Computer games can be used in schools as they have already been used in management training to provide this practice—to condition [*sic*] him to the world he must face." The concluding sentences of the book read:

> To put the matter briefly, if secondary education is to be successful, it must successfully compete with cars and sports and social activities for the adolescents' attention in the open market. The adolescent is no longer a child, but will spend his energy in the ways he sees fit. It is up to the adult society to so structure secondary education that it captures this energy.

Quite apart from the question of whether we adults have any moral basis for feeling so superior—or being so manipulative—Coleman's methodology leads to extremely serious problems of interpretation. His questionnaire data just do not seem to tell us the *kind* of thing we need to know in order to decide whether his arguments are convincing.

Through nearly all his sample, Coleman finds that "personality" and "reputation" are what youngsters feel get them into "leading crowds" in schools. Athletic ability is most highly prized in boys, popularity or recognition as a social leader for girls; these are what they want to be remembered for. In most of the schools, cars are very important to the boys. The superficiality of all this he finds objectionable; and he interprets it as evidence that the adolescent society has come between the youngsters and the scholarly purposes of the school, which it ignores or rejects. One theme that gives the work unity is the superiority of athletics to scholarship by every criterion of the adolescent society, whether as a source of status, self-esteem, or just plain visibility. This finding is so much emphasized that it is convenient and economical to focus on it as illustrative of the interpretive difficulties that arise.

Some of the items of the questionnaire on which Coleman's conclusions draw most heavily are worded in such a way that the kids have no chance to be much less superficial. Boys were asked: "If you could be any of these things you wanted, which would you most want to be?" The choice *given,* and the percentages making each choice, were: jet pilot, 31 per cent; nationally famous athlete, 37 per cent; missionary, 6 per cent; and atomic scientist, 26 per cent. For girls, the corresponding choices were: actress or artist, 19 per cent; nurse, 26 per cent; model, 34 per cent; schoolteacher, 21 per cent. Coleman cites this as evidence that the kids go for glamor. But this is unfair. Not only is the wording of the question an invitation to a daydream choice, the choices given do not include anything creative in a humanistic way. I would rather be a nationally famous athlete than the other three myself; one does no harm to subject peoples, and Congressional committees assume that athletes are patriotic Americans, which is a convenience. And the girls can only express a dream of high status in "glamor" terms because the other high-status roles in our society are not distinctively feminine and Coleman did not list them. If any of these kids wants to be a Supreme Court justice, or a poet, he didn't get a chance to say so.

Similarly, the boys are asked "Which of the items below fit most of the *girls* here at school? (Check as many as apply): friendly, catty, hard-to-get-to-know, mad about clothes, active around school, boy-crazy, studious, out for a good time, and snobbish to girls outside their group." Another item for boys reads: "Suppose you had a chance to go out with either a cheerleader, or a girl who is the best student in class, or the best-looking girl in class. Which one would you rather go out with?" For girls, "star athlete" replaces "cheerleader." The good student comes in a poor third, with good looks and athletic ability overlapping in the data and perhaps in the minds of the youngsters. But Socrates himself would have had a particularly hard time figuring out what to do with this question.

Coleman does establish beyond a doubt that the image of the athlete is far more highly esteemed throughout his sample than that of the scholar or good student, and his recommendations are designed to correct the value system that such preferences represent. "If the bright scholar is no longer merely a grind working for good grades, but becomes the captain in brilliant moves of strategy or discovery (as he is in the adult world), then his image will again become an attractive one." In view of the time it takes to print and distribute a book, this statement must almost certainly have been written during the Eisenhower administration.

I would submit that, interpreted in their total relationship to American society, Coleman's findings may be more a credit to the adolescent society than an indictment of it. He himself points out that the top achievers in the American high school are probably very far from being the ablest youngsters, because the brightest and most perceptive quickly learn to shun this particular competition. He also cites the recent and highly suggestive findings of Getzels and Jackson that teachers prefer youngsters who manifest their ability in conventional rather than creative ways. Coleman's policy proposals are intended to improve just these matters; but it is the level and conception of scholarship the youngsters have actually experienced in the high school as it now is that have led them to rate it way below athletics.

For in their experience sports are at least real and manly; the competences they demand are true competences. They are a lot less likely to be phony than the scholarship. I have seen boys from a tiny Louisiana high school, who had just defeated a major city high school team in a basketball tournament, come striding out of their locker room after the game, dressed once more in their farming clothes, and they looked magnificent. A girl who would not have dated one of them at that moment would have had to be singularly unimaginative. I have never seen these boys as they come out of their class in "Problems of Democracy," if they have one in their segregated high school, but I expect they look sheepish. They seemed to be the kind of boys who would know when they had been cheating.

Even within adult society, un-Greek as we are, athletics retains its place in the unconscious as something genuine and comparatively pure. When basketball players sell out, the public is shocked. When business executives are indicted for collusion, it is wearily amused. Coleman makes a far better case for the isolation of the adolescent society than he does for its triviality. Both its isolation and its triviality are largely responses to the greater triviality and corruption of much of our adult society. Their isolation is but an imperfect defense against our triviality; but it is the best they have, and the only way "teen-agers" have of gaining a little time and space in which to work out such meanings as their lives possess. I am reluctant to see this defense breached.

I am afraid Ginzberg's *Values and Ideals of American Youth* exemplifies some of the kinds of compromise that I think drive adolescents to take refuge in athletics. The volume has something of the character of an all-star spectacular to promote interest in a worthy cause. The title is grossly misleading; most of the papers included in it have nothing specific to do with the values and ideals of American youth. Many of them, simply as papers, are nevertheless excellent. The best of them are either summaries of current research in their author's special field of competence or—as in the papers by Urie Bronfenbrenner and by Margaret Mead—thoughtful and original analyses of the implications of such research for character and personality development in adolescents and young adults. Few of the contributors bother to be that analytical; they describe developments in their specialties.

The book is divided into three major parts: Development and Adaptability, Problem Areas, and Values in Transition. This last is most closely related to what the title promises, and is least empirical. Some of the authors don't know how to behave themselves in a universe of subjective discourse, and celebrate their freedom from the need to be scientific by writing campaign oratory like:

> A decision made in the area of the moral should be a true decision based on the eternal verities. Since democracy is predicated on the ability of an individual to make choices based on reason, the fate of democracy will be determined by the success we have in creating decision-making values that are ethical, meaningful, consistent, and consciously chosen.

But some of them use the occasion of the Conference to write compassionately of youth and to express a sensitive general understanding of the social sources of its plight. One of these papers, that of Joseph Sittler on "The Interior Aspects of Change," is notable.

What is wholly lacking in the volume—besides focus—is the kind of thoughtful analysis of values in their human context that is neither empirical nor normative, but critical and heuristic. Perhaps one cannot be heuristic at a White House Conference without causing widespread embarrassment. But I suspect that an R. H. Tawney, or a Karl Mannheim, or a Harry Stack Sullivan could have managed it. The writings of such men are as daring and as disciplined in their handling of ideas as in their handling of data, though they are very careful not to confuse the two.

In neither of these two books does the life of the adolescent as a particular human being become manifest as an *idea,* in the sense that the life of Swann or Madame Verdurin becomes manifest as an idea in *Remembrance of Things Past.* He remains a datum, and while a competent and resourceful analysis of the relationships among data, such as Coleman has made, may be very useful, what it yields is something less than a picture of the adolescent society, because the adolescent society, like Parisian society at the turn of the century, is a complex pattern of relationships among individuals.

1961

Mental Health in the Metropolis, the Midtown Manhattan Study (Volume I)

By Leo Srole, Thomas S. Langner, Stanley T. Michael, Marvin K. Opler, and Thomas A. C. Rennie

The Midtown investigation, beyond any question, was large in focus, goals, strategy, and operational scope," the senior author of this book asserts in his epilogue. So, indeed, it was. Sampling a population of 110,000 residents in a mid-Manhattan district described as a "sociographically well-delineated residential area near the epicenter of New York City's hub borough of Manhattan," the study employed several massive procedures for data collection. If the reader is at all interested in the results of this important and highly publicized research, it is important that he understand these procedures with some precision; because some of the more widely accepted implications of the study depend, I believe, on a partial misunderstanding of its data.

The authors are meticulous enough in cautioning the reader. "The keystone of the entire study was the Home Interview Survey," in which 1,911 residents were selected as a rigorously randomized sample of the 110,000; 1,660 of these were actually interviewed, which is a highly satisfactory proportion in such a study. Demographically, Midtown checks out as virtually identical with the rest of Manhattan, except that very few Negroes and not many Puerto Ricans live there. Like the rest of Manhattan, it contrasts sharply with the other boroughs in having a much smaller proportion of children and a larger proportion of single individuals. And, as the authors literally stress by their italics: "Throughout the volumes of this Study, the data must be evaluated *as a rating of mental health based on the rating psychiatrists' perceptions operating through a questionnaire instrument.*"

This is the heart of the matter. The authors are at some pains—they seem almost obsessive-compulsive—to examine the weaknesses and biases of their procedures honestly. Indeed, it may well be as a case-study in self-conscious research methodology that this book will have its greatest value; the chapters in the prologue on design are as subtle in their self-questioning as the musings of a Dostoevsky character, though Dostoevsky's work enjoys the advantage of translation into excellent English. But more is at issue here than the validity of the questionnaire, or of a process in which mental health is assessed by psychiatrists who have never seen the patient from whom data were gathered. It is true, as the authors note, that the questionnaire procedure, thus applied, precludes any assessment of mental illness in the usual psycho-dynamic terms. But it also commits the authors implicitly to a position as to the *nature* of mental illness and of its social function.

Under these circumstances, the questionnaire functions as an inventory of symptoms. The symptoms selected *are* valid signs of emotional disturbance even though, by themselves, they reveal very little about its nature. The reader must agree, I think, that the individuals rated as "Impaired" by the instrument doubtless were. There is more doubt, however, about those rated "Well," "Mild," or "Moderate." The mental health of the comparatively well-educated and well-to-do probably shows up on this instrument as better than it actually is, because the language of the questionnaire is essentially one long working-class whine.

The authors of this Study guard very carefully against introducing class bias. They discuss their precautions in detail in Appendix H: among others, "so far as it was practically possible, it was our policy to assign each interviewer to respondents of the SES (socio-economic status) range and ethnic background closest to his family or professional experience." Yet how could even this precaution avail against a questionnaire that asks "stomach upset pretty often," "Felt weak all over," "Bothered by sour stomach several times a week," "One drink is one too many." There seem to have been no questions about piles or getting up nights; there were certainly none about the stock-market, or bad schools, or civil liberties, all of which are good, sound points of crystallization for middle-class anxiety.

Settling for a working-class frame of reference is usually justified as necessary to yield comparable results; vocabulary and concepts must be limited to what all the respondents can understand. But, on the basis of the much more sophisticated treatment of Hollingshead and Redlich[1] in the New Haven Study, which the authors frequently cite, it seems obvious that the terms—and the symptoms—in which different social classes express their illness are *not* mutually comprehensible. Indeed, this is a major source of difficulty in their efforts to live together.

What the Home Interview Survey primarily observed then, it seems to me, was the tendency for life in Midtown to make people nervous. It does. One of the genuinely comical aspects of the book is the authors' efforts to reconcile their findings with the much lower incidences of mental illness reported in studies of other populations. The authors write as if they assumed that it is the *discrepancy* that must be explained, since their readers could hardly be expected to believe that people in Midtown really *were* sicker. New York remains, however, a wonderful place to visit.

The most important findings of the Study, and the most stressed, are the positive relations between mental health as here observed and SES; and the negative relation between mental health and age. Nobody could cavil at these findings. In one subway trip out of three, at least, one encounters a poor, old man or woman in obvious distress and often apparently psychotic; the younger and richer, though not always more agreeable, do clearly more frequently have their wits about them. Mr. Srole, in his epilogue, "Sociologist's Sight Lines: Retrospective and Prospective," expresses his compassion for these victims and his insight into the sources of their degradation in the characteristic language of the volume: "In the stigmatize-rejection mechanism here considered pathogenic for its objects, we confront the entire evaluative apparatus of the society's status-allocating system." Who would deny it? *Mental Health in the Metropolis* does not exaggerate the plight of the aged poor in Midtown. Dante himself could not have exaggerated it. But it does, I believe, grossly underestimate the impairment of the "more fortunate."

Partly, the reason lies in the tendency of the questionnaire to enumerate diffuse suspicion and physical symptoms, which are essentially lower-status modes of expressing anxiety. As Hollingshead and Redlich put it: "the class V [lowest] neurotic behaves badly, the class IV neurotic aches physically, the class III patient defends fearfully, and the class I-II patient is dissatisfied with himself." The Home Interview Survey would, I believe, respond more sensitively to the symptoms of classes III-V than to classes I and II. But a much more basic source of distortion than any bias in the inventory of items is the fact that it *is* an inventory—that it takes account of symptoms rather than of character and personality.

The most serious consequence of starting with a catalogue of symptoms is that the authors then perceive mental health as wholly normative. Their formal definition of mental health is sound enough, and not normative: Rennie, who guided the Study for four years prior to his untimely death, explicitly conceived mental health in dynamic terms. But the concept drops out in the methodology, and leaves the Study staff studying not mental health, but adjustment.

What is lacking in the work is anything approaching Erich Fromm's conception of a socially-patterned defective character. Socially-patterned defectives don't have symptoms; they *are* symptoms. As long as they are functioning in their accustomed society they are not nervous and they are not seen as inadequate; they succeed. Until thalidomide blew up, Dr. Kelsey almost certainly showed more nervous symptoms than her Food and Drug Administration superiors or the salesmen who were pressuring her. Yet we still believe, with some reason, that integrity is a sign of health, and the strength to maintain it under stress, when the stomach turns sour and the palms sweat, a sign of greatest health of all.

This consideration strikes, I feel, at the plausibility of the authors' central inferences. They emphasize, for example, their disagreement with what they take to be sociology's—as exemplified by Seymour Lipset's—position that social mobility is often both a source and an expression of emotional stress in the form of anxious striving. These authors, on the contrary, find the best mental health among the successfully upward mobile and the poorest among descenders in the social scale. They interpret this observation—undoubtedly correctly—as circular; not only are achievement and promotion soothing and gratifying in themselves; but nervousness, rigidity, and passive hostility are formidable barriers to advancement. Success, certainly, is partly the acting-out of a self-fulfilling prophecy. Confidence leads to success, and the confident are not nervous. But they are not necessarily healthier than the worried.

So the implications drawn by the authors of *Mental Health in the Metropolis* must, I think, be interpreted with reserve. But the work nevertheless remains exceptionally impressive both in its scope and in its methodological rigor. Its most impressive finding—and this one seems unimpeachable—is precisely the one that has received most publicity: the incredibly high rate of impairment in Midtown generally. Eighteen and one-half per cent of the respondents rated as Well, and this is probably an overestimate. Nearly a quarter are Grossly impaired, 36 per cent show Mild, and 22 per cent Moderate symptom formation. The cliché, it appears, is right. So marked an evolutionary development must have some adaptive value. You don't have to be crazy to live in New York, but it helps.

1962

1. A. B. Hollingshead and F. C. Redlich, *Social Class and Mental Illness: A Community Study* (New York, John Wiley and Sons, 1958).

The Children of Sanchez

By Oscar Lewis

This book is altogether superb. Professor Lewis does what he undertakes to do dramatically yet unobtrusively, and with a degree of taste and craftsmanship that is unlikely to be fully appreciated however much the work is praised, because the format is unfamiliar to most readers. Only a social scientist who has worked with recorded interview materials knows what is involved in editing these in such a way that the life and character of the speaker are revealed and made clear to the reader. It is a measure of the author's skill that most readers may well think that Jesus Sanchez and his sons and daughters wrote the book while Professor Lewis, after introducing them briefly, just took down what they said.

By letting the central figures tell their own stories at first-hand, Lewis gives the work an immediacy and vividness that are completely compelling. This is a book that will reach almost any reader on his own terms, whether he is looking for an adventure story, a complex and subtle account of human development and disintegration over thirty years' time, or a basic anthropological study. Moreover, since Manuel, Consuelo, Roberto, and Marta are siblings and involved in the same events, Lewis's Rashomon-like technique of presenting portions of the account of each consecutively and independently fills the book with moments of revelation as we see how each participant is blinded and paralyzed by his own character at crucial junctures in his destiny.

So it is possible to read *The Children of Sanchez* as if it were an unusually profound picaresque novel, a detailed and fugally intricate picture of Mexican social life in the lower—though not quite the lowest—depths, or as an unbearably pathetic human document. It is even possible to take it as a soap opera of unparalleled lubricity; for while Mr. Lewis's treatment of his materials does not encourage this, the Sanchez family does. Most middle-class readers, I predict, will feel revulsion as well as pity for them and their difficulties.

When one finally finishes the book, the last lines of *Othello* come curiously, and not altogether sympathetically, to mind:

> No more of that. I pray you in your letters,
> When you shall these unlucky deeds relate,
> Speak of me as I am; nothing extenuate,
> Nor set down aught in malice: then must you speak
> Of one that loved not wisely but too well;
> Of one not easily jealous, but being wrought
> Perplexed in the extreme; of one whose hand
> Like the base Indian, threw a pearl away.
>
> LODOVICO: O bloody period!

It may be well for the reader to accept this and not wear himself out trying to see the Sanchez' as lovable. Despite Lewis's obviously deep respect and concern for them, and despite the fact that (except for a thirty-page introduction) the whole book is their personal narrative, they are not really the occasion for writing it; and its subject far transcends them.

What Lewis is concerned about, both personally and professionally, is poverty. He is perfectly explicit about that in his introduction:

> In the nineteenth century, when the social sciences were still in their infancy, the job of recording the effects of the process of industrialization and urbanization on personal and family life was left to novelists, playwrights, journalists, and social reformers. Today a similar process of culture change is going on among the people of the less-developed countries, but we find no comparable outpouring of a universal literature which would help us to improve our understanding of the process and the people. . . . This situation presents a unique opportunity to the social sciences and particularly to anthropology to step into the gap and develop a literature of its own. Sociologists, who have pioneered in studying urban slums, are now concentrating

their attention on suburbia to the relative neglect of the poor. Today, even most novelists are so busy probing the middle-class soul that they have lost touch with the problems of poverty and the realities of a changing world. As C. P. Snow has recently stated: "Sometimes I am afraid that people in rich countries . . . have so completely forgotten what it is like to be poor that we can no longer feel or talk with the less lucky. This we must learn to do."

Lewis has certainly learned to do both, and in the process has defined for himself a special professional interest within anthropology of the greatest and most general human significance:

> To those who think that the poor have no culture, the concept of a culture of poverty may seem like a contradiction in terms. It would also seem to give to poverty a certain dignity and status. This is not my intention. . . . I want to draw attention to the fact that poverty in modern nations is not only a state of economic deprivation, of disorganization, or of the absence of something. It is also something positive in the sense that it has a structure, rationale, and defense mechanisms without which the poor could hardly carry on. In short, it is a way of life. . . . The culture or subculture of poverty comes into being in a variety of historical contexts. Most commonly it develops when a stratified social and economic system is breaking down or is being replaced by another. . . . It seems to me that the culture of poverty has some universal characteristics which transcend regional, rural-urban, and even national differences. . . . Although this is not the place for an extensive comparative analysis of the culture of poverty, I should like to elaborate upon some of these and other traits in order to present a provisional conceptual model of this culture based mainly upon my Mexican materials.

In the next two pages of the introduction he does so; and the narratives of the individual members of the Sanchez family brilliantly illuminate his observations. Abstractly stated, the characteristics of poverty have lost their power to shock; "frequent use of physical violence in the training of children" and "a strong predisposition to authoritarianism" do not sound too bad until their victims talk about what actually happened to them. All modern life, to be sure, is made bearable by pretending that experiences are identical with the rubrics under which they are classified for administrative purposes: this is Eichmann's Law. There is very little left of this illusion after the Sanchez children have told the stories of their lives to early middle age, each revealing through his personal biases and omissions the full horror of what he has helped inflict on the others. The father, Jesus, is not very appropriately named; in his rigid, upright malevolence, sexual exploitativeness, and combined responsibility toward property and suspiciousness and callousness toward people, he is a character wholly at variance with the New Testament. As for his sons and daughters, each emerges, through hundreds of pages of narrative monologue, as a unique and engrossing personality. Lewis has rendered their highly colloquial argot into an English which seems not merely to retain the Spanish character of the original but to distinguish and illuminate the young speakers themselves.

We leave them in the middle of their lives, perhaps no more trapped than ourselves and certainly no less aware of being trapped, but in danger and discomfort that we could not bear for a month. Neither can they, of course; the damage is irreparable; they are still there and nothing important has changed, except themselves.

And not for the better; there are no incidents in which the Sanchez' transcend their condition or their character. This is not to say that they emerge as squalid, Erskine Caldwell caricatures; on the contrary. They retain, on the whole, much more courage and a little more dignity than people generally do; but the circumstances of their lives make it clearer than the circumstances of ours do that this is not enough for survival. Our novelists usually try to protect us from too much reality by drawing the poor—when they draw them at all—as either buffoons or tragic heroes; and, indeed, it is hard to see what else could flourish under the conditions Lewis depicts. The Sanchez', unfortunately, are neither.

The Children of Sanchez, however, resembles a novel less than it does a Breughel painting. Vivid and minutely detailed, it is so masterfully organized that it remains completely lucid and its pattern is never obscured. The book is deeply moving, in parts earthily comic, and extremely colorful; but the color, brilliant as it is, never makes the picture cheerful. The Sanchez' have their times of revelry, fervor, and passion; but not tranquil joy or affection. Dionysus blesses them from time to time; Apollo never. The commonplace picture of life among the poor as roughly tender and warm, to which so many middle-class people wistfully contrast their own pallid comforts, is shattered by Lewis's observations. None of the five central characters relates any experience of sustained, mutual emotional acceptance, though they form relationships that last for years. Even the world of Jules Feiffer is cozier.

This clearly is their tragedy. There seems to be a vicious dialectic at play. Among these poor, the people like Roberto who remain loving and affectionate take such a beating that they have no self-confidence left; they never learn how fine they really are and spend their lives in flight. Thus, Roberto as a young man:

> I missed my mother then, and I still miss her. Since her death I felt I could never be happy again. Some people feel relieved when they talk about their troubles, but I've told this to many people and it has never helped. I feel calm only when I run away, when I go off as a vagabond, when I am alone in the country or up in the mountains. I believe if my mother were still alive I'd be very different. Or perhaps I'd be worse.
>
> . . . .
>
> I wanted to make a kite of my life and fly it in any field.

Those like Consuelo, who drive themselves to acquire enough education and middle-class habits to hold on to respectable life by their fingernails, become too angry and exhausted to respond to love when they find it; while her comments on her brother, Manuel, who also is troubled by aspirations, leave both of them hanging in full view:

> Of the three, Manuel had the hardest heart. He was never there when he was needed and even if he were, nothing concerned him. He reminded me of a person walking backwards in darkness, without setting foot upon solid ground. He walked

> and walked and got nowhere. He just moved his legs to give people the impression he was doing something. His gaze was fixed upon little stars shining in the firmament. He tried to catch them and when he managed to get one, he would sit down there in the infinite emptiness and play with it until the dazzling light lost its power. Then he would leave the dead star floating in the air, and go irresistibly after another.

Others, like sister Marta, simply and shortly descend into sluttishness, turning every proposition life makes to them into something dishonorable by their intense—and usually shrewdly justified—suspicions. One of the minor revelations of this work is how little good sex does the children of Sanchez, even though it seems to take up most of their attention and energy. D. H. Lawrence, surely, learned even less than usual from his Mexican experiences. For the people of the *vecinidade Casa Grande,* sex is no primal source of renewal. They use it as *rentiers* use the stock market; as a distraction, a *raison d'être,* a status symbol, a defense against anxiety, and sometimes for the sake of revenue and security. Of course, it makes them very nervous. Lewis writes:

> This method of multiple biographies also tends to reduce the element of investigator bias because the accounts are not put through the sieve of a middle-class North American mind but are given in the words of the subjects themselves. In this way, I believe I have avoided the two most common hazards in the study of the poor, namely, oversentimentalization and brutalization. Finally, I hope that this method preserves for the reader the emotional satisfaction and understanding which the anthropologist experiences in working directly with his subjects but which is only rarely conveyed in the formal jargon of anthropological monographs.

How brilliantly he has succeeded! The effect, however, is devastating. Sentimentality and brutality are two aspects of the same pathetic fallacy. When both are avoided we are forced to see the children of Sanchez in all their alienation.

Compare lovable Alfred Doolittle, lustily singing "Get Me to the Church on Time!" in nostalgic tribute to the non-respectable poor, with Jesus Sanchez, the real article:

> Another man would be in jail by now! But I value my freedom and never looked for unmarried girls. No! All my women have already been married before I lived with them. Otherwise, there would be complications. If they had been virgins, I would probably have had to marry one of them in church or by civil law, or I would be in jail for twenty years!

Our alienation is not very different, but we feel betrayed by it. Though we continually fail one another miserably as sources of love and devotion, our culture nevertheless continues, feebly, to assert that these should exist. Education has done this much for us, anyway; we still have an idea what a hero or a lover would look like if they made them any more. Being the sort of people we are, we use the recollection to pity and delude ourselves, but we still possess it.

The children of Sanchez must manage without these necessities. They know that they have been cheated, and their resentment is perhaps the most potent political factor of the 20th century. But they are prevented by the culture of poverty from formulating precisely what they are deprived of; they do not really believe that it exists. At least, not enough do at any one time to support each other by trust and devotion. This, alone, is what has saved the rich so far. We have always been able to assume that the poor would be jealous of us for the wrong reasons.

1962

The Hiroshima Pilot

By William Bradford Huie

In the last sentence of his book, Mr. Huie declares: "I believe the story of Claude Eatherly and his publicists curiously illuminates the time in which we live." How true—how very true—this statement is, and how livid the illumination. I have no independent source of verification of the account Mr. Huie unfolds. I cannot judge the accuracy of the book; but I must take it for what it is. There isn't, unfortunately, much doubt about that.

Mr. Huie's summary of the public record, which I accept, is clear. Claude Eatherly, a former Major in the United States Air Force, was the commanding officer of a weather-scouting aircraft assigned the duty of observing weather conditions in Hiroshima on August 6, 1945. He flew over the city, reported that the weather was lovely, and was 225 miles away by the time Colonel Tibbets actually dropped the bomb. He had nothing to do with the selection of the target, and was too far away to see the flash of this primitive thermonuclear device, much less to inspect the damage it inflicted. Huie tells us that Eatherly flew only one more mission—a similar reconnaissance of a city that was not bombed—before his discharge.

Subsequently, in civilian life, Mr. Eatherly has certainly had serious problems of "adjustment." Everyone who knows him seems to have found him likable; but he passed bad checks and confessed to two attempts at post-office robbery, though he was acquitted of these on psychiatric grounds. He has attempted other robberies, in a bizarre manner; and on September 13, 1960, his brother who, by Mr. Huie's account, had patiently tried to help him throughout his difficulties, filed an application to have him committed indefinitely to the Veterans Administration Hospital in Waco to which he had often been confined previously. The judgment rendered was ambiguous, holding Eatherly to be mentally ill and requiring hospitalization, but not finding that he needed a guardian. He was returned to the hospital, left it seven months later, and was living in Galveston, Texas, on an authorized "trial visit" away from the hospital in March, 1962, when Huie sought him out. Huie relates that Eatherly asked him to write a book about him, and also asked for $500 for cooperating. A few days later Huie agreed to do so, warned Eatherly that the book might not be favorable to him, and paid him the $500. "I had already written his check, and I had also written four letters for him to sign." The letters were to the Office of Public Information of the Air Force, the Director of the Veterans Administration Hospital in Waco, and to the Chief Legal Officer of the VA in Washington and, *mirabile dictu,* to J. Edgar Hoover. They authorized these officials to make every record bearing on Eatherly available to Mr. Huie, and Mr. Eatherly signed them. In retrospect, the judgment of the jury at the lunacy hearing that Mr. Eatherly did not need a guardian seems not to have covered all possible contingencies.

There is no point in summarizing here the squalid, highly circumstantial account that follows of Eatherly's petty crimes and imprisonment, the collapse of his marriage, and his sojourns in the mental hospital; whether it is true or misleading, it is soap-opera. Mr. Huie's interest in Major Eatherly seems to me justifiable. The Major has become a hero in England, and, of course, in Communist countries, where his legend is deliberately exploited. He is believed to have been the actual commander of the mission that dropped the first atomic bomb, and his subsequent derangement is attributed to his unbearable burden of guilt. Mr. Huie makes a far more plausible case for the interpretation that Eatherly suffered from neglect rather than from guilt, and made up his guilt in order to dramatize himself. Where "pacifists"—the print of the book hisses when Huie uses this word—portray Eatherly as committing bizarre crimes in order to court punishment for his guilt, Huie sees him as seeking to appear more deranged than he is in order to avoid imprisonment and increase his disability pension. And so it may be. Mr. Eatherly has corresponded with and sometimes worked with the people who have portrayed him as a hero, as he did with Mr. Huie; and he seems to have made no effort to correct their untrue statements. The most egregious and unjust of these is that he is a prisoner in a hospital, prevented by the authorities from declaring his guilt. Edmund Wilson's brief comments on Eatherly in *The Cold War and the Income Tax* did give me that impression.

What makes it so unjust is that if the book—despite Mr. Huie's efforts—has a hero, it is the Veterans Administration. With a moral sensitivity I would not have believed possible for a bureaucracy, it has, by Mr. Huie's hostile account, maintained through the course of its unrewarding relationship to its difficult charge a concern for Major Eatherly and a respect for his rights that commands my astonished admiration. Both in Waco and in Washington the authorities responded to Mr. Huie's letters of authorization by pointing out that, since, in their professional judgment Mr. Eatherly was mentally incompetent, they could not accept them, and refused Mr. Huie access to Eatherly's records. Mr. Huie responds:

> I consider this sort of secrecy dangerous, improper in the United States, and I told them so. But Dr. Middleton and Mr. Brickfield insisted that the law gave them no other course. Dr. Middleton invited me to visit the Waco hospital, to inspect it from basement to attic, and to talk at length with Dr. McMahan [the director of the hospital]. But only with Dr. McMahan, and *not* about the medical record. . . . The VA decision did not prevent my obtaining most of the pertinent information about Eatherly. The decision did, however, force me to employ a device which is abhorrent to me. To this point, I have named the source of whatever I have reported. But from this point [p. 93] I must resort, in a few cases, to quoting only the informed source.

Mr. Huie resorts, as well, to innuendo and animadversion. His particular target is the psychiatrist who was placed in charge of Eatherly's case in the spring of 1956, whose testimony was largely responsible for Eatherly's acquittal at his trial for postal robbery in December, 1957. This physician, whose full name Mr. Huie repeats from time to time in case the reader might have forgotten its implications, was Dr. Oleinick Pavlovitch Constantine. "Fair, stocky, strong-faced, amiable, he is unmistakably Russian. In appearance and manner he reminded me of General Zukov." Even as a child, Oleinick Pavlovitch seems to have been offensive, since the Red Army drove him, along with certain other children, out of the country at the age of nine. The fact that his father was a Baptist set in train the events that ultimately brought the boy as a medical student to Baylor University, and hence to Waco, where he settled, and where, ultimately, he met Mr. Huie. Samarra would have been a lot shorter trip.

Mr. Huie is particularly suspicious of Dr. Constantine's change of Eatherly's diagnosis from "anxiety reaction" to "schizophrenia"; which increased his disability compensation and influenced the postal-robbery jury to acquit him. Huie insists that he is not himself a psychiatrist, and regards Constantine's diagnosis as questionable because other psychiatrists at the hospital disagreed with it. But Eatherly was Constantine's patient, and if one wishes to write a book about a man the meaning of whose life depends on the validity of psychiatric diagnoses one must know something about the uncertainties inherent in the field. Mr. Huie does not even seem to grasp the idea of ambivalence in human behavior: he attacks Eatherly's sincerity and consistency, and insists that if Eatherly were really crazy or guilt-ridden he wouldn't goof-off about it. In his initial telephone conversation with Mr. Eatherly, and before he had met him, Mr. Huie told him, "I'm only a reporter. The only thing about you which interests me is the truth." But his suspicious contempt for his subject makes this statement quite untenable. Here is Mr. Huie's account of their first meeting.

> His appearance was no surprise. I've visited too many jails and mental hospitals not to know that the "disordered" man today often looks "just like everybody else." Eatherly is six feet tall, and smokes cigars. His jaws have fleshened, to make his face round; and his forehead slopes backward to curly, reddish receding hair. He had arrived in an old-model car, and his dress

> was ordinary. He doesn't appear alert, but I sensed calculation in his manner. He seemed distrustful, watchful; each word is a maneuver.

Then, later, when Huie was checking out one of Eatherly's check-passing episodes:

> Every criminal has what police and the television dramatists call his "MO"—his "mode of operation"; . . . I studied Claude Eatherly's MO.

But a far more serious defect in the book than its hostility toward its subject is its moral obtuseness. And this, paradoxically, makes the book really an important document of our times—an incomparable bit of authentic mid-century Americana. From this point of view, Major Eatherly almost vanishes; he recedes, at least, into the background that made the entire series of events perhaps inevitable. Take, for example, these comments from two different letters to Huie from former members of Major Eatherly's crew, which Huie cites to show how normal American young men react to peripheral participation in the historic events at Hiroshima:

> We have three children, all girls. . . . We live in a lovely home overlooking the village and facing the Green Mountains of Vermont. . . . We have lived in Ukiah since 1946 when I got out of the service. We have a nice home, swimming pool, patio, etc.

Or this verbal comment on Eatherly by a third crew member:

> He was a swell guy to drink with and chase girls with. He always carried the book with plenty of girls in it. From Wendover, Utah, we used to race in two cars over that hundred miles to Salt Lake City. The Skipper and I would pass the whiskey bottle back and forth, from one car to another, at eighty miles an hour. Certainly it didn't occur to me that there was anything abnormal about the Skipper.

Or Huie's:

> Every one of the 1800 men in the 509th thought he had some role in the *support* of Hiroshima. . . . These are proud Americans: they are proud because they think they "ended the war."

> And "Hiroshima" to these men means, not a city, but the *attack* on Hiroshima.

Or these remarkable words in which Mr. Huie, speaking to Eatherly, "tried to make retraction easier for him":

> Hiroshima was something different; it wasn't another air battle like Schweinfurt or Ploesti. It was a deliberate demonstration of terror. The men who ordered it were well-intentioned men who thought they were acting in the name of humanity.

Yet, there are people who call *Dr. Strangelove* satire. Patriotism is an admirable human quality even in 1964. But it has gotten a bit tricky to handle, and requires, I think, rather more intellectual dexterity and compassion, for others and for oneself as an American, than Mr. Huie brings to bear in the book he calls, with heavy irony, *The Hiroshima Pilot*. I share his disgust at Mr. Eatherly's willingness to allow his life story to be distorted and misrepresented in foreign countries. But indignation on this point is beyond me.

It isn't Mr. Eatherly, after all, who has harmed our moral reputation. The people who criticize us for imprisoning and attempting to silence a remorseful man—as they have been led to believe we have done—at least do us the honor of believing we might have produced one. They do not despise us primarily for what they think we did to Major Eatherly; I wish they did. They hate us for what we did in fact do to Hiroshima—I mean the city, and its people, not the attack. They hate us for being, so largely, the kind of people who could have spoken of it as Mr. Huie does.

But we did do it, to a nation already defeated and attempting, through the Russians, to sue for peace. One of Mr. Huie's recurrent complaints against Major Eatherly is that he misrepresented his combat record when, in fact, he had never been under fire: "The Japs had nothing to bother you at that altitude by July, 1945," one of his crew members remarked. This is not a factor that could reasonably be held to augment the guilt of a minor officer in the Air Force. But it does augment Mr. Truman's guilt, and ours.

Eatherly, certainly, is no hero, and he may be as miserable

a creature as Mr. Huie makes him out—though Dr. Constantine seems to have been guided closer to the truth by a mixture of compassion and professional competence. But even if Mr. Huie has painted Mr. Eatherly accurately, I am afraid that he has still not recognized him.

Just what did we expect, anyway—something more dignified than a poor, publicity-seeking, middle-aged man too weak to defend his country's reputation at some small sacrifice to his own? Is it distressing to find the victory—and the victors—of Hiroshima mockingly exploited by a man who passes bad checks, figures small angles incompetently, and makes an inextricable mess of his life? Does the promise of the nuclear age merit a more stirring betrayal? On the contrary, I find it reassuring that the gods, after all they have been through, have retained their sense of proportion. Everyone, even in America, is eventually served by precisely the Fury he has summoned.

1964

The Mature Attitude

I SHOULD LIKE to begin this analysis by re-making three points about which there is considerable agreement among most persons who have considered the attributes of maturity. The first of these is that the mature individual can certainly *not* be recognized by any *particular* set of beliefs or convictions which one may expect to find in all such persons. There are no ideological tests for maturity; there is not and cannot be any series of questions through which those entitled to call themselves mature might be identified by their common answers.

The second is that there is, nevertheless, a relationship between personal maturity and a fundamental style of life which may be called virtuous, and has been called this since the time of the Greeks. We do recognize the mature individual through the net attitude toward the experience of living which that life-style expresses. It is in general a humane and responsible attitude, even though it may lack specific components of any particular prevailing moral ideology.

The third point is that maturity means, not the end of growth, but the condition in which growth is most fruitful. Before an individual—of whatever species—achieves a degree of maturity, most resources must be spent on development of a stable apparatus for living. When this has been realized, resources then become available for his prime functions and purposes. But stability in maturity is never static. It is completely dynamic; the mature individual is one whose energies are most fully absorbed in being himself and fulfilling his purpose, which is a very active state indeed.

It seems evident then, that attitudes characteristic of maturity must be attitudes toward life itself, rather than toward any given issue. Persons, to the degree that they are mature, do hold in common a characteristic orientation toward life, although there may be no area of agreement among them on particular ideas. This orientation is observable, not as the background of their activities, but as a part of the pattern which they create for themselves in the process of living. As they grow, and grow more experienced, the pattern becomes richer and more subtle. It also becomes more clearly defined in their every act of being.

This pattern of living, itself, constitutes the attitude of maturity. In order to discuss it, we must use the word attitude in its sense of a customary posture or position, as in "receptive attitude" or "a defiant attitude," or even, "I just don't like his whole attitude." It is not sufficient, and would lead to confusion, to limit the concept of "attitude" in this context to that of a belief or emotional response.

When we speak of a person's attitude toward Negroes, we should not refer merely to whether he is prejudiced against them and how much. We mean rather the condition assumed by his entire self when a question concerning "the race issue" arises and he has to do something about it. I think that personal maturity is indeed revealed by certain common characteristics of attitude in this sense, regardless of the particular issue which may be involved or the way the person decides to vote on it. In this paper, I shall examine these characteristics, and the dynamics which seem to underlie their operation.

Four Facets of Maturity

There are many ways in which these characteristics might be defined. I think it will be fruitful to discuss four of them, which I shall call *awareness, objectivity, emotional responsiveness,* and *civility*. I am using these terms very much in their usual sense; but I am concerned with certain of their implications which are not always stressed, so I had better explain what I mean by them and how I think they are operative in the mature attitude.

Awareness

By *awareness,* I mean simply the power a person has to know what is going on around and within him, and to take conscious account of it. There are two rather clearly distinguishable aspects of this. Awareness is, on the one hand, a matter of education and intelligence. One cannot be aware if one is simply too dull or ignorant to read the signs.

I recall that when I was beginning graduate study in chemistry it was necessary to undertake an organic synthesis for which the only available published procedure was in Beilstein's *Handbuch der Organischen Chemie.* My German does not amount to much, but it was good enough for me to tell how much of what to mix, and how long to heat it to get what I wanted.

Beilstein, like most German reference works, is pretty exhaustive, and also summarizes the side-reactions which accompany the synthesis, although they don't usually matter in routine work. One notes that they occur—the German and English names of chemical compounds are usually enough alike to present no great problems—and goes on about his business.

In this synthesis, Beilstein said, large quantities of *Blausaure* would be evolved. There is no substance which is called "Blue acid" in English, but it sounded pretty and rather *gemütlich,* as acids go, so that as I began setting up the apparatus in the open laboratory I was rather looking forward to it. *Blausaure,* as my major professor told me shortly after I began heating my mixture of reagents, is hydrogen cyanide. In scientific work, there is no substitute for systematic knowledge and, equally, for precision.

On the other hand, awareness is equally a function of ego-dominance and emotional well-being. It is not enough to see the signs, and be intellectually qualified to interpret them. One must also be willing and able to allow them to penetrate and to *accept their implications.* So much of our energy seems to be taken up from day to day in trying to communicate with people who show quite clearly by their defensiveness that what is going on has got through to them, but who are totally absorbed in the crucial task of remaining unaware of it. Most responsible people, I believe, by the time they are middle-aged, cannot help but recall several disagreeable occasions on which they have been injured or betrayed by persons who were resolutely unimpeded by insight as they carried out their destructive purpose as steadfastly as a wasp building a nest. Some of us have even known individuals so twisted in their perception of reality as to believe we were acting that way ourselves.

In calling *awareness* an aspect of maturity I am asserting that a mature individual approaches life with the capacity to perceive, and to permit himself to understand, the complexities of his involvement in it. I do not, however, wish to imply that one achieves this condition simply by hanging around on the surface of the earth for a quarter of a century or more. Nor, certainly, do I wish to imply that stupidity, ignorance, or malice may be the more easily condoned by relating to them flaws in the process of growth.

One of the few really unpleasant consequences of the influence of psychoanalysis has been the tendency to evade moral judgments by taking refuge in neurosis. The bad guys of history, from Heliogabalus to Hitler, were doubtless all, in my terms, immature; but this is not the slightest reason why anyone should have put up with them. It does follow, however, that it is the capacity of the human being for growth which spares most men their character and their destiny. This, I think, becomes increasingly clear as we examine the other three aspects I have attributed to the mature attitude.

Objectivity

The second of these is *objectivity.* This is a conception closely related to the psychodynamic aspects of awareness just discussed; but it goes much further. By *objectivity,* I mean the capacity of the individual to break through the skin-barrier without confusion; to discern the properties of external reality without attributing to it the properties he would wish it to have, or believing himself to be responding to it when he is actually responding to his own needs and feelings. All aspects of maturity have moral significance; the objective person does not bear false witness, which is not the easiest of the Commandments to observe.

This conception of objectivity implies nothing whatever about detachment or impartiality. An objective person, if he sees a man beating a dog, will not confuse the dog's feelings with his own feelings about the dog. He will not confuse his objection to the beating with his delight in seeing himself as the kind of man who *does* object to it. But he may also be too forthright to permit such considerations to sickly over the native hue of his resolution; and it will reflect nothing on his objectivity if he goes right ahead and slugs the man—so long as he does it because he saw something real which really made him angry.

In the world in which we live, it is probably impossible and surely undesirable for an objective individual to be dispassionate. There are only two ways in which he can remain so, and each involves a serious failure in objectivity. He can stay dispassionate if he does not see what the external world is like; if he does not really believe in Suez or nuclear fission. This is a common form of detachment, reaching peak perfection in waxy catatonia.

Or—and this is even more common and more serious—he can stay dispassionate through a kind of reverse solipsism, attributing to himself the feelings and moral attitudes which he detects in the external world, making use of adaptive anxiety to achieve ethical neutrality. This is the garden variety of conformity, on which the modern state seems largely to depend for cohesion. It is good-humored and makes life easier; why should Big Brother waste effort watching us, when we are so cautiously watching ourselves for him? It leads to the tolerant and well-rounded view—the patience to give equal TV time to the murderer and to any confused liberal who still wants to step out of line and speak for the victim. This may be tolerance, but it is not objectivity; and it is not maturity.

Reality being what it is, objectivity should lead *to* passion —not away from it. This is not a particularly novel point of view: ". . . a true knowledge of good and evil," Spinoza wrote, "cannot restrain any emotion insofar as the knowledge is true, but only insofar as it is considered as an emotion."

Modern life, however, treats knowledge of good and evil precisely as if it *were* an emotion; and rejects the emotion as a subjective state having no valid relation to reality. We distrust people who "get too involved." We use the word *disturbed* as a synonym for *sick,* and mean by both *unbalanced.* By treating genuine and deeply felt devotion or indignation as if it were neurotic *per se,* we alienate people from the most important meanings of their life and forestall their growth.

Emotional Responsiveness

It is in the strongest possible agreement with Spinoza's view that I have designated *emotional responsiveness* as a fundamental aspect of the mature attitude. Real men and women love and hate. They may not be easy to get along with, but you can count on them. They love and hate with awareness and objectivity; they understand their world, and they respond to it according to their own values.

What is involved in this emotional responsiveness? It is difficult to analyze, but at the root of it are clearly two traits: self-respect and empathy. The kind of self-respect which is needed is remote indeed from the categories of clean-living which one learns in scout camp; it is equally distinct from the grandeur of minor princes. It is effective to the degree that it is unconscious.

This is true not merely because unconscious processes tend to influence us more powerfully than conscious decisions. Nor is it true merely because conscious self-respect so easily turns priggish and alienates us from real experience of other persons and of the world.

It is true because what people have in common as human beings is largely the stuff of presymbolic experience. What we respect in ourselves, if we are to be capable of genuine response to other persons and life around us, must be a humanity which existed before it was molded and embossed by our particular lives, in our particular series of social roles, in our particular branch of Western culture. Our particular branch of Western culture is very often cheap and nasty. While it gave us the tools with which to communicate with one another, and the terms in which to do so, it has often weakened us in our use of them.

If we have retained a respect for our personal share in common humanity, no matter what shape we are now in, we have the basis for emotional response to any man. Not, to be sure, with love. The day is late, and there are shadows which were not cast by lovable persons. But we have the basis on which to respond to some men with love, and to all with authenticity. The instrument of this response is empathy.

Empathy is the capacity, also unconscious in origin, to feel with other persons, to sense their emotional condition. Unlike awareness and objectivity, it probably does not increase with age. A small child does not know enough to interpret reality accurately, and cannot distinguish reliably between himself and the outer world. But infants, perhaps unfortunately, are connoisseurs of emotional climate; they have a lot of sensitivity to lose before they are fit for adult life. Those who lose least of it in the course of development are able as adults to fuse understanding and feelings into a degree of perception which is "miraculous." Saints are recruited from their numbers, which tends to keep the quality of miracles from descending to the merely magical.

Empathy, to be sure, is the source of compassion in human affairs; and as such is highly prized. More attention should be given, I think, to its function as the source of precision as well. Our common humanity knows quite well that mankind can be tricky as well as noble—is most human when it is being both at once, with a complexity which may defy analysis but not detection.

If the capacity for empathy has been retained as awareness and objectivity have developed—then we know, and we are no less compassionate for knowing. We know exactly. As we comfort the widow in her bereavement, we can accept the unexpressed release along with the very real grief. We can spank our children when we must without expecting them ever to quite forgive us. We can watch the candidates for public office assert their fellowship on television, and know that the cold clutching at our hearts is functional rather than organic; we need not send for Dr. White quite yet.

Through self-respect and empathy, then, we respond with feeling to other persons and to the common situation which binds us together. We view this situation with full awareness of its meaning; and we can distinguish our role in it from that of other persons and other factors. We can act; and when we act, we know what we are doing and why, from the bottom of our hearts.

Is there more to the mature attitude than the habit of approaching life in this spirit? Although this would make a very good average, I think there is one more necessary attribute. I have called this final essential characteristic of the mature attitude *civility*.

Civility

Civility, like emotional responsiveness, involves and is derived from self-respect and empathy. But it contributes to maturity something distinct, which is the complement—even, in a measure, the antithesis—of emotional responsiveness. Civility is the virtue which makes civic life endurable. It functions to preserve the integrity of individuals who must pass their lives in a changing succession of ambiguous groups; and it does so in part by keeping a distance between people. Its purpose is not isolation, but privacy; and it works through understanding—not concealment. In a private home or a good Continental hotel, one does not lock one's door. People don't come barging in. But if they do, there must be locks; and if they break the locks, there must be guns.

Among civil persons, one needn't lock one's mind or one's heart. One's neighbors know when they are welcome there. Some may become lovers; the others, knowing themselves no less welcome than before, quietly note that the hours for unexpected visits have been altered. This gives them more time to cultivate their own gardens. What they grow they may send to the fair if they wish to compete for a blue ribbon or an honorable mention. But if there is no honorable mention for this class of event, they may still enjoy it among themselves. They are aware; they know what is going on; they are responsive, and responsible. They trust one another, even though they have been acquainted for years. There are no spies.

These are the sort of persons whose attitude I call mature. I need hardly say that they do not dominate modern society. Modern society makes enormous demands on the maturity of those who would live full lives in it; but it does not encourage any aspect of maturity.

The conditions of contemporary life make it very difficult to become aware. This is usually attributed to the complexity of our society; but it is by no means self-evident that our society *is* more complex than that of the renaissance or antiquity. It is certainly more intricate and has more moving parts. Our difficulty in becoming aware seems more nearly due to a built-in obscurantism.

The administrators of our communications, being themselves among the most rapidly moving parts, are neither willing nor able to pause and give account of the total apparatus. The mass media have come to function rather like the specially designed industrial lighting developed during World War II, which concealed installations more effectively than detailed camouflage ever could.

Objectivity is opposed by the dominant processes of cooptation and interlocking veto-groups which characterize American society. Every individual, that is to say, who tries to do anything or get anywhere is reminded frequently and forcibly that what other people think of him is more important a determinant than his own goals and values. Under these conditions, it takes the soul of a saint in the hide of an elephant even to remain certain that one has a separate identity of one's own, and that the distinction between subject and object is meaningful.

To be fair, one must note that our culture has in some degree taken account of its disastrous tendency toward alienation by institutionalizing powerful therapeutic forces, like psychoanalysis, to countervail against it. But they are not sufficient to redress the balance. The great threat to our objectivity remains that which caught up with the college president in Randall Jarrell's delightful *Picture from an Institution,* whom Jarrell describes as so well adjusted to his environment that it was difficult to tell which was the environment and which was the president.

Emotional responsiveness suffers from the decay of the Kantian imperative. In a society in which individual advancement is more highly prized than love, in which people compete for status, and home is a good place to be from, the Kantian imperative doesn't stand a chance. We use other men as a means, and seldom as an end withal. How dare we love or hate, when we never know who may be useful? We seek rather to understand one another, not in the fullness of our hearts but as one might a 1950 car, which will still give pretty good service if we know its quirks and don't try to push it too hard. Ultimately, if we are doing well, we may not even trade it in. People are sometimes sentimental about cars.

But it is civility which seems to encounter the most formidable checks, and to be most continually breached. There is in modern life a truly Panic quality, malicious and goatish. We are appalled by the hostility in which we dwell together—but so much that we sometimes fail to notice that it is rancid as well as bitter. There is no dignity in it. The gossip at dusk trills over his Martini, and sages and statesmen are stoned through the streets like yellow dogs. On every enduring monument one finds, as Holden Caulfield noted, an ugly word crudely chalked.

It is noted in the *Times*. A few months ago there was an exemplary issue. It had in it ugliness and terror enough; British boys had been hanged in reprisal for the hanging of Greek boys; Algeria was in a state of civil insurrection; Prime Minister Eden was being pilloried because a British Naval officer had lost his life while engaged in an act of inexplicable espionage on behalf of what must have been, in terms of British traditions of decency toward guests, a peculiarly foreign power. But the story most symbolic of our times contained no element of tragedy. It was, in fact, about the only really funny thing in that day's paper.

An unknown transport plane, wandering over the Gaza strip, was intercepted by the Israeli air force and forced down at Lydda airport. There it proved to be British. The plane, that is, and the crew were British. The passengers were Rhesus monkeys which had undertaken the journey to London to permit their livers to be used in the preparation of Salk vaccine. They were recognized as unusually public-spirited monkeys and no more anti-Semitic than most, and were dispatched again toward London and Destiny without let or hindrance when it was found that their papers, such as they were, were in order.

Well, the monkeys made it; so, perhaps, one ought not to give up. Though immature—the livers of elderly monkeys are not suitable for Salk vaccine—their behavior throughout the incident was composed and detached; they did not permit themselves to become involved, and the cloud of suspicion soon passed.

The role of man is harder to play. The casting is often poor, and the direction—if there is any—rather inept. The whole drama has too much spectacle and too little characterization and development. The same situations are repeated in every act.

But it must be noted that the monkeys did not invent the vaccine. We did. I don't think we have very sound grounds for pride in our superior technical proficiency, which is an ambiguous virtue. What is important is that we were able to see some reason for inventing it in the first place. We do object to children being paralyzed. We do try to change what we object to. We do perform miracles—not only of technology, but of organization and intellectual continuity—in the effort. Even when, having spent our lives scaling apparently insurmountable technical obstacles with final success, we find ourselves bemired in the Department of Health, Education, and Welfare; we do not despair.

Despair is not a component of the mature attitude.

1957